The
Changing
College
Classroom

Philip Runkel, Roger Harrison,
& Margaret Runkel, Editors

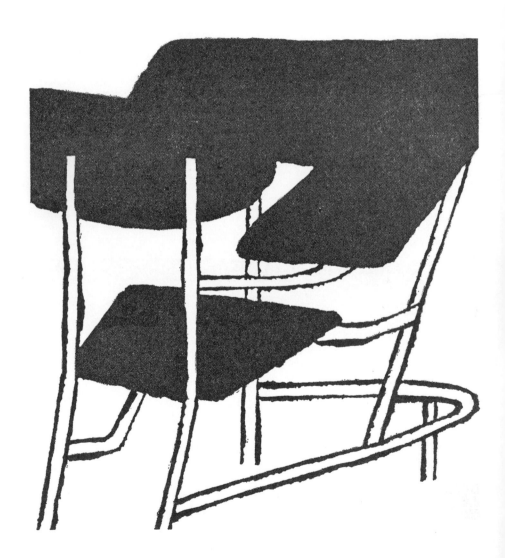

THE CHANGING COLLEGE CLASSROOM

Jossey-Bass Inc., Publishers
San Francisco • Washington • London • 1972

THE CHANGING COLLEGE CLASSROOM
Philip Runkel, Roger Harrison, Margaret Runkel, Editors

Published in Great Britain by
Jossey-Bass, Inc., Publishers
St. George's House
44 Hatton Garden, London E.C.1

Library of Congress Catalogue Card Number LC 70-92896

International Standard Book Number ISBN 0-87589-047-4

Manufactured in the United States of America

JACKET DESIGN BY WILLI BAUM

FIRST PRINTING: November 1969

SECOND PRINTING: January 1972

Code 6919

THE JOSSEY-BASS SERIES IN HIGHER EDUCATION

Consultants

JOSEPH AXELROD, *San Francisco State College*

MERVIN B. FREEDMAN, *San Francisco State College
and Wright Institute, Berkeley*

PREFACE

The Changing College Classroom is about innovations in college teaching written by some creative college teachers to describe work they, themselves, are doing. They display the faith and hope possible when human beings deal with their common concerns as human beings. In these classrooms, teaching and learning are the common concerns of teacher *and* student.

Historically, the nature of learning, the role of the university, and the characteristics of the educated man have been the concern of philosophers. The training of college and university teachers has had limited attention from professors of higher education. Learning theory is the domain of a specialized group of psychologists who do not necessarily apply their research to the field of college teaching. Professors of educational psychology do not themselves train other college teachers. By and large, college and university teachers acquire whatever skill they have in the art of teaching by following selectively the practices of their own college teachers, or attempting to practice what they read.

The professional literature on the problems of improving col-

lege teaching is not extensive, but recently several collections of essays have made notable contributions to it (Lee, 1967; Dobbins and Lee, 1968). Case studies of classroom teaching at the college level are difficult to find in the literature. We hope that this book of reports of actual experiences will add significantly to this latter kind of literature.

This book has been in preparation during some of the most turbulent and disruptive months in the history of American higher education. Administrators and faculties have responded in various ways to the pressures put upon them. One common thread, often overshadowed by the nature of the confrontation itself, runs through most of the public and private statements made by those responsible for teaching and administering colleges: some student complaints are legitimate; some things need changing.

A former president of the University of Minnesota and the University of Oregon has this to say about change (Wilson, 1967):

. . . [Students] have been taught so much about change, have seen so much change themselves, that now almost anything seems possible. Yet the world they inherit is or seems to be only a web of undesirable improbabilities; considering what their mind teaches them about man's ability to force his environment to respond to his will, they consider a good world to be possible. Little wonder, then, that they find their real world intolerable. Like Job, the young intellectual sees himself as life's finest product assailed by life's greatest and most unreasoned ills. And, like Job, he would like to escape his sorrows; he wants even more to understand his world than to escape from it. If the campus were really listening, it could hear the student crying, as Job did: "Teach me and I will hold my tongue." And, if we heard that cry, the act of teaching would be honored on the campus, and it would be cultivated there.

Students have things to tell us about the process by which they are educated. And we need to listen not only to their ideas but also to their pain and frustration. We have included in Part One essays by two of the most articulate leaders in the educational reform movement spearheaded by students. Against these expressions of dissatisfaction with traditional teaching and learning modes, we present papers describing what teachers who are also dissatisfied with old ways have done to change their classroom teaching.

The innovations described in Part Two differ from those described elsewhere (for example, Baskin, 1967). When we began to collect papers for this book, we sought only those by teachers who had made some change in the traditional student-teacher relationship in the college classroom. (This ruled out lecturing via television, new administrative roles for students, and numerous other interesting innovations on campus.) From our experience, we felt that changing the relationship between teacher and student would almost inevitably bring with it a change in the relationship among students themselves, and their experience would increase the resources useful to the group. We discovered far more classroom innovations of the sort we were looking for than we were able to include in one book. Each contributor reported his experience in greater useful detail than we have included here; our authors urge interested readers to correspond with them.

Each of the chapters in Part One suggests desirable changes in the theoretical assumptions on which teaching and learning rest. The

chapters in Part Two deal to some extent with the theoretical framework around which the experimental teaching was planned. The chapters in Part Three analyze in detail the theory expressed or implicit in
these experiences. The last chapter in Part Two also presents a systematic analysis of the roles of the teacher in the learning process.

The Changing College Classroom is for all who are confused,
anxious, or angry about what goes on in the college classroom. It is
therefore a book for deans, college presidents, heads of departments,
trustees, students, parents, professors who teach others how to teach,
and for those long-suffering, underpaid workhorses of the university,
the graduate teaching assistants. But especially, it is a book for teachers who are not satisfied with the results of their own teaching and
want some ideas about what to do to alleviate their own dissatisfaction.

For one reason or another, we were not able to use all the
papers we solicited. The overriding reason was our desire to make it
a short, readable book rather than a reference book. All the papers we
considered were interesting and all dealt with the central problem. We
are especially grateful for the gracious and cooperative attitude contributors showed in the face of what must often have seemed to be
arbitrary editorial decisions.

We hope a place will be found in the professional literature for
an increasing number of accounts of actual teaching—frank reports of
attempts to bring students and teachers together as human creatures
seeking to teach each other and learn together.

Eugene, Oregon   PHILIP RUNKEL
September, 1969   ROGER HARRISON
                                                 MARGARET RUNKEL

Contents

The Authors

JOHN D. W. ANDREWS, *assistant professor, Policy Sciences Program, State University of New York at Buffalo*

MEYER M. CAHN, *professor of higher education, San Francisco State College; associate, National Training Laboratories Institute of Behavioral Science, Washington*

SAMUEL A. CULBERT, *assistant professor of behavioral science, Graduate School of Business Administration, University of California at Los Angeles; associate, National Training Laboratories Institute of Behavioral Science, Washington*

SOLOMON CYTRYNBAUM, *lecturer in psychology, Uni-*

*versity of Michigan; as of January 1970, assist-
ant professor of psychology, Yale University*

NEIL FRIEDMAN, *assistant professor of sociology, Bran-
deis University; formerly director, Freshman
Social Science Program, Miles College*

J. RICHARD HACKMAN, *assistant professor of administrative sciences and psychology, Yale University*

ROGER HARRISON, *Development Research Associates,
Cambridge; fellow, National Training Laboratories Institute of Behavioral Science, Washington*

ROBERT E. HORN, *president, Information Resources Incorporated, Cambridge*

MALCOLM S. KNOWLES, *professor of education, Boston
University; associate, National Training Laboratories Institute of Behavioral Science, Washington*

LEONARD M. LANSKY, *professor of psychology, Univer-
sity of Cincinnati; associate, National Training
Laboratories Institute of Behavioral Science,
Washington*

RICHARD D. MANN, *professor of psychology, University
of Michigan*

MICHAEL ROSSMAN, *theorist and organizer of youth
movement for radical educational change,
Berkeley*

PHILIP J. RUNKEL, *professor of psychology, and research associate, Center for Study of Educational Administration, University of Oregon*

JOHN A. SEILER, *associate professor and assistant dean for the M.B.A. program, Graduate School of Business Administration, Harvard University*

ORON SOUTH, *director, midwest division, National Training Laboratories Institute for Applied Behavioral Science, Kansas City*

NORMAN SPRINGER, *professor of world classics, Saint Mary's College; visiting professor, New School for Social Research*

WILLIAM R. TORBERT, *graduate student in the Administrative Sciences Department, Yale University*

PHILIP R. WERDELL, *leader in the educational reform movement of National Student Association; member of Transition Associates, Washington; former editor of* Moderator

The
Changing
College
Classroom

PART ONE

There is an ideal that has long been basic to the learning process as we have known it, one that stands at the very center of our modern institutions of higher education and that had its origin, I suppose, in the clerical and monastic character of the medieval university. It is the ideal of the association of the process of learning with a certain remoteness from the contemporary scene—a certain detachment and seclusion, a certain voluntary withdrawal and renunciation of participation in contemporary life in the interests of the achievement of better perspective on that life when the period of withdrawal is over. It is an ideal that does not predicate any total conflict between thought and action, but recognizes that there is a time for each.

George F. Kennan
(in a speech given at Swarthmore)

The classical ideal of learning stated by Kennan (1968) has an almost archaic ring to it. The ideal of the ivory tower has not enjoyed wide acceptance since business, government, and industry began to look to institutions of higher learning for technological, scientific, and practical help earlier in this century. As a people, we have begun to take more seriously the point of view expressed by Gardner (1969). No group rejects the former and adheres to the lat-

CONFLICT

How curious . . . that in all of history, with all the immensely varied principles on which societies have been designed and operated, no people has seriously attempted to take into account the aging of institutions and to provide for their continuous renewal . . . The society capable of continuous renewal will be one that develops to the fullest its human resources, that removes obstacles to individual fulfillment, that emphasizes education, life-long learning, and self-discovery. In these matters—our record is uneven—brilliant in some respects, shameful in others . . . We are still far from having created, for either black or white, an educational system that produces self-discoverers and life-long learners.

John W. Gardner
(in a lecture given at Harvard)

ter more than the young intellectuals. The point of view of the young intellectuals is set forth by the two authors whose chapters follow. In their opinion, institutions of higher education are indeed aging institutions, in need of renewal or reform if they are to live. Both authors suggest alternate models of teaching and learning that have been used outside of formal college classrooms. Both are critical of the theoretical basis on which they believe traditional higher education rests, as are many of the other contributors to this book.

Philip R. Werdell

Teaching and
Learning:

If American colleges and universities are to take teaching seriously, they must provide for student development; they must make the private needs and concerns of students a dominant thrust in their policy.[1] The priority for teaching calls for an alliance between educators and student innovators, for more concern for how college graduates act as well as for how much they learn, and for major innovations in the approach to student learning. A highly developed democratic society must shape its educational institutions according to the conflicting needs of individual members of a highly diverse student body and of a society in which individuality flourishes.

[1] This chapter is somewhat abridged and edited from the article originally entitled: "Teaching and Learning: Whose goals are important around here?" in Charles G. Dobbins and Calvin B. T. Lee (Eds.), *Whose Goals for Higher Education?* Washington, D.C.: American Council on Education, 1968. Copyright, American Council on Education; used by permission.

I

The Basic
Process

Mass higher education is already upon us. By 1970, it is estimated, half of the population between eighteen and twenty-one will be in institutions granting degrees. With the growth in numbers of students, there is already a shift from small, sectarian, residential colleges to vast, urban, commuter universities as the principal purveyors of higher education. It is expected that by 1970 most college students will be in major metropolitan centers and will commute to institutions enrolling more than five thousand undergraduates. If these trends continue (and I assume that they will), the multiversity will become the chief means of higher education in the United States.

While the small liberal arts colleges are hustling for funds, facilities, and faculties (and regional alliances, so that they, too, can become multiversities), the multiversity is searching for an indentity. Its growth has been rapid, and its direction and goals defined strongly by interests large and powerful enough to command attention. Business expects the multiversity to train managers and technicians. Government expects it to supply consultants and to perform research. Labor expects it to provide a less expensive degree. Cities expect it to offer extension courses as well as being the intellectual and cultural center of the city. The faculty expects it to extend the traditional undergraduate curriculum and to provide more graduate assistants. Administration of a multiversity is, almost by necessity, a holding action: in the face of conflicting demands and purposes, balance among the competing forces is reluctantly substituted for the more difficult task of molding an institution that best fosters diversity among its students.

During the 1950's educators began heroic acts of self-analysis and self-criticism. Three major collections of research papers offered, at the end of the decade, a resounding indictment of higher education. By this time the United States had become the most powerful country in the world and had committed itself to increasing involvement in international affairs. Yet Bidwell's (1962) *Report on Undergraduate Education in Foreign Affairs* stated that "seniors emerge from . . . college with hardly any more acquaintance with foreign affairs than when they entered as freshmen." In the latter half of the decade, it was becoming apparent that the technological revolution was rapidly creating new societal environments. Yet Jacob (1957) could shock the educational community with his findings that "the college student does not significantly change his view of himself or the society in which he lives as an undergraduate." Many of the country's most distinguished educators offered well-documented findings, in Sanford's (1962) *The American College,* that, in essence, intellectual development and personal development were inextricably intertwined, but that higher education was not dealing adequately with the former because it was not dealing at all with the latter. The verdict was clear: teaching and learning in American higher education are provincial, structurally stagnant, and psychologically simplistic.

A wide range of experimental programs has successfully produced better models of teaching and learning but, for most students, undergraduate education continues to be an extension of the goals, requirements, and methods developed a century ago in response to the industrial revolution. Research demonstrates the great need to reevaluate and reform the approach to student learning, but educators have not succeeded in translating the results of research into broad-based reforms.

An alliance between educators and student innovators could bring to bear a combination of professional expertise and student organizational ability on the task of reforming American higher education's approach to student learning. I have purposely left the labels *educator* and *student innovator* undefined; they would include those who provisionally accept the discussion above and those who are willing to enter into such an alliance.

The condition that would foster an alliance between educators and student innovators is precisely that same condition necessary to a reform of higher education's approach to student learning: student academic freedom. Frankel's paper, *Rights and Responsibilities in the Student-College Relationship* (1966), contained as cogent and concise an argument for student academic freedom as any student has made:

> The right of students to present and to consider points of view of their own choice outside the classroom and the right to do so as an intrinsic part of their collegiate experience, is a necessary condition for students' own free inquiries. The granting of this right cannot be construed as a matter of pedagogical policy, subject simply to the determination of the faculty. It is properly regarded as the recognition of a constitutional right of students, a right they require as a protection against pedagogical domination.
>
> The second reason the view is mistaken that students have no academic freedom in their own right is implicit in [the fact that] students are a part of the educational process, contributors to it and not merely beneficiaries of it. They do as much to educate one another as teachers do, and sometimes they educate teachers. . . . The college has an obligation, insofar as its resources permit, to make its facilities available to students for such inquiries. In doing so, the college does not grant students a privilege. It responds to their legitimate claim, as members of an academic community, to contribute to its activities (p. 242).

The need for a strong policy of student academic freedom is

most urgent when students take responsibility for their own education. It is implicit then that a student must be allowed to make his own mistakes: lacking opportunity to build on his failures, he also lacks opportunity to develop his own successes.

A *Joint Statement on Student Rights and Freedoms* has been endorsed by the United States National Student Association, the American Association of University Professors, the National Association of Student Personnel Administrators, the National Association of Women's Deans and Counselors, and the Association of American Colleges. This statement calls for the safeguarding of minimum rights: freedom of speech, an uncensored student press, right to lawful assembly, confidentiality of student records, due process, and a voice on faculty and administration decision-making bodies that affect the lives of students. Until this policy is effective on campuses, it is unlikely that educators and student innovators will be able to begin an effective alliance. From meetings of students, faculty and administrators, on a campus which works toward such a policy, cooperative efforts might be made not only to assert the rights of students but also to begin reforming higher education's approach to student learning. Without such efforts, confrontation remains always imminent.

Colleges and universities are growing rich in knowledge and poor in understanding. Oversimplified curricula in most American colleges and universities are based solely on a search for knowledge and truth. A problem is solved when the true, correct, reasonable answer is discovered and verified. Knowledge is transmitted when the intellectual analysis of a problem is organized into a lecture, paper, or book. The primary goals of teaching are to transmit an organized body of knowledge to the student and to help him to develop critical judgment. It is assumed that, when a student has amassed a large body of knowledge and acquired a highly developed analytical ability, he is prepared to deal with the problems of society and to pursue further learning on his own. He is left to solve for himself the formidable problem of integrating learning and living.

The goal of an alliance between educators and student innovators should be to develop teaching and learning models which help the student in the increasingly difficult and increasingly important task of integrating learning and living. While cognitive learning should have priority, the process of integrating learning and living clearly demands new emphasis on other kinds and styles of learning. Specifi-

cally, the curriculum must offer experiences in the creative and speculative uses of the intellect as well as analytical uses. Specifically, the
curriculum must offer practice in dealing with people from diverse
backgrounds, of various life styles, with differing goals, as well as
practice in understanding their problems from a distance. Specifically,
the curriculum must offer challenges to act on the basis of what one
understands as well as theorizing about ideal solutions. In short, the
curriculum must introduce to students a variety of styles of learning
as well as a variety of bodies of knowledge. In no other way will a
generation of students be prepared to use what it has learned to solve
the problems of society. In no other way will the student learn that
the pursuit of knowledge and truth is personally relevant: before he
can become a self-directed learner, he must understand that learning
can be self-actualizing.

Until now serious criticism of higher education has tended to
be polarized. On the one hand are those, both educators and student
innovators, who maintain that higher education must assume responsibility for meeting important social needs and that these needs have
been deliberately or inadvertently misrepresented. On the other hand
are those, both educators and student innovators, who maintain that
higher education must first pay attention to the development of the
individual student, and that it now does not. Ironically, one criticism
cannot be met without meeting the other. Teaching and learning models that attempt to integrate learning and living must be relevant to
both.

The following examples of teaching and learning models have
three purposes: to demonstrate that some less analytical styles of learning are as necessary to develop citizens who can cope with major social
problems as they more obviously are necessary to individual students;
to show how these less analytical styles of learning call for risks,
settings, attitudes, and rewards different from those in the traditional
academic structure; to record where such teaching and learning models are being constructed today in multiversities.

PROBLEMS OF THE FUTURE

Education is commonly regarded as education for the future
in the sense that the past and present are prologue. But this avoids a
crucial problem: many aspects of the future cannot now be antici-
pated. Technology in this century is rapidly and radically reshaping

the entire society. In less than a half-century, the airplane as means of transport has changed the rules of warfare, politics, and business. The time from Rutherford's discoveries about the atom to Los Alamos and Hiroshima was only thirty-five years. The first landing on the moon occurred less than a decade after the test run of solid-fuel missiles. How far away is the fusion of man and machine, now that artificial organs, hormone producers, transistorized brain supplements are reality in the laboratory? (Toffler, 1965).

It is difficult even to anticipate scientific and technological advances, let alone to understand their social implications. Yet there is probably no greater social need to which higher education must respond even if it cannot make definitive predictions, much less find solutions. It can, however, provide students with skills for such learning and encourage rigorous practice in their use. A prime skill is that of creative speculation and synthesis.

Even the best academic seminar seldom encourages creative speculation and synthesis; rather, it furthers analysis of existing information. The communication is discursive, the tone is argumentative, the teacher is assumed to be an authority for whose approval there tends to be informal competition, the grading system reinforces informal sanctions against playing a hunch or speculating about the implications of observations. There is a strong, implicit assumption that the student cannot be trusted (Rogers, 1968).

The challenge to higher education is to expose every student to learning experiences, including highly personal free association, more conducive to developing his creative capacities. If a group is involved, the tone should be open and gentle, the attitude should be cooperative and mutually reinforcing. There should be rewards for daring articulation of experiences and theories. The operating principle should be that of suspended judgment (Osborn, 1957).

A variety of teaching and learning models to foster highly sophisticated creative thinking have been developed by educators and student innovators. The Institute for Creative Education at the University of Buffalo has developed a basic course, Applied Imagination, and the basic techniques have been applied to courses in a variety of subjects. Major innovations have arisen from the student-initiated Experimental College at San Francisco State College and from the Campus Dialogue program of the University Christian Movement. At San Francisco State, students were encouraged to design their own courses.

They have produced some highly imaginative approaches to subject matter, and a unique array of courses (*Moderator*, 1966). In the Campus Dialogue program, an essay called a "dialogue focuser" is used to initiate free discussion about new approaches to the problems of education, poverty, and technology (Kean, 1967).

American students today have lived since birth under the threat of the Bomb, have been continually exposed to television coverage of world crises, and have increasingly been able to travel abroad while still in college. They should be gaining a new concern for, and knowledge of, world affairs. Yet the complexity of international problems leads most students to believe that little they learn or do can matter. They will gain little from their "educative experience" as long as they travel in the comfortable company of other Americans, limit their trips to Western Europe, and have little prolonged contact with natives of developing countries. A student may become highly involved in international crises through intimate, on-the-spot television coverage, but when he can take no comparable involving action he will become frustrated or indignant and thus resignation will set in. Every student is concerned that a few people in positions of power could annihilate the world in a matter of hours. Yet because the individual student sees little that he can do to prevent this, he seldom even discusses the subject. Instead, he becomes fatalistic (Groves, 1967).

The traditional curriculum, even if transplanted to another country, will not fulfill the need for exposure to people from other cultures and for practice in listening, even if not with empathy, to their opinions and aspirations (Abrams, 1965). Two elements would be missing: first-hand association with others and the opportunity for intense, personal encounters. Teaching and learning models that might be adapted by colleges and universities are to be found in the work of the Human Relations Laboratories developed by the National Training Laboratories, and in the Training Program for Peace Corps volunteers. In the former, a heterogeneous group enters a two-week retreat to focus upon sensitivity training and interpersonal relations (Bradford, Gibb, and Benne, 1964). In the latter, volunteers are given intensive orientation to one country by a variety of teaching and learning techniques but relying heavily on association with native instructors (Rossman, 1966). The leading student innovation in intensive cross-culture experience is the community tutorial movement in which the new culture is not that of another country but of the *other*

America, the culture of poverty. Students leading these programs have developed a sophisticated orientation to ghetto life, and have developed models for facilitating relationships between student tutors and the children and even with the children's parents.

In today's mass society it is difficult to develop a sense of personal power. It is only through the individual's self-renewal that a mass society can develop social mechanisms for its own self-renewal. Higher education cannot reform the entire society, but its institutions can prepare students to deal with other institutions which can tackle large problems. Crucial to the undertaking is the ability to act from a sense of personal power and knowledge gained by practice in acting on the basis of what one understands, especially when it has been contrary to the formal and informal rules of society or of its institutions. The traditional curriculum is itself an institutional system. It may prescribe rules and procedures, which encourage passive learning, but not action based on the student's own ideas (Rogers, 1968). Higher education is challenged to offer every student an action curriculum, to offer learning experiences in which he can test the consequences and practicalities of ideas in which he can decide which subjects and styles of learning are relevant, experiences in which he can generate his own ideas and select the concerns and problems he will pursue.

Models for action curricula are plentiful. In the Antioch College work-study program, the student alternates academic study with work every three or six months (Stickler, 1964); the Dearborn Program at the University of Michigan integrates internships in business with technical training (Stickler, 1964); the five-year B.A. at Yale allows a select group of students to undertake an independent project abroad between their sophomore and junior years; Eastern Michigan University offers a varied program of work abroad in cooperation with the Peace Corps. Within a single course, an action component even on a mass scale is possible: every student (as many as one thousand, three hundred) taking Introductory Psychology at the University of Michigan has an opportunity to choose work "in the laboratory of everyday living" (Cytrynbaum and Mann in Chapter Fourteen). Student initiative in all of these is obvious. Student participation in the civil rights movement and in urban community action projects was an improvised action curriculum. Models to integrate students' action

concerns with more cognitive learning are now being developed by the
United States National Student Association (Steinberg, 1966).

Research into these teaching and learning models indicates that
they do not disrupt or even displace the curriculum's traditional concern with developing analytical abilities, and that experience designed
to help a student develop his creative ability, social skills, and ability
to act on the basis of what he understands supports and stimulates the
cognitive learning of the traditional curriculum. The creative education models developed by the University of Buffalo Institute for
Creative Education have demonstratively produced improvements in
practical problem-solving and stimulated further reading and study
(Osborn, 1957). The group dynamics and sensitivity training models
of the National Training Laboratories and the Western Training Laboratories have facilitated dealings with others and understanding of
oneself and have furthered purely intellectual pursuits (Schutz and
Allen, 1966). Students in action curricula have consistently fared at
least as well on standard academic tests as those who have not participated in such programs (Stickler, 1964). New techniques of teaching and learning in higher education would give students more opportunity to pursue their personal development, and would help assure
society of a supply of college-educated people better able to cope with
new and complex problems. But the new techniques would not dimin-
ish the important quality of the traditional pursuit of knowledge and
analytical skills.

NEW MODELS

The greatest public service higher education can perform is to
develop persons prepared to help solve society's problems, who can
articulate new needs, develop new directions of learning and doing,
and chart new goals. Only they will be able to assume new roles as old
ones become obsolete. Only those who have gained confidence in their
own identity and direction can chart new goals for society. The challenge is to develop self-directed learners.

The development of a self-directed learner is subjective and not
to be forced. Speeches about student apathy and the need for student
participation in their own education may raise the issues, but they do
not help the student to discover what *he* is committed to learn. Nor
can self-directed learning be cultivated in an atmosphere into which

other thinking and working press; smaller classes may encourage a better understanding of the subject, but they do not help the student to decide what he wants to learn. This cannot be achieved for the student by anyone else; student-members of educational-policy committees may draw attention to student problems and concerns, but committees do not help most students to learn to articulate their own concerns. The institution can develop self-directed learners only by innovating new teaching and learning models through which students can learn their own learning process, learn what they want to learn, and learn how to communicate this with other people. Each of the following models of teaching and learning methods could become fully operational without revisions or reforms in the traditional curriculum, with minimal financial commitment by the university, and without adding new educational requirements for students. Equally important, each is based on innovations that students have formulated in recent years and found successful, and each stems from a longer experimentation by educators. They have been adapted to undergraduate education, and are proposed as a practical, fundamental beginning for an alliance between educators and student innovators.[2]

The Reference Group is designed to help a student to focus on his own learning process. Nowhere else in the institution is he encouraged to work deliberately, nowhere else is he reinforced in this primary task of education. The Experimental College is designed to help a student discover how he can best learn what he wants to learn. It encourages the student to formulate an intellectual framework for studying concerns that now lie outside the formal curriculum and to inquire into traditional subjects immediately relevant to his interests. It is a focal point at which he may attempt, by integrating learning and living, to learn what he chooses to learn. The Individual Growth Program is designed to facilitate communication by placing the vast potential of the computer at the service of the individual student. For the first time the computer would be used to categorize information for the student rather than to make him a category of information.

The Reference Group: At the beginning of the academic year,

[2] The Reference Group is modeled on the Student Stress Program of the United States National Student Association. The Experimental College is modeled on a student program at San Francisco State College. The Individual Growth Program is modeled on a series of experiments with the Facilitator model made by me and several others working with Transition Associates, Washington, D.C.

each student is assigned to a Reference Group, which is fairly small (eight to fifteen students, to facilitate group discussions), and which includes upper- and lowerclassmen, one or two faculty members, and a mixture of personalities and backgrounds. One upperclassman has previously been trained in a group-dynamics laboratory. During the first week of school the group meets intensively to become acquainted and to begin work. The task is not that of a traditional academic seminar but, rather, that of helping all members to learn about themselves —how they learn, what they want to learn, and how to articulate their progress. Attendance is voluntary, and assistance is given to those who wish to change groups or to pursue their goals in a different manner. Students who drop out are offered counsel. The group is encouraged to continue working together throughout the academic year, but must decide for itself how to do so. Alternative ideas and models for working together are fed to the group by the trained upperclassman, who himself meets regularly with other upperclassmen similarly engaged. The training program and the meetings of the upperclassmen are conducted by a small number of creative, skilled professionals.

The Reference Group may be started within a freshman class, perhaps through progressive reform of freshman orientation. The faculty should participate from the beginning, for one goal is to have the group replace faculty advisers once work has got under way. The only financial outlays are in salaries for the small professional staff which runs the program and possibly in pay for the upperclassmen trained in group dynamics. The staff should be responsible to a board comprising faculty members, administrators, staff from the mental health services, and a diverse group of students. The overall program may well be developed at a series of week-end retreats of the staff and the board.

As the Reference Group could bring a personal excitement and relevance to abstract but basic elements of education, it is worth speculating about the possible educational rewards.

Intensive personal experiences that cut across normal social and friendship lines could lend a sense of community to an otherwise fragmented society. Students and faculty would meet on a basis meaningful to students. The training in sensitivity to others and in group work would carry over to other relationships. Each participant would acquire experience in meaningful communication, and the experience gained in cultivating a group dynamic would facilitate organizing new, autonomous groups. As the group continued to meet throughout the year, students could bring up problems as they happen and explore solutions with others who may have the same problems; students might well meet problems which they can handle better, having discussed them already. Upperclassmen would not only bring their own experience to lowerclassmen but also would learn through teaching. The groups would efficiently and continuously examine the total educational experience. Students would be encouraged to bring new ideas, as well as personal problems, to the group. Possibly, many of the cases could be recorded and made available to other groups.

The Experimental College: The Experimental College should be initiated by the students, and is a logical outgrowth of rewarding experience of Reference Groups. The philosophy of the Experimental College is best expressed in the introduction to the Fall 1966 catalog of the Student Experimental College at San Francisco State College: "The idea is that students ought to take responsibility for their own education. The assertion is that you can start learning anywhere, as long as you really care about the problem that you tackle and how well you tackle it. The method is one which asks you to learn how to learn, so that you can set the highest conceptual standards for yourself. The assumption is that you are capable of an open-ended contract with yourself to do some learning and capable of playing a major role in evaluating your own performance. The claim is that if people, students, faculty, and administrators, work with each other in these ways, the finest quality of education will occur."

Students would participate in the Experimental College in addition to taking their formal course load. There would be no single experiment. Each participant would set his own learning conditions; each organizer would be free to set different contexts for different participants. In one central course those who wished to could evaluate the different student experiments. These evaluations would be presented to standing committees and departmental bodies of the university administration and to the Reference Groups. Enough has been done in experimental colleges to make some thoughts about potential educational rewards possible.

The absence of grades would force a student to decide what he wants to learn. The necessity for self-evaluation would help him decide what subject matter was most relevant for him. Student-initiated courses would force the participant to consider not only what he wants to learn but how best he can learn it. Such reality testing would provide concrete experiences for discussions in Reference Groups and would give the student an opportunity to learn from his own mistakes. The absence of requirements would allow a student to begin learning at a point most interesting to him, and would give him time to relate his personal needs to the subject matter and the style of learning he chose. In this way he would be likely to become excited about, and committed to, the learning process. Student-initiated courses would allow students to structure an intellectual framework for studying concerns that normally fall outside the limits of the curriculum—including personal problems. The Experimental College would provide a focal point for the integration of learning and living. Students who accepted leadership in the Experimental College would be assets to the governing bodies of the institution because of their intimate knowledge of student concerns and abilities, their firsthand experience in educational organization, and their access to continually fresh funds of teaching and learning models, which might be more or less successful than the formal curriculum.

The Experimental College would identify problems in the institution's curriculum through attempts to improve the relevance and effectiveness of learning. The number of students who might attend is not less than the number whose educational needs remain unfulfilled by the institution. An Experimental College might develop new teaching and learning styles which the institution could use as models in a process of individual and institutional self-renewal.

The Individual Growth Program: When a student comes to college, he would take a number of tests designed to disclose his plans, interests, problems, and needs. A computer would be programmed to offer him a printout of organized lists: of courses (in a variety of possible sequences); of faculty members with teaching styles particularly suited to his learning styles; of books or references to annotated bibliographies; of students, faculty, and persons off campus with similar interests and concerns; of work-study programs geared to his abilities; of summer jobs and other educational opportunities. Lack of information about a particular interest or concern would be noted, and the student supplied with a standard explanation of how best to pursue independent study, to organize a course in the Experimental College, or to find assistance. Should his interests or needs change, he could, with a shorter questionnaire, obtain new information. Students would help develop new questionnaires whenever they felt that the information elicited by earlier questionnaires was not relevant. The information questionnaires would not be kept unless the student asked that particular data be made available to others. Although the first computer programs would be crude, it would be worth the university's while to employ a programmer, a specialist in questionnaire design, and students to refine the program. Once established, these programs could be used in other institutions so that students could find out whether their interests and needs might be better served somewhere else. The Individual Growth Program is more than a feedback of information. Creatively used, it might produce a number of educational rewards.

Faculty advisers, whose knowledge outside their own fields might be limited, would be relieved of the chore of helping students select courses and informing them about the intricacies of sequences of study. Students would not have to rely upon perhaps inadequate information. The adviser's time would be available for the more difficult, important task of discussing, in Reference Groups, students' approaches to learning. The Individual Growth Program's most valuable service would be informing students of others who have similar interests and needs but no one with whom to work and learn. A student who had learned to organize his own learning experiences in the Experimental College would profit greatly from others with similar interests. In larger institutions, a student is often wise to choose most of his courses according to teacher rather than content. The Individual Growth Program could refine this process by offering information about teachers in terms of their effect on individual students. Listings of courses and teachers would become available for students' perusal as soon as the information was approved, and possibly this would make the scheduling of courses more flexible. Students seldom think of summer jobs and activities outside the university as being intricately connected with their courses and extracurricular activities. From the Individual Growth Program, students could obtain information about summer jobs and other off-campus activities, such as unrelated courses, travel, volunteer services, that they seldom connect with the formal curriculum.

The computer is invading education. Almost universally it is used to store information (the memory banks full of student test scores), to centralize (the numerous IBM cards filled out at registration), and to standardize (the teaching machines) individual students. The Individual Growth Program would do what is long overdue— place the computer at the service of the individual.

Higher education can criticize society most effectively by acting upon the major criticism it has been making of itself. It is crucial that the institution of higher education, especially the multiversity, should begin by building teaching and learning models to reinforce and assist students to become self-directed learners. In doing so, the institution would develop a self-renewing mechanism for itself and for those who are ready to participate in the process. Individual, and institutional, self-renewal would become more than an educational slogan: it would become a dynamic, working process intrinsic to the identity of the institution. With its new identity, the institution would not only be more responsive to the individual needs and concerns of its students but also be more active and effective in the development of a freer world.

Michael Rossman

Learning and
Social Change

I want first to talk about the failures of the university, not analytically, but evocatively. For we now have available much percep-
tive analysis of the social and human failure of the university and,
behind that, of the failure of our entire educational system. But no
one listens, by which I mean that this analysis seems to have no impact upon our actions. This in itself is one of the crucial failures of the
university, and because of it we all may die.

In 1965 there were five ghetto riots; the following summer
there were twenty; in 1967 there were eighty. At this writing, a year
after the Kerner Commission's Report (1968), the first fact of life
in America is that the root causes of racial violence have not changed.
The hungers and pain we have chosen to create move toward a desperate awakening. I say chosen because none of this is accidental. As
many analyses point out, it comes as a natural function of what America is. And the least cynical and bitter thing I can find to say of this

II

The Problem
of Authority

is simply that the social structure we have constructed to deal blindly
with our numbness, our anger, and our greed is on the point of col-
lapse; we shall have to find another way. Halfway around a world
we are trying to dominate culturally and economically there is the
war. Many Americans feel that it is not only immoral but badly run
and dangerous. It begins to press unbearably upon our lives. All this
is no more accidental than the ghetto situation; at home and abroad,
America is acting out her nature. These are simply the most dramatic
present examples, although they may not be the most important. If the
analyses which say that this is so are correct, we shall have to find
ways to change America's nature, or we shall die.

Universities are not irrelevant to these problems. They do research for chemical warfare and make profits as slum landlords. Their
campuses keep blacks out and let the army in. Men with prestigious
academic credentials are the architects of our foreign policies and do-

mestic neglect. So the university is a deep and willing accomplice in practices that mean disaster for us all. This sad relevance is not surprising, for the university, far from being made of ivory, is cut from the very center of the American fabric of assumptions, motives, and institutions. But what is truly terrifying is the deeper irrelevance of the university. For it simply does not equip us with the tools to begin to solve the critical social problems of our time. It does not produce the knowledge we need; its sociology and political science have not informed us usefully. It does not help us acquire the skills we need. Its graduates, taken all together, do not know how to control their government in a way which ensures the satisfaction of their needs within a healthy society. Indeed, few of them seem to have the sense that the government is a thing to be controlled. This is not to say that the university—or the entire educational institution—produces no useful knowledge or skills. But historical judgment is clearly being made upon our educational system: too little, too slowly. Whether now it is also too late is not clear. Nor is it clear what we are to do if it is not.

Many good people, even some who recognize that we are flirting with genocide at home and abroad, still feel that it is not the university's function to serve as a tool to make the tools to solve the society's problems. They do not reply directly to the contention that our society has no other institution which fills or can fill this function. They do argue that the university's basic purpose is quite different: to preserve and transmit the intellectual heritage of our culture, and to train new workers in those vineyards. This ideal of the university was formed in an earlier, ivy era, when higher education served to train a narrow elite in a narrow spectrum of skills. Now it is the morning after a night of change and we are suffering from a cultural hangover. Suddenly America has become a technological culture heavily committed to universal, liberal, higher education. In this new time the university is a new institution whose nature is hidden under the rhetorical cloak of an old purpose.

Those who try from scratch to analyze its present function find that the university trains people in skills that the technological economy and culture find most immediately useful. And, if the educational system is the society's main socializing mechanism, the university also functions as the delicate and crucial last main segment of this mechanism. Beyond this, there is little clear and useful discussion of what the university's function ought to be, or might be; of whether it serves its present functions well; or indeed, of whether it should serve them quite differently. We do not know what the institution is *good* for. All we know now, if you grant that the institution itself extends far beyond the classroom walls, is that almost all of the young of the culture's main class spend a crucial part of their development within its boundaries—and that, if education is the process that ought to give people the ability to meet their individual and social needs, our education is disastrously inadequate.

The disaster is more diffuse and less dramatic on the personal level than on the social level, but no less massive. If you take our literature seriously as a barometer of the inner weathers of America, you will read that mostly we lead lives of uncertain frustration; we are vaguely and powerfully dissatisfied, without knowing why or how to change our lives. All the other guides to our condition, from the literature of social psychology through divorce statistics to the tests in the *Readers' Digest,* confirm this. Your secret nightmare, if you are young, is that sense of emptiness.

It is appropriate, in serious talk about the function of the university, to mention matters which form the topics of midnight bull sessions in undergraduate dormitories. In these sessions we speak and try to learn about the matters which are most important to us in our full personhood. Later, looking back on that constant delicate web of conversation that forms what we might call our nighttime university, we recognize its importance and place it more accurately as part of our university education. The tragedy is that we carry on that conversation so badly. We rarely realize this, having few visible standards of comparison. We rarely connect this dimly sensed failure with our powerful sense of dissatisfaction. Nor do we realize how strongly the conversation of the nighttime university is influenced by what goes on in the daytime university. All that is clear is that the university's failure to provide us with the tools to meet our needs is much the same on the personal and the social level. We have little sense of control over our selves or our contexts; and we are not much good at talking to ourselves or each other. All this is another sort of death.

The background then is this: our culture is moving toward crisis on all its pain-filled levels. Neither as individuals nor as social beings are we very good at changing our behavior to satisfy our needs. We measure learning by changes in behavior. Whether we decline Spanish verbs or create a nonviolent society, this seems to be a useful description. If we extend this operational view to say that we are what we do, changed behavior is equivalent to changed identity. So learning, behavioral change, and identity change are alternative names for the same human process. These three terms seem interchangeable on the social level also. To say that a society or an institution learns, is to say that its subinstitutions and processes behave differently; that its identity changes since this identity lies in the actions of its parts upon its persons. When this change is great enough it is often called a revolution.

But there is an intimate connection between these two levels of learning, the individual and the social. The importance of the connection is clear. For we who are numb to inner lives, which we cannot control, are also numb to feelings about the far foreign flesh that chars beneath our napalm, and to the pain that swells to riot bursting in our black ghettos. The connection is simple and deep. It derives from the fact that the *individual* and the *social* are but different perspectives, or levels of description, of a single human complex; not separate but conjugate, in the sense that each prepares the shape of the other and carries this shape within itself. There are other such pairs of conjugate perspectives which fit intimately together: *personal* and *cultural, private* and *public*. Individual learning and social change are two faces of a single coin. Their interconnection is deeper and more natural than this trite metaphor conveys. So it is not surprising that the skills of the individual learner parallel the group skills of the society which is able to change; that the problems involved in changing private behavior mirror those involved in changing public behavior; or that the processes by which individuals and cultures reconstruct their identities are closely similar. Given all this, there is a potential power in talking rather abstractly about the skills of learning and the problems of building changed environments.

It seems useful to think of a good learner as someone with a certain set of skills. He knows how to formulate problems. He can identify the relevant information and resources available in his environment. He is able to choose or create procedures and to evaluate his results. Beyond this, he has a set of higher skills that we might call *metaskills*. Described loosely, they include the ability to know what he wants (or needs) to learn; the ability to see clearly the process of his own learning; and the ability to talk with others to help learn these metaskills. Given all this, he is able to create useful knowledge. He is an autonomous learner, for he directs himself. These skills and meta-skills are somehow natural: little children are wizards at accomplishing useful learning. If older children and their institutions were equally skilled, we would be less involved than we are with failure and death. The problem is that we construct environments that stunt and warp the development of these skills.

Consider the university as it now exists. By its very nature it forms an environment that inhibits the development of autonomous learners. For teaching, in higher education, is generally taken to mean a particular way of conveying information which is already known. It is based on the assumption that the student must have a certain quantity of knowledge before he can question what is known or before he can create new knowledge. His arrival at graduate status is usually, but not always, accepted as proof of minimum preparation. So the creation of knowledge, usually comprising either research or scholarship, becomes an expert's job. The teacher's task is to transmit knowledge; the student's task, to learn it.

In this model of education, problems are identified for the student by experts and authorities who also define and supply the problem-solving approaches. Relevant information is labeled as such by authorities; they evaluate methods and results by comparison with known solutions. Described this way, the reason for calling it an "authority-centered model" are obvious.[1] This model is more or less suited to the university's hallowed mythical purpose: the transmission of the culture's intellectual heritage. It served (and still somewhat serves) to train scholars to order, preserve, and present established knowledge.

The university's current main function—to service a technological economy and culture—is quite different, but this earlier model of education still seems compatible and it still persists. It trains people for a style of technical expertise, and prepares them for preestablished social and technical roles. The man educated in this mode makes himself useful in immediate, limited, and necessary ways. He is prepared to deal with the problems whose nature is well-defined and which can be approached from within an already-formalized discipline or style of thought. Training in this model generates a particular notion of the nature of useful change: it is conceived as a linear, continuous

---

[1] For an extended description of this model and a countermodel, see Harrison and Hopkins (1967). This essay has helped to clarify my thought about learning.

advance within the existing organizations of knowledge, technology, and society. It is explicitly not revolutionary.

Well-defined problems must be dealt with, and linear advance should be effected whenever it is appropriate. Any notion of education must include some version of expertise, some development of the indispensable sense of what it is to "know in depth." But the authority-centered model at best equips its products to function well within the bounds of a discipline. The trouble is that all real human problems are transdisciplinary. Even the designing of a building requires the integration of a whole spectrum of skills, of which structural engineering is the least important. Our increasingly uninhabitable cities testify to how poorly we accomplish even this. In fact, authority-centered education is not particularly well-suited for the university's present function of servicing a technological society. Not only are its products unable to cope well with the problems such a society generates—the inner problems, the social problems, the foreign problems—but also, and more immediately, it prepares these products less and less well for their social and technical roles, the task for which the university is supposedly designed. There are two reasons for this growing failure of the authority-centered learning system to satisfy even its own goals. One is that the jobs for which it trains are changing. The direction of change is from animal husbandry to social worker: that is, the jobs are becoming increasingly transdisciplinary. The other reason is that the nature of the society's jobs and roles is changing fundamentally. The increasing rapidity of social, technological, and intellectual change means that the traditional notion of a job, as involving the application of fixed kinds of knowledge to fixed kinds of problems, is becoming unreasonable. (This is reflected in a limited but striking way in some fields of engineering in which a graduate's knowledge is outmoded within five years unless he undergoes an almost continuous retraining.)

Taken together, these trends suggest an appropriate set of skills: those of the learner who must constantly be redefining and re-creating his competence so that he can deal with problems that cannot be isolated from the social environment (and thus become targets for attack by experts). He must develop information and resources from the entire social environment. He must define the problems themselves and generate relevant approaches to them. He must be concerned, not so much with verifying established truths, but with the social processes involved in dealing with people's attitudes, with reconciling conflicting information, and with searching for imperfect but viable solutions that can result in action. Hence, he must be able to establish his own criteria for success. These skills are necessary not only for solving real problems, but also for directing one's own learning as a process of continuous change to satisfy one's goals and needs. They are the skills of the autonomous learner. Ironically, they are precisely the skills which are inhibited by authority-centered learning and by the system of education based on that model.

There is always a problem of how to set limits on the expression of energy. Sometimes limits can be generated flexibly from within the energy itself, permitting great freedom of expression. More often, limits are imposed from outside, with less flexibility. We have a particular style of doing this, in America, which I will call the authority complex. It permeates our culture.

In America, authority is typically exercised as a function of fixed and centralized roles in an hierarchical system. Its face is always benevolent, but its power lies in coercion by some framework of punishment and reward. It controls energy and change to satisfy its own needs—in particular, to preserve the status quo of power relationships, and to ensure that its own nature and form do not change. The consequence is always some form of cultural imperialism, in which the identity of the controlled individual or group tends on all levels to become an image or extension of the authority's identity.

The authority complex is visible throughout the university. Advisers police permissible study lists. Dorm mothers police permissible hours and clothing and sex. Deans police permissible political activity. Professors police permissible readings and methods of learning. In each case the justification is "for your own good"; the effect is to inhibit autonomous adulthood. One consequence is the lack of a range of behavior in any of these domains: people in college look, think, and act alarmingly alike. In fact, if you measure the existence of freedom by the presence of diversity, it would seem that the authority complex inhibits freedom as well.

Our culture's central failure is its inability to help its people and itself learn how to learn. The root cause of this failure is the culture's style of handling authority. Rather than learn to change our culture, we must change our culture to learn. It is a bootstrap operation; it may not be possible, but some people are trying to learn how to begin, and trying to define a science of beginning. The prevailing model of education is knowledge-centered in that it assigns roles to participants on the basis of their relation to this knowledge. The expert makes it, the teacher owns and transmits it, the pupil absorbs it. In any given learning group, these roles are assigned relative permanence. Given his expertise, his bankroll of knowledge of a certain subject, the teacher becomes the figure of authority in a class, and authority becomes permanently vested in him. This *role-defined authority* harms autonomous learning, partly because almost always it evokes the authority complex. This is true even when the teacher is not embedded in a system of tests, grades and similar punishments. For we know only one main way of relating to authority in this culture. We are conditioned, and our expectations tend to create a punitive framework whether or not authority has a whip in its hand. (This is one of the main stumbling blocks in creating groups with more flexible patterns of authority.) Considering teachers and students generally, it seems that the lesser part of the framework of punishment and reward running through their relationship, in class and out, is expressed formally—as in graded tests. The greater part occurs in a generally wordless dialogue of approval, reproof, glance, and gesture, in which both parties participate equally. Those who have experimented with a model in which there is no fixed authority—as we did in the experimental programs at the University of California at Berkeley and at San Francisco State College—are amazed to discover what happens to cardboard *C* students when they cannot find someone to play the game of "stay in your *C*-student role." After they get over their initial confusion they often abandon the role and become significantly more independent and creative.

In the field-theory of learning,[2] in which the self-directed learner plays a prominent role, we take the behavioral view that knowledge is what a learner creates, and learning is the evolution of appropriate responses in a context. Then it seems more useful to configure the roles of expert, teacher, and pupil back into a single field and try to understand what does or should go on in the field in which the learner is embedded. To begin with, the field must be viewed from the learner's perspective. From this perspective, for someone simply to hang knowledge up in the air of a lecture hall and expect the learner

[2] For ideas about field theory I am essentially in debt to a fragmentary and abandoned grant proposal written by Cynthia Nixon for the San Francisco State Experimental College in 1966.

to incorporate it into his personal patterns of thought and behavior seems unrealistic and inefficient. This is teaching in name only. The real teacher or leader is the person, or group of persons, who acts on the learner's environment—the field situation—so as to draw from him new and appropriate behavior.

There are two important things to be said about the idea of a learning field. First, all the elements of the field are seen as being active. Each contributes to producing a change-inducing (or retarding) climate or field. Each necessarily is changed by any change in the field, including those it initiates. This model is both more accurate and more worthy than the current one, in which change is largely thought of as the result of action-at-a-distance, or teaching-by-telling, originating from a static central source (the teacher, the administration, the departmental structure) which does not change in the process. This model is more useful for making change than the current one, which is constrained to regard students as neutral, irrelevant, or even hostile elements in producing a learning field. Because of this flaw in the current model, the largest single teaching resource in the daytime university—the students themselves—is almost completely wasted. When students are used, it is with the explicit title of apprentice teacher, as if, to share their knowledge, they had somehow to become a different species. But students are, in fact, active agents of change. There are few schools where significant change is underway; at most of these, students have initiated it. In the institutional landscape, and in the classroom, we are having to think anew about agents of change. This brings me to the second point about field theory, which is that its broader perspective of agents of change helps us to create a different style of exercising authority. In a group context, learning displays itself in the ability of the group to go on. Awareness of the group and of individual styles of learning, and of the emerging nature of a problem, is used to produce appropriate behavior; deliberately to change the group's learning field. Thus the learner, in going on, consciously shapes the direction of the group's development. Alternatively, the learner is the group's leader; and the central problem in the design of a learning group becomes that of good leadership—possibly a different notion of leadership. Usually the function of guiding a group's development, however badly, is called teaching. Now, like *individual* and *social*, *teaching* and *learning* are alternative, interdependent descriptions of a single human process. And so learning, in our sense of leading, involves not only the creation of knowledge, but also the conjugate part of this process: the communication of thought and behavior to others so that they can use it.

Therefore, since the goal of each member is to be able to take on the group's leadership when appropriate, he wants to develop the ability not only to learn and present information, ordering principles, and basic assumptions, but also to facilitate the learning process for others by clarifying problems, unblocking difficulties, and so on. This demands attention to a wider spectrum of skills than those usually involved in the roles of teacher and student. It requires a sense of the individual learning patterns of the group's members and a deep sensitivity to group dynamics: to all the concerns that arise when you think how intimately we impinge upon each other in a group where people are changing. In fact, the spectrum of skills involved in this model is broad enough to suggest that good learning makes possible creative and appropriate action not only within one's work, but also, and simultaneously, upon the quality of one's life.

A learning group organized in this style begins as a set of students who have some idea of what they want to learn and how they want to learn it. They may decide to recruit more learners to fill out the group, and, if needed, people to serve temporarily or permanently as resources of knowledge—for example, technical experts or group-process specialists. The core of people whose previous learning fits them for the function take the leadership at first, by beginning to present the ordering principles of a body of knowledge. They direct their leadership and the group's work so as to invite the active participation of the others in affecting the directions of inquiry and study and in providing additional knowledge, old or new.

Two factors encourage a response to this invitation. First, work that is self-chosen is a powerful internal motive. The model takes seriously the notion that people will choose to learn what they are enabled to choose to learn. Second, each participant begins with a beachhead of leadership which he can then expand. He is the authority on his own precise position in the learning field: on the state of his learning, on the group's ability to satisfy his needs, and on his ability to elicit appropriate behavior changes from others. This authority is significant in a group centrally concerned with mutual participation in a field of mutual interaction where it provides a common denominator of leadership. In such a group, authority is inherently distributed rather than centralized.

The motive in designing this learning group is to set in motion a conversation between leader and others that uses authority in a flexible and participatory fashion to generate its own limits from within. The model assumes that the group is sensitive enough to its processes to discover a conversation that develops naturally once the metaskills are freed from the demands for conformity from an overbearing authority. In such a learning group, the ability to assume leadership is expanded by watching others lead; learning is catalyzed by watching others learn. This suggests that the best resources are advanced students who are capable of recreating learning experiences they have only recently experienced, or people skilled in this way of facilitating learning. It does not imply that these facilitators need be experts in the specific material being studied. It does suggest that the best way to help others learn may well be by displaying raw chunks of developing understanding, with all their sloppy edges dangling, and all the ego-danger this involves. (People who have spent a long time actively playing authority roles or being subjects of authority generally find this quite difficult to do.)

This brings us to the last essential element of this model, and I state it strongly. What is needed is love. You cannot learn with people you do not care about enough to care for in some essential way (as, for example, their being who they are). That kind of caring is not dramatic, but is indispensable. Most of us are not good at it; we need to work hard, in every learning group, at creating the atmosphere of trust on which the group's successful functioning largely depends. It is imperative that each member be perceived and perceive himself as learning and responsive, rather than as playing a stereotyped role which rigidly limits his growth. His exposure to good examples of behavior-change (learning) on the part of others in the group may lead him to feel that the rules governing his behavior and the group's behavior have been expanded. That is to say, he may indeed have his mind "blown" by an example, and his self-limiting set of expectations enlarged. But there must still be an atmosphere of trust in the group for him then to be able to make a statement, a guess, a touch, or an attempt in the open space of his enlarged expectation. The act of learning is always an act of freedom in the sense of being an attempt to move freely, in an unstructured space, creating one's own structure and behavior. You cannot move freely when you're hung up in satisfying other people's expectations, or when you feel you have something to lose. What is needed is trust based on a willingness to let, and to help, people be who they are, so that they may be able to take genuine risks in a search for learning. There is not much of that in the standard college classroom.

PART TWO

In the current controversy and conflict on campuses the forgotten men are the faculty who wish to teach and the students who wish to learn. No matter what the outcome of political conflicts and power struggles, the focus of attention must eventually come back to the relationship between these participants in the teaching-learning process. The question of how this process is to be made more effective is only partly a political one; it is very largely a question of the technology of teaching and learning. The authors of the following chapters sought new ways of asking the question. These chapters show concrete examples and proposals that can be put into practice by individual teachers without awaiting the outcome of attempts to change the struc-

NEW PRACTICES

ture of the educational institution. They are case studies demonstrating what is possible, using, in most cases, only what any educator has at hand: himself, his subject matter, his students, and his understanding of teaching and learning. Since the older conceptions of teaching methods have yielded no significant differences in academic achievement (McKeachie, 1968; Dubin and Taveggia, 1968), there seems little reason for college teachers to hesitate to adapt to their own styles whatever innovations and new conceptions among these chapters seem attractive. All of the authors will welcome requests for further information; some have additional evaluative data to offer.

Meyer M. Cahn

Teaching Through
Student Models

In these times, as colleges increase their enrollments, the teacher
becomes aware of at least two important issues. One, class size, has
recently been dramatically argued at Berkeley. There, as elsewhere, the
student is threatened with becoming a statistic and the classroom becomes more and more a place where he is endlessly spoken at. The
other issue is not so well known. In junior colleges, which are in many
places providing at least two years' worth of universal college education, there is a classroom atmosphere that falls further short of providing effective communication. At least in the university, lectures
often consist of ideas, facts, summaries and issues which the student
can condense into notes, and later discuss with his campus colleagues.
In the junior college, the student is often far from ready to perform
these tasks. His aptitude for college work—as shown on scores of national tests—is low. Many junior-college students have severe reading
problems. In some colleges more than half are unable to pass the ordi-

III

City College
of San Francisco

nary college-entrance English tests. That many of the students are really not motivated to do college work—or even to be in college—is of greater concern. There are others who are extremely able, are highly motivated, and are hungry for this new opportunity to grow and develop.

The City College of San Francisco has classes for the students who have not passed the basic English test. The teachers have been challenged to develop special courses that take their problems into account and still enable them to enjoy the college experiment. In some cases this challenge has inspired the development of courses that are considered to be more useful than traditional courses not only to these but to all students. Films, field trips, photographic essays, group discussions, and other means have been used to explain the subjects more effectively. I developed a course in which I attempted to deal with the challenges in a way that was novel for me as well as for the students.

37

In the early part of the course—before the experiment phase began—this class of about twenty-five students met in-the-round, and presumably we covered our material through discussions led by the teacher. The course material consisted of philosophical essays, short stories, poetry, paintings, architecture, and music. Actually, no more than a handful of talkative and enthusiastic students participated in these discussions. The others remained observers, and apparently rarely studied until examinations were announced. They simply sat in class— surreptitiously uncomfortable, feigning interest and knowledge, but unprepared to participate. I never quite knew who my real partici- pants were. The whole thing seemed patently dishonest. These stu- dents were not really studying, nor were they learning how to study. Though physically present, and technically a part of the school, their hearts and their selves were far removed from this experience. They forfeited the opportunities which the in-the-round arrangement is de- signed to encourage: peers talking to peers in a free manner, peers learning from each other, peers judging peers. There was little oppor- tunity to deal with their erroneous views of both text materials and the statements by the more verbal students and the instructor. Their com- ments, both written and oral, frequently revealed such gross miscon- ceptions that it was difficult at times to know where to begin—without long and arduous individual tutoring.

In general, there was a lack of personal commitment to the whole enterprise. This would be difficult to accept in any course; in a humanities course dealing with man's destiny and his significant modes of expression, this lack of commitment was particularly tragic. Surely this could not go on, even in an educational system that toler- ates all sorts of meaningless activities and somehow permits student lethargy to become the norm in an arrangement that looks like an ordered system of graduated accomplishment.

At least the beleaguered teacher might make a brief experi- ment, an attack on student ennui, on lack of commitment, on the lack of genuine activity commensurate with their youthful spirit and latent abilities. My objectives were: I wanted the students to be honest about their own position in the class. If they were active students, they were to be active students, genuinely playing this role with all its risks and rewards; if they were observers, they were to play this role and accept its benefits or losses. I wanted the discussions to be per- sonal, to reflect the concerns and understandings of the students themselves. I wanted the students to experience the glow and excitement of becoming deeply and personally involved—with people, ideas, questions, and issues. I wanted them to know this excitement and to glory, if possible, in the aftermath of knowing that this experience had caused them to change for the better, had caused them to grow in powers that they would relish and treasure.

For many years, I had dreamed and talked about a college which divided its student body into students and observers, each clearly designated by goals and behavior. Students would sit with the teacher and communicate with him and each other; "observers" would watch. Now was the time to see if there were merit to the idea. No one would give me a college to experiment with, but the class was mine, and the failures were mine. First I changed the seating plan. Instead of a circle, we had a U-shaped seating arrangement. A table for

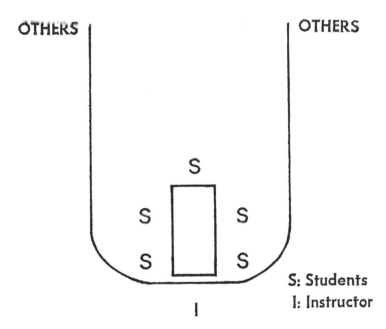

OTHERS   OTHERS

S

S   S

S   S

S: Students
I: Instructor

I

five students was brought forward to facilitate a small group discussion between the students of the day, and the instructor.

To become students class members signed up for a particular panel discussion. The opportunity was made available to everyone. The first three panels were on Nietzsche, Existentialism, and an autobiographical essay by Tolstoy. The first two panels were filled (five for each) but we could not quite staff the third. When the entire class was canvassed, the procedure was repeated. During the semester, some people eventually sat on six or seven panels. Gradually more and more class members consented to sit on panels. Each person decided whether and when he would sign up. Late in the semester, when some of the habitual observers decided to enter the panels, there was more than casual drama in the decision itself—the class not only recognized this, but facilitated in subtle ways the success of such ventures.

Students of the day were given about a week to prepare for their panel assignments. They were expected to study the essays and other materials in depth, to consult special articles, books, newspapers, journals, and any other appropriate or interesting source. The panel members on art (Van Gogh, Rouault, Kandinsky, and Klee) were asked to bring reproductions, books, and other helpful art materials or reports of experiences. Visits to art galleries were encouraged. Students were asked to become experts on their assignments, and many of them took pride in this challenge. They pressed harder, some told me, than they had ever done before, but liked it. Their industry was stimulated partly because they would be exposed to the judgment of the rest of the class (all sessions were taped). There is no doubt that many of them did not enjoy the position of doing unsatisfactory work under these conditions. As one student put it: "I find the panel a motivation to learn. I mean, I have to learn the material not only because I'm interested in it, but I'm going to be on the spot if I don't know it. I've already committed myself to sit down at that table with other people who are supposed to know that material, and I have to use what I learned against, or for, anybody—against somebody who might challenge me, you know. So to me, it's a motivation to learn . . ."

Perhaps in our traditional classes we too seldom expect open and judged performances from our students. The instructor carries the main burden of making limited judgments based on examinations, term papers and verbal recitations—which seem to have gone out of style or to have been abandoned as class size has grown. Students have become apathetic onlookers. When the burden is transferred from the instructor to the student; when the student, not the teacher, is to be seen and judged, he must do what the teacher usually does. He must prepare thoroughly if he is not to be embarrassed before his peers. In such classes he is likely to become excited; other students like him are excited; the teacher becomes excited. Here are the makings of a lively and meaningful hour. When students, in a discussion that engages their feelings, sense that others are interested and absorbed, the level of performance and satisfaction is raised even higher. Add to this the natural enthusiasm and energy of youth which is, in this case, directed toward a positive, personal and immediate learning goal and the classroom becomes an electric, intense place. Initially the students show the same tension that new teachers experience. As they learn to work in this way and acquire greater polish and ease, they loosen up and even allow some humor to creep into their discussions; some develop grace and style in the process.

Having established the job requirements for students, and implied that all others would be observers, we found that we needed another category, that of the intermittent participant. This included people who had something to say about the subject under discussion, who had special information or special experience they wanted to share. It also included the congenital talkers who simply must speak. The intermittent participants, "those who would like to join in the discussion from time to time," sat on both sides of the instructor. To permit panels to get well into their own discussions, the intermittent participants could not join in until twenty minutes had passed. Often this proved painful for enthusiastic students—and often we overlooked the rule if events were exciting.

Initially, the observers were ignored. It was hoped that they would find their role unpleasant and would, in time, abandon it. Although all but one or two eventually entered at least one panel, it became apparent that some class members would continue to confine themselves to the observer role. In small group discussions, the quiet ones find it more and more difficult as time passes to enter the discussion. Though they may want to speak, they need something special to say in order to justify a change of behavior after such a long silence. We attempted to counteract this through new rounds of panel assignments, and through direct and indirect encouragement. There must have been a great deal of informal outside discussion about the entire class experience; I cannot say how these outside discussions influenced the observers to change roles. In time, the intermittent participants and the observers were given additional responsibilities. They were asked to judge the performance of the students, to make written comments about their contributions, to express any disagreements they might have with the participants, and to evaluate and grade the students.

This carried the potential for valuable feedback for the students. It turned out to be an important element in knitting the class together as a group of people communicating, learning, and feeling that they were being critically judged as they did so. All the basic elements of performance, exposure, judgment, and activity were present.

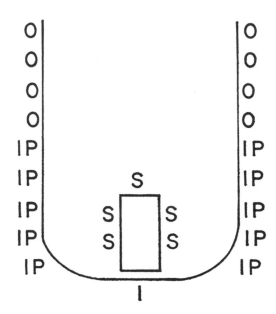

O: Observers
IP: Intermittent Participant
I: Instructor

FINAL SEATING ARRANGEMENT

Besides the personal feedback to each student, peer judgments offered another advantage. We could now safely and reasonably reduce class tests. Each class session was a test, not only of the performer, but also of the judge. More class sessions could be devoted to discussion; more reading materials could be dealt with, and the setbacks to morale that customarily follow formal tests were forestalled. Our situation more closely paralleled the future life of these students in that they were being judged every day on everything they were doing. Class life was really one long test. The anxiety and energy usually devoted to preparation for being tested were funneled into every-day experience, thus giving it a force and drive that gave it the excitement of an experience that counts.

A group meeting is hard to report. One needs to be on the scene to sense the frustration, the good will, the interchanges, the surprises that develop in groups. Looking across the table at each other, answering each other, doing business—school business of the highest order—made all of us respond to a higher common denominator than we had thought possible. The level of interchange was admirable and mature. Students gave each other attention and respect. If the instructor spoke, they listened with almost frightening intensity—the teacher was teaching. All of us were experiencing a higher level of achievement than we had come to expect in classrooms. Compared with similar classes I had taught, this class was more highly motivated; its members freer and more intimate. Discussions were continued beyond the classroom, and there was a fine intensity to them. Often they began before classtime. What were the forces at work here?

When we attempt to assess educational methods and results, we often find it almost impossible to cite specific cause for any apparent improvement. Improvement is often the result of the teacher's enthusiasm for the situation. It may have been that the personalities of those particular members combined happily to yield splendid results. More than once I considered whether we might develop a tentative hypothesis about student models of behavior and use and test such models with other students in a classroom setting. The importance of models in our daily lives is difficult to quantify, although we know a few things about models and their meaning for behavior. We know that infants and young children are particularly vulnerable to the models which their parents set before them. The process of identification, which is probably the extreme of modeling, works its way quite effectively into the personality and hence affects the future behavior of offspring who share an environment with the parent. We are learning more and more about the effective force which other associations have upon the child, and upon the adult. There is a powerful and lasting effect of enduring relationships among children of the same age. Teen-age associations and teachers also make their imprint upon the personality of the growing person. With a broadening circle of associations, it becomes apparent that, as one moves out into society, there are affects which result in behavior of one sort or another. The cultural anthropologist might call it acculturation; the educator might consider it simply the result of socialization. We do not yet know much about imprinting except for what we have learned in the laboratory about animals and their behavior. Possibly humans, too, are imprinted behaviorally in a massive conditioning, which leaves them quite markedly changed, by interaction with certain people at certain vulnerable periods in their lives. We do know that human beings affect each other as they interact, sometimes quite profoundly, and that the lasting effects of this interaction affect future behavior more than is commonly realized.

If the models with whom the growing person interacts are so vitally important to behavior, we might well ask a few questions about models in education, questions such as: What models are generally found in the classroom? What responses do these models evoke? How do these models correlate with our objectives in education? Do these models create problems of social expectations, freedom of the individual, spontaneity and individual differences? Are our usual models good? I cannot answer these questions, but I believe them to be germane to educational experimentation.

In the traditional classroom, the teacher is the main model to be observed by the students. In one way or another, students find themselves interacting with this model—some intimately and successfully, others distantly, with less success. Recognizing what we know and feel about age-mate relationships and their importance, we cannot dismiss the models set by peers, models in which we have the behavior of those students who made themselves known in one way or another, perhaps by exemplary behavior, perhaps by some degree of antisocial behavior.

Another model, one which deserves more attention, is the general group tone which sets forth group expectations to its members. The values, goals, and procedures of the group are translated into everyday behavior by its members in unmistakable terms—limited by the group's cohesiveness. It may be that this element of group expectation distinguishes different schools and classes from each other and accounts for the degree of effective learning that takes place. This is not to say that the teacher does not contribute to group expectations, but rather to emphasize the fact that not only the *dominant members,* but *all* members make their impact on the class. Eventually the group tone is set, and group expectations become clear to all.

The experiment described in this chapter was the behavior exhibited by the better students as they spoke, thought, and responded to the materials at hand with a sense of commitment to the whole enterprise of education. It was a model set by peers for peers. Peers were interested; peers studied and read as widely as they could; peers showed enough concern to relate school materials to their own lives. The model incorporated thinking, challenging, and being challenged in a forthright manner, working together to achieve an understanding of the subject and, at times, drawing on the teacher's knowledge and views for clarification of the issues.

The students who were interested exhibited interest and were the most active; the less interested were less active. These roles were fluid; a student could determine his own status—student, intermittent participant, or observer—on any given day, and would then have to play the appropriate role. If he chose to be a student he had to come prepared, to be interested, to think about the materials even before the discussion began. Thus the student was responsible for his own condition. He was free to choose his role, knowing the responsibilities, the rewards, the risks, and the status which accrued from his choices. He was not automatically a student by virtue of admission to the class. He had to earn this status. He had to see how difficult it is to maintain this role. Perhaps once a week, or once every two weeks, a young person can be a genuine student in a large or medium-sized class. On other days he may be only an intermittent participant, or perhaps just an observer. Pity the traditional classroom which relegates these young people primarily to the role of observers. Pity the potential students. Pity their parents. Pity the community. Pity an educational system which says it cannot do otherwise.

We developed new roles not only for the students, but also for the teacher. There were no lectures; there were few formal presentations of material. The teacher was not expected to present the learning materials to the students. It was assumed that the students could do this for themselves, and that they could was proved time after time. The teacher could and did elaborate upon the materials as the need for it grew out of the context of the discussions.

The role of the teacher was, perhaps principally, that of organizer. He was responsible for seeing that at any given moment there was some significant learning experience for all participants—students, intermittent participants, and observers. He was the manager of the experience. In addition, the teacher had to stimulate students to the point where a high standard of learning activity was set and maintained. He could accomplish this by direct challenge, by reinforcing exemplary behavior, or by setting an example as a good participant himself in the group discussions. When high standards of learning activity were not present, it was his task to point this out. Careless, listless, impersonal, unnecessarily argumentative, or uncommitted students were dealt with openly; it was pointed out that such behavior was below the standard of the group. When discussions were exciting and to the point, when personal but relevant ideas were introduced, when the argument ran hot and dealt with private concern illustrating commitment to the materials at hand, then the teacher reinforced this behavior so that students would be encouraged to behave in this way and to provide a satisfying model for all to share.

Apart from organizing the setting and stimulating the participants, the teacher was mainly a discussion leader. Students had to be trained not to engage in one-to-one conversation with the teacher, although it was most natural for many of them to do so since most conventional classroom discussions are not group discussions at all, but short conversations between certain students in the class and the teacher. To encourage and facilitate group discussion, I used various methods to disengage myself from the conversation. To encourage the speaker to direct his comments to his own group I would not look at him. After an opening question, I tried to remain silent long enough to get the discussion well launched before I made any comments. Some students always wanted to speak directly to the teacher rather than to other students; this probably tells us a good deal about their bondage to authority figures. One of the real tests of the teacher's ability as a discussion leader lies in the handling of questions directed to him. When he skillfully redirects the questions to the group, he usually finds that students can answer questions satisfactorily. I found this true when students began to feel liberated from their passive role and to enjoy their active one. When they were actively engaged in discussions, as in the smaller groups, they were more than ready—they were eager—to take on questions that seemed beyond them. When the questions were unfathomable, an unbelievable amount of curiosity and concern was directed toward the teacher who was then able to perform a unique and needed function for the group.

When the discussions were good, observers watched with an

impressive intensity. At times their participation as listeners was rapt. When I asked them, after a particularly lively discussion, if they minded their role, one student replied, "No, not at all. I felt I was right in there myself. I wasn't actually talking, but I was there. Do you know what I mean?" I had hoped that someone would say something like that. But it was not always this way. Some observers were concerned about their role although they were unwilling to become active participants. I found it necessary to assure observers that they could submit papers, and some of them wrote weekly papers outlining and discussing the essays and assignments. After about ten sessions, though, I felt that I had to know more about the observers. Were they unhappy? Did they feel ashamed? Was this a debilitating experience for them? I wanted to check their morale, and to find out why they chose the role of observer. I wanted to assure them that I was concerned for their welfare and that I would like to help turn the experience into a fruitful one for them. The ten observers comprised 40 per cent of the class, too high a proportion of the entire group to be taken lightly. I decided to see what I could find out by talking directly to them as a group. The observers seemed relieved to be alone with me, and I, too, was pleased. I tried to draw them out so that I could discover what kept them from speaking in class. After a halting, difficult opening, they tried to give me their reasons: they would rather listen than speak because they did not feel comfortable with the materials; some were frightened of the brighter students in the class beside whom they felt inadequate; some were afraid to speak at all. They were chieflly concerned that the readings were difficult and they felt behind others with, apparently, some earlier experience that gave them the advantage and confidence to be active participants.

I was impressed with the general friendliness of this group. When we had finished discussing their role, I felt that they were relieved to have clarified their position in the class to one another and to me. When I asked them to suggest other ways of contributing to the class, they asked only to do some extra work to hand in. I presented other alternatives. They could listen to the tape-recordings and report, to the class, the discussions which, after all, were quite fluid and somewhat unpredictable. One observer was willing to try this. I suggested that two observers, who accepted this bookkeeping with relief, record the evaluations of the panel discussions.

We parted in good humor, but not until one of them, who had

said nothing up to this point, proposed rather vigorously that I meet with the observers in this fashion one half hour a week to deal with them separately and at their own pace. He was not supported by the others, one of whom said vehemently that this proposal was nonsense: if we were talking about discussing subject matter, the observers could do this in class; if we were to practice speaking with one another, the conversation scarcely deserved this priority. There it ended, but I am sure that there was more to this problem.

Later it turned out that the observers had other motives. One who had been submitting excellent papers and finally entered the discussions toward the end of the semester admitted that he stayed out of the panels because it was easier. When students questioned him, he said, "Don't you always take the easier way? I do." The class disagreed and clearly told him so. Another observer who entered the discussions late made students reconsider their cajoling efforts to get him in. In his evaluations, he gave no student more than a D: he felt that most of them were being duped—by the authors and their ideas, by the teacher, and by one another. Students were sometimes tough in their reactions to the observers and their passive roles. When grades were discussed, one student said: "It's like some people not being able to do their homework, just like some people can't stop murdering . . . you have a handicap. Sometimes you have to pay for it; sometimes you don't. We're trying to figure out whether they should or not. Some of you people are trying to say that these people can't; that their problem is like a sickness. But you can attribute a lot of things to a sickness . . . murder, robbery—all kinds of things. It's always the 'poor little kid whose mother didn't like him, didn't treat him right.' You can always explain things away by talking about 'those poor people.' But in the end they have to pay for it. You have to pay for their handicaps. You can't just write them off and say 'I'll excuse them; I'll excuse them; I'll excuse them.' I mean, sometimes you have to pay."

As in almost any group which criticizes itself, the active participants were often concerned about the less active ones: The talkers made well-meaning efforts to invite the observers to perform tasks of importance; sometimes all discussion was set aside as they dealt with this. "The observers can tell us what we're doing wrong," was one proposal. "They can give us suggestions." Modifications of the help that the nontalkers might give to bring them into contact with the entire group were developed. Some class members objected strenuously to being labeled nontalkers, and, indeed, objected to any description that set them apart from the rest of the class and its accomplishments.

A concern for moral issues wove like a thread through the discussions; this moral theme seemed to be one of the most significant aspects of the entire experience. Time after time I noticed that students themselves took a position of moral leadership which led to interchanges relating directly to their own lives. One such instance grew out of a discussion of Herbert J. Muller's *The Uses of the Past*. Muller says that, in an age notorious for its skepticism and irreverence, we have a "continued need of an adventurous spirit—of still more creative thought, bold, imaginative, experimental, self-reliant, critical of all infallible authority." We asked ourselves where any of us had exhibited those qualities in our school work. One student replied, "I can't think of where I have been bold, but I can sure think of where I wish I had been bold." When questioned, Roger recounted that one of his teachers had maneuvered out of her class a student who had challenged her authority and judgment. Now in this humanities class he was saying, "I wanted to challenge her on this—and on many others things [but did not] want to be thrown out of class, too—or get an *F*." At this point leadership moved to a strange corner of the room. Mark, a boy who was not noted for his scholarship, but later became one of the most influential class leaders, took Roger to task for his fears and his failures. He did it softly but effectively. "Using her way," he said, referring to the teacher, "all you could lose would be a grade, or at most, one semester of your life. Using your way, you get your self-respect—and that's forever." Mark's moral message made a deeper impression on the lives and feelings of those students than anything I could possibly have said. During the silence that followed, the moral implications of the issue were being deliberated by all those present—not only by Mark, Roger, and me.

We often speak of spontaneity, play, naiveté, and trust as qualities of childhood. We forget that young college students have their own special qualities which can transform their world into a place of enormous importance. My class had these qualities. Their intensity, and their quick acceptance of it, made the spirit quicken. Some facts they knew, and they could account for this knowledge. They could question their colleagues with the challenging innocence that young people use with great effectiveness when given half a chance. They kept searching for truths as though this were their business—as it is. They argued. Young people argue beautifully, sometimes around the barberry bush and back again, given the opportunity. In their evaluations, although they were consistently tough, they gave credit where it was earned. At first glance one might assume that it was the subject matter which lent itself to inspired talk. The subjects included the philosophies of Kierkegaard, William James, Tolstoy, Sartre, and Existentialism; the work of such artists as Van Gogh, Rouault, Kandinsky, and Klee; the writings of Kafka, Faulkner, and some modern poets. However, it might also be argued that students of this grade level and cultural background would not easily become involved in such challenging work. More than one critic of this course has said that the material was irrelevant and too difficult for college students of their caliber. However, I am convinced that there was no magic in the subject matter that would have stirred these particular students. Nor was the material itself irrelevant to their interests—*once they became involved.*

It was exciting to see these young people struggling with ideas, to see them hammering away at meanings, catching them, losing them, moving adroitly like detectives sometimes, and falling flat on their faces at others. Often they moved with remarkable speed and efficiency. Their memories, as they repeated what others had said, were astoundingly accurate. Their feedback, as they reminded each other what they had said earlier, was startlingly honest. Candor seemed natural to them, and they applied it with ease. It was a tough experience, not a soft one. These young people seemed to be able to take it. Apparently they take it all the time, and we teachers too often do not see. No teacher can help catching fire when the fire of youth illuminates a problem. When the teacher catches fire on the rebound, he feels a force long since gone that must surely be his own youth returning to help him. He must surely be grateful for this—grateful to everyone, the students, the observers, the school, the community—everyone. For now he has found the spark that sent him into teaching, the thing that some have said would never be felt. In this case the feeling was so strong that it could not be denied.

Neil Friedman

Experiment on a
Black Campus

In the late 1950's, white America rediscovered the Negro. In the early 1960's, it rediscovered the poor. Starting with fewer infantry-men than Gideon's army, the civil rights revolutionaries pushed the federal government into declaring war on poverty. In both cases, grandiose labels disguised reformist protests and programs which have achieved modest successes. At the present writing, both glorious movements seem dead. It looks as if the undeclared war in Vietnam has ended the declared war on poverty.[1]

The civil rights and antipoverty movements were responsible for focusing attention on upgrading the education of youth of the

[1] The work of the following staff members of the 1966 Freshman Social Science Program helped me: Walter Draude, Diane Liff, Ronald Kaiman, and Bruce Rappaport. The writing of this paper was supported by the Division of Behavioral Science Research, Tuskegee Institute. Another version of this essay appears in the *Journal of Negro Education*.

IV

Miles College

Negro poor. This attention has outlived the more dramatic demands of both movements—perhaps because education is the most tame method of social change. In any event, we are still in the midst of innovations in what is euphemistically labeled "the education of the culturally deprived." One such program is the Miles College Freshman Social Science Program initiated in 1966.

Miles is a private, unaccredited, church-related Negro college on the outskirts of Birmingham, Alabama. Its one thousand students commute. Many hold down forty-hour-a-week jobs. Many come to Miles only because academic, financial, or family conditions keep them from escaping Birmingham. The largest major field at Miles is education. Between 5 and 10 per cent of its annual graduating class of about one hundred goes directly on to graduate school.

Before 1965, incoming Miles freshmen could take courses in communications, world history, math, science, language, religion, physical education, and effective living. In 1965, a course in English was introduced to supplant communications. In 1966 social science supplanted world history. (Lucius Pitts, Miles' President, and John Munro, now Dean of Freshman Studies at Miles, were instrumental in beginning the freshman program.) The world history course was really a course in western, white civilization. It studied the world as if Europe and America were the only existing continents. The textbook started at the beginnings of man and wended its weary way up toward the present. Students dropped off like flies at various points along the way. Faculty morale was low. Trained historians with esoteric specialties droned away to large, resting and restless introductory classes. Students at Miles talk freely of the profound dislike for history they had cultivated in high school; this dislike emerged from that world history course intact or reinforced. Miles' students were not visibly enthusiastic about western, white civilization—neither the course nor the reality.

For many Miles students, the world history course had been their one and only general education course in social studies. The course had been copied, most likely, from a classical curriculum whose aim was to acquaint majority-group students with their heritage and thus produce liberal, knowledgeable, well-rounded human beings.

For several reasons the course at Miles was failing to realize its dubious objectives. For one thing, exactly what the relevant and engaging heritage of the Miles student was had become highly problematic. Enthusiasm for Negro (black, Afro-American) history was far more obvious than any for white western history. To be mundane: one cannot liberally educate students in a course that puts them to sleep. Moreover, in a rote memory and content-oriented course, students could not begin to develop the diverse skills that they could develop in a course that exposed them to the questions and techniques of various social sciences. Finally, the world history course had been in no way pragmatic. The social science course tried to be pragmatic in the best sense: to increase student awareness and involvement in contemporary social issues so as to increase the student's control of his world. We felt that a course that introduced some of the methods, concepts and questions of the various social sciences—always in the context of the student's real life concerns—could better serve him than world history had.

A recurrent theme at Miles is that students are not motivated. Essentially, this means that they do not throw themselves into the educational activities designed for them by their teachers with anything approaching the verve and elan that they save for other, usually frowned upon, activities. We felt that students would be better motivated if they could identify with the material they were studying. As Cuban (1967) has noted, there is no evidence as yet that teaching them Negro history produces more mentally healthy Negroes. On the other hand, it is difficult to deny what one sees: Negro history motivates Negro students in a way that Greek history does not. This is not to say we taught only Negro history; we probably taught too little of it. What we did was to present material, whatever the topic, in a way that made students feel part of it. To take two examples: the duties of a circuit court judge were taught through a play about the trial of a Negro accused of killing a white; the methods of historians were studied by reading conflicting interpretations of Reconstruction.

The world history course had forced Miles' students to run the gauntlet. Almost perversely, it exposed the student's every weakness. Miles' students are poor readers, they were given a huge textbook; poor at note-taking, they were placed in large lecture classes; weak in writing about abstract ideas and nonexperiential topics, they wrote voluminous essays on long ago and far away subjects. For students who have, so far, existed on the academic margin, who have fragile self-esteem and a greater than average fear of failure, this approach is bound to be self-defeating. We tried, in freshman social science, to ally ourselves with the students' strengths to fight their weaknesses. Unfortunately, Miles' students are usually described in terms of atrocity statistics: this many broken homes, that many low reading scores, delinquent backgrounds, and so on. However, if one looks at them, one also sees considerable strengths. Riessman (1962) has done the best job of cataloging the strengths of students like those who come to Miles. They are on the whole stronger in motor skills than in ideas, wiser in the ways of the world than in the ways of the classroom. We tried to teach through media that use these strengths: role playing, audio-visual materials, fieldwork, skits, group debates and discussions. We found that, generally, students talked, wrote, and learned best, when they had recently had an experience they could talk, write, and learn about. Learning by doing was therefore an early step in almost everything we studied.

Why did we not simply replace one year of history with a few months each of sociology, politics, history, and economics? Why did we not organize our courses along disciplinary boundaries? We felt that such an approach would make some sense only if we were training students to become professional social scientists. At Miles this would not have been a contextually realistic goal. We decided instead to show how the social sciences can work together to illuminate various aspects of the same subject matter. By selecting as our units various social issues, we tried to define and approach reality, not in the terms with which academicians slice up the pie, but in terms of topics that would increase the students' social awareness and involvement.

Attempting to involve students in that amorphous residue called world history conveniently obviated, for Miles, issues of involvement in community life. In this respect, the world history course was symbolic of the college's predicament. Miles is usually spoken of as a community college. Primarily, this means that it takes students from the Negro school system and sends them back to teach in the same school system, thus serving the community. In reality, like most Negro colleges, Miles' overall attitude to the ghetto is a mixture of fear, disdain, and uneasy separation. The school administration is most sensitive to the black bourgeois element in Birmingham and so, despite its rhetoric and its reluctant sponsorship of some anti-poverty programs, it is basically unresponsive to the call for producing students trained to attack ghetto problems. Much of the faculty's effort goes into helping students escape, like prisoners of war, one by one from their humble origins.[2]

One guiding principle of the social science course was to invent exercises that sent students out into their communities physically and to study topics that involved students in community issues emotionally. For example, students attended their neighborhood civic league meeting the night before the November election. They drove neighbors to the polls. They collected jokes, folk tales, and superstitions from older people in their communities. They monitored neighborhood antipoverty elections. Our entire unit on poverty was concerned, however unsuccessfully, with community organization. We

[2] This attitude helps explain progressive education's failure to make a significant impact at colleges like Miles. Progressive education begins by starting where the students are. Many Miles' faculty cannot start where their students are because they consider that where the students are (their life situation or life style) is shameful, sinful, and contemptible. A criticism of the freshman social science course reflected this viewpoint. One experienced teacher told me we were sending our students back into what she was trying to help them forget.

attempted to orient our students toward involvement in the problems and struggles of their brothers and sisters.

Each member of the freshman class had to take social science. On the basis of a reading comprehension test, the four hundred students were divided into twenty sections—two honors, eight regular, and ten slow. Some of the usual inflexibility of such a track system was eliminated by our policy of moving students up or down as the year progressed. The nine staff members taught two or three sections each. All but one of the original staff members were white. Seven were graduate students who had taken a year out to teach. Six Miles upperclassmen acted as teaching assistants; one taught a section. Classes met five days a week for an hour each day. The students received eight credits for the full year course.

Each section studied four units during the year. The first three units were: politics—the 1966 Alabama elections; economics—poverty; methods of social science. For the fourth unit, each teacher could develop a unit of his own choosing. Ten of the twenty sections studied Negro history.

We chose to teach politics first because Alabama was having a volatile gubernatorial election in the fall of 1966. We studied the election to increase the political sophistication of our students and to show them how they, too, might get political power. We hoped to teach those principles of political science that would increase their know-how in politics. We decided to focus on the qualifications, duties, powers, and campaigns for four offices. Two of these were the statewide races for governor and senator. The other two were county contests for circuit court judge and board of education member.

We began by drawing and writing four cartoonlike handouts that described the qualifications, duties, and powers of the four offices. The idea for such presentation was taken from voter education materials prepared by the Student Nonviolent Coordinating Committee (SNCC). Our material was written simply and illustrated vividly; its content was purposely propagandistic. We felt that students might care about these offices if they knew just what their incumbents could do for (or to) them. Excerpts from a trial that was acted out in class illustrate our general approach:

The State Versus Jack Jones

Narrator 1:   In order to understand the powers of a circuit
                 court judge let us follow a made-up case through
                 court. We will focus on those choice points where
                 the judge's decision can decide the fate of the de-
                 fendant.

Narrator 2:   Here are the facts of the case. Jack Jones, a Negro
                 male, shot and killed a white policeman in Jeffer-
                 son County.

Judge: We have a jury here that has been selected from a
                 list of all those persons who voted in the 1960
                 election. Does either the prosecuting attorney or
                 the defense attorney wish to challenge any jury
                 member?

Attorney for   Your Honor, I contend this entire jury should be
Mr. Jones: disqualified since it contains no Negroes and the
(Defense   list from which it was drawn contained no Ne-
Attorney):   groes.

Judge: Motion denied.

Defense   I then ask that juror Number 3 be removed be-
Attorney: cause he is well known for his anti-Negro feelings.

Judge: Motion denied.

Prosecuting   Your Honor, this is really an open and shut case.
Attorney: Jack is a mean nigger; we all know that.

Defense   I object to the use of the term "nigger" to refer
Attorney: to my client.

Judge: (*in bored tone*)' Objection overruled. Continue.

Prosecuting   As I was saying, Bill, uh, I mean, Your Honor,
Attorney: everyone knows Jack. He is 6'2" and 220. Patrol-
                 man Cracker, rest his soul, was 5'8" and 160. And
                 he was a good man; why he was nephew to the
                 deputy police commissioner . . .

Defense   Objection . . .
Attorney:

Judge: Overruled . . .

Prosecuting   Thank ya! I will call just one witness . . . Would
Attorney: Miss Southern Belle please take the stand.

We spent about three weeks on this material. At the same time, we began taking field trips to local campaign headquarters. Our students listened to white workers extol the virtues of their favorites, asked pointed questions (Why was the county board of education foot-dragging on integration?) and then wrote papers on what they saw, heard, and felt during these trips. White candidates came out to Miles to speak to the students (an unusual event) and, in class, we discussed their presentations. These class discussions and papers examined the trips and visits from both the political and the interracial perspective. The intersection of the two was often most fascinating. Sometimes we analyzed the manouvers by which white candidates endeavored to retain control of situations despite students' efforts to take control. Sometimes we analyzed the various inhibitions that kept students from taking control. Each section discussed what the man said about the office he held; but it is worth mentioning that the interracial situation created by the trip or visit became itself fertile ground for personally meaningful discussion.[3]

When we knew what each officer did, we next had to find out how one gets on the ballot to run for the office. The staff wrote a five act play about five ways of getting on a ballot. Study questions suggested relevant comparisons among them. A portion of the act describing the Lowndes County Freedom Organization (whose president, John Hulett, addressed the students later) captures the play's tone:

Act III—*The Mass Meeting*

First   We have seen how established political parties
Narrator: select candidates in primary elections and con-
            ventions. But your choices are not limited to the
            choices offered by established political parties.

[3] One of the latent functions of the Negro college has been to insulate its students from the white world and vice versa. Such insulation is, at this point, a profound disservice to both parties. We tried to make the fence surrounding Miles a membrane permeable from both sides. Two important hours for one of my sections were the hour we all ate downtown at Britling's Cafeteria after visiting Democratic campaign headquarters and the next hour spent in class discussing our feelings and actions in the cafeteria.

Second Narrator:	Citizens of Alabama can hold a mass meeting.
Third Narrator:	This really happened in Alabama this year. The Lowndes County Freedom Organization held a mass meeting and picked candidates to run under the symbol of the Black Panther.
Hulett:	We are here to form a third party. I think we have to do this because we have to form our own power structure.
Third Black Citizen:	I don't know if this is such a good idea. I mean, there are Negroes in the Democratic Party.
Hulett:	*Rich* Negroes . . . They are there only for personal power. They get into positions of power and then just walk over their black brothers and sisters. (*Cheering.*)
Fourth Black Citizen:	I don't like the black panther symbol. That seems to say there's no place for whites. Some whites have helped us.
Fifth Black Citizen:	Things have been white for too long now. Why can't they be all black awhile? I've lived my whole life in Lowndes. I've been fired from my job, thrown out of my house, and beaten up. I need a black panther on my side.
Sixth Black Citizen:	And also, illiterates will see that black *cat* and know they are voting for a *black* cat . . .

What do you do once your name is on the ballot? You go out and campaign. So the students next got involved in the three steps of political campaigning: polling, campaigning, and getting out the vote. Students first administered a lengthy political-preference poll, the results of which were discussed in class. They then used the poll results as they went out and campaigned either for the candidate of their choice or for a bloc vote. (At this point we were working closely with the Negro leadership of Birmingham, which was urging a bloc vote.) On election day, all Miles freshmen were excused from classes to take voters to the polls. Students had identified those in their areas who were going to vote for their candidates; now they were to be sure that those people did vote. Students were assigned to precincts and boxes, with a student captain for each. On the evening of election day, fifty students met to watch and discuss the election returns.

The remaining two weeks of the political unit were taken up with other speakers and discussions of the election results throughout the country. The unit ended with the students' reading a political glossary, written by the staff, which attempted to show that the concepts of political science actually come from practical experiences of politics —some experiences that they had now had.

We had studied the elections because they were there. We studied poverty because it was there. Unfortunately, elections are quadrennial carnivals while poverty is more enduring.

In the poverty unit, we wanted to emphasize an action-oriented approach to poverty. We wanted to study three things: who the poor are, why they are poor, and what can be done about poverty. We also wanted to introduce a book, *The Other America* (Harrington, 1962) so that we could begin to move the students away from their too-heavy dependence on oral tradition. Most of all, we wanted to keep uppermost in everyone's mind that we were studying the categories and causes of poverty in order to do something about it—and it was our inability to do something about it that kept the poverty unit from succeeding. As one staff member suggested, "We really need to go out and organize a community but this seems, unfortunately or not, out of the question in terms of time and resources." Our compromise was to read about various community organizations that successfully fought poverty.

The unit failed in its grand objectives. Basically, the staff sank deeper and deeper into a collective depression as the sheer weight of the poverty problem became clear. *The Other America* proved to be a book directed to a middle-class white, Anglo-Saxon, Protestant (WASP) audience. It did not rouse students. Disengaged from concrete community activity, our thinking on community organization and the psychology of poverty was expressed in much too sophisticated terms. Our students were never, on the whole, convinced by our analyses of the strengths of the poor. This is not to say the unit was a total waste. We made our best use of films in this unit. *Harvest of Shame* brought to life Harrington's chapter on rural poverty. Films showed better than we could say what poor people could do for themselves. Scene-by-scene analysis of films by the class proved another way to bring out our students' articulateness.

Staff-written essays giving six different possible causes of poverty led to some heated class debates. We were also able to link brief field assignments to large issues. A field assignment, to do comparative shopping in various kinds and locales of stores, led to discussions of credit, ghetto stores, ghetto economy. Comparisons of various kinds of local and federal antipoverty programs led to discussions of participatory democracy and the federal system. The two honors sections monitored the Jefferson County antipoverty program's election "of the poor by the poor" and discovered how corrupt the voting really was. Then the classes were faced with the question of what to do with their findings. The antipoverty agency had held the election in order to get funds released from Washington. Our class had devastating evidence that the voting was a fiasco. But class members also were aware that there were people in their communities who knew that the students had been monitoring the election, people who felt it best for the funds to be released, people who wanted the funds under any conditions. After some soul-searching, these future intellectuals had an important emotional experience: they sold out.

The poverty unit dragged on into the second semester. The staff then came to an impasse. In retrospect, the conflict appears to have been clear: should we study Vietnam or Negro history next? (The solution would have been to do first one and then the other.) But at the time we compromised by doing, as a group, a unit on methods of the social sciences followed by a free choice unit in which each instructor could do a pet project.

The way we approached methodology illustrated again our action (in many senses of the word) orientation. Methodology can and usually is taught with reference to a philosophy of science textbook on problems of measurement, validity, and so on. We started differently. We asked ourselves what research methods we had found fun to learn about and to carry out. We wanted to teach how social scientists go about gathering their information by having students go out and gather some—and enjoy doing so.

We began by having the students administer a Social Distance Scale in their own neighborhood. We discussed how to do the survey, the principles behind it, and then analyzed the results gleaned from it. One class administered a distance scale of its own design to whites. Moving to anthropology, students again went out into the community to collect and analyze folklore, music, jokes, proverbs and superstitions. They were trying to infer what they could about a culture from these bits and pieces of it. One class sat through *Blow Up* twice and then reported what they learned about England's mod set from it. Another successful assignment was to give students fifty proverbs from an unknown culture and have them, using only the proverbs, describe the culture. The methods of the historian were illustrated by having the students compare the differing assumptions, examples, and inferences in two opposing historical views of Reconstruction.

We concluded the methodology unit by studying the social psychology of conformity for a week. The main event was a staged experiment in which particular students had either to conform by giving wrong answers to arithmetic problems or stand alone before the entire class and give the correct answer. Students saw a film on conformity, read a *Scientific American* reprint on it, and discussed the class experiment and its implications.

Looking back, we found this unit entertaining but superficial. It would probably be wise to start a course like this with such a unit. The quick jumping from one topic to another keeps things from getting too deep and too dull too fast. In the meantime, as the teacher gets to know his students better, he can ease into the more substantive and controversial units which require more than the usual amount of rapport between teacher and students.

Ten of the sections studied Negro history for their free choice unit. Here I will say something about the different materials we used for the slow, regular, and honors sections.

The predominantly white staff had been playing all year with the idea of doing Negro history. One year at Miles had convinced me that *The Autobiography of Malcolm X* would be the one most successful book any instructor could assign. We were, however, involved in a curious, but not, in the Negro college, unusual, paradox. A predominantly Negro college was doing painfully little to foster black consciousness. (The faculty once voted down a motion to institute even an elective course in Negro literature.) A predominantly white social studies staff was eager to do so but felt, shall we say, unequipped for the endeavor. The whole irony pressed too sensitively on our complex feelings about being, as white teachers, in a superior relation to black students who, we were hoping, would break out of their traditional inferior relation to whites. The only compelling answer that ever came to the recurrent question, "Who are we to be teaching Negro history to Negroes?" was, "If we don't, who else here will?" Eventually, some of us decided that white people should teach Negro history if no black people on the faculty were going to do so.

Fortunately, the students seemed to care less about our color than we did—at least, they did not let it interfere with their enthusiasm for Negro history. The slow sections, for whom material usually had to be laboriously staff-written or rewritten, were able to use *The Freedom Primer* put out by SNCC and *The Zenith Books* on Africans and Negroes.[4] Both sources glorified the enduring culture and history of black people in Africa and America. Teachers did different things with these materials, but it really did not seem to make too much difference what we did as long as we let the students have the books and answered their questions honestly. The regular sections used *Before the Mayflower* (Bennet, 1966) which was a hit. One honors section tackled with great success a highly motivating introductory assignment: "Go to three high school American history books and see how many of the Negroes listed below are mentioned in each one. Also see what is said about those mentioned. Find out from some books in our library who the other Negroes were and what they did. Then write about a five-page paper comparing the image of the Negro in high school history books and the image you have after reading the other books. Include in your paper a chart showing which Negroes are mentioned in each school text. In the paper discuss the causes and effects of omitting certain people from the school textbooks." The list was: Allen, Attucks, Banneker, Bruce, Bunche, Carver, Devine, Douglass, DuBois, Garvey, Revels, Salem, Turner, Vesey, Washington.

OUTCOME

Those were the bare bones of our program. One or two other important aspects of the year's work have to be noted. The freshman social science program at Miles acquired a reputation for being "where the action was." This was very important. A lot has been written about the effeminate nature of ghetto schools and how they force their

[4] The Zenith Books are published by Doubleday Anchor Press. They would be excellent for junior high, high school, and junior college students.

best students to prove their real manhood elsewhere. We certainly did not solve this problem. But we did consciously try to be dramatic, relevant, militant, and irreverent in the hope that some of Miles' dramatic, relevant, militant, and irreverent students could identify with the course and so educate themselves.

In this effort the administration played an important, though somewhat involuntary role. Early in the year we scheduled our four hundred students—except those who did not wish to do so—to attend the Wallaces' first rally, at the Birmingham Municipal Auditorium. We knew this was not a routine assignment. We had planned carefully for it and had spoken to Wallace's campaign manager, the city police, and other Birmingham officials. Our students were armed with suggestions of things to look for at a political rally. In a dramatic meeting, on the day of the rally, the college's president called the class to the auditorium and canceled the assignment. I had the opportunity to disagree with him publicly on the matter. About fifty students later attended the rally without incident.

The meeting was to prove, in many ways, a crucial moment for the program. What it did most immediately was boost our morale as a staff and let us close ranks with the students against the stodgy old administration. At the time, the dramatic confrontation did wonders for developing student interest. However, because the meeting seemed to pit Negro administrators and faculty against a small group of white trouble-makers, it brought into the open a political problem which plagued us throughout the year. Our reputation for irreverence endeared us to students but estranged us from fellow faculty and administrators. In two telling cases of mistaken identity, we were blamed for others' derelictions.

Our success with Negro history was also aided by an apparently fortuitous event. Stokely Carmichael spoke on campus just as we were starting the unit. His brilliant evocation of the need for black people to know their history did far more than we could have done to introduce the topic. (I have often thought that tapes of that speech should be made available to any group starting to teach Negro history.)

We also tried to be innovative in our use of Miles students as section leaders and, again, ran afoul of the administration. We felt that good Miles seniors could work well with a class either on their own or along with a regular teacher. One senior led a section on

Negro history; the regular staff member (white, male) became her assistant. We did not make as much use of such aides as we would have liked to, but our experience did suggest that Pearl and Riessman's (1965) ideas about new careers for the poor have validity.

We should make clear that our program was something less than an unqualified success. Perhaps my biggest personal disappointment was Miles' inability to adjust to our innovations and our inability to handle the resulting controversies. Our public relations effort was poor; we had a bad image. Some people at Miles called us communists; some Negroes exploited the racial issue ("don't listen to those bad white folk") to sabotage our efforts at building race pride. Looking back, I am still saddened and amazed that our rather mild program evoked such extreme responses.

Miles College is teaching freshman social science again this year. Ultimately, whether or not the program will ever be truly significant depends upon the road the college itself takes. It should come as no surprise by now that black colleges find themselves caught in curious dilemmas. Their students are cultivating their black consciousness. They are militantly attacking authoritarianism and paternalism—black and white. But the curricula and administrations in these colleges too seldom cope with these developments. Where are the courses that encourage community involvement? (I do not mean social work.) Where are the programs that analyze and deal with ghetto problems? Where are the courses in African and Afro-American literature, art, music, culture? Where is there a major in Afro-American studies? Where are administrations ceasing to be benevolent despotism and recognizing student power?[5]

Miles College freshmen still have to look forward to an antiquated version of higher education. One year of real learning is not enough. Perhaps the students themselves will have to reshape their curricula to fit their nascent interests. Whether or not the college adapts will be the best test of what it has learned from freshman social science.

---

[5] To add to the list a slightly different kind of rhetorical question: Where is there a course on the civil rights movement? Where is there a black college in the deep South that is actually integrating? Tendencies in all these directions are too few.

Robert E. Horn

Experiment in
Programmed Learning

The descriptions in the 1965 Teachers College summer catalog were not much different from a thousand other course listings, but the twenty-five graduate students found themselves in a unique learning situation—a prepared environment containing twenty learning stations.[1] I greeted each student, asked him to fill out administrative forms, and invited him to have a look at the learning station area of the room. "You mean we just wander around until we find something we want to study?" was the usual question. "Yes. Here's a list of possible objectives; they might be of some use to you. The room will be open from eight in the morning to four in the afternoon every day. We will have a group meeting most days right after lunch." The stu-

[1] This experiment would not have taken place had it not been for the invaluable assistance, enthusiasm, and support given me by Philip Lange. I am indebted to Matthew Miles and Kenneth Herrold for valuable comments and advice.

V

Columbia
University

dents moved around the part of the room containing the learning stations while I watched from a lounge chair on the other side of the room. For a long time I had wanted to try out this kind of instructional systems design to see what kind of learning took place when students had substantial control over such factors as the amount of time they spent on various aspects of subject matter and the sequence in which they set up their own learning. I wanted to see what would happen when this self-directed study took place in an information environment specially designed for such study. When the experiment was over two weeks later, I was satisfied that this kind of instructional systems design had many advantages, over more conventional designs, for the educational needs of coming decades.

For several years I have taught courses in elementary and advanced programmed instruction, educational technology, and instructional systems design. I have become increasingly disturbed because the

LEARNING STATION DESIGN FOR TWO-WEEK COURSE ON
INSTRUCTIONAL SYSTEMS AND PROGRAMMED
INSTRUCTION AT TEACHERS COLLEGE

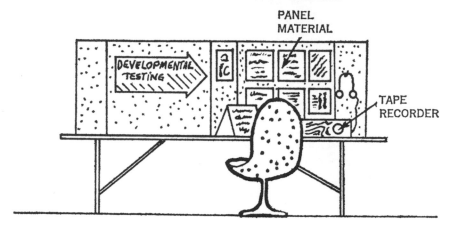

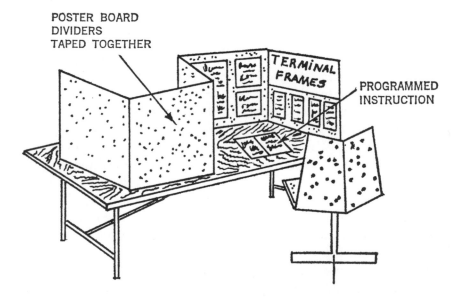

courses were not being designed to meet the needs of all the students
who took them. Everybody who took the course got the same sequence
of lectures, assignments, and exercises, and yet, not only did the stu-

THE INFORMATION ENVIRONMENT—FREE ACCESS
LEARNING STATIONS

THIS ROOM WAS AN ORDINARY COLLEGE CLASSROOM
ARRANGED LIKE THIS

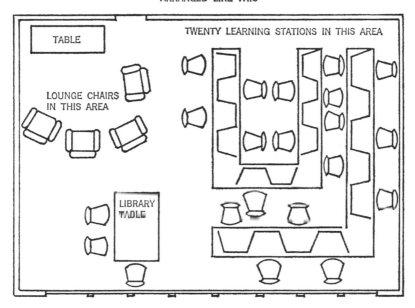

dents vary in age and ability, but also they differed widely in background, experience, and interests. Training directors from industry, free-lance writers, publishers, editors, college professors, high school administrators and teachers, and elementary school teachers were all in the same class. I had tried a number of conventional methods to individualize instruction, as well as some novel ones (Horn, 1964), but felt that I had not yet solved the problem of designing an instructional system that enabled each student to pursue his own learning path, to meet his own learning objectives.

With Michael Spock, director of the Children's Museum in Boston, I had been working on designs for museum exhibits and had explored the notion of informal learning—the learning that a person does when he does not have to (Horn and Spock, 1965). The museum display was impressive as a behavioral influence, the architecture of environment design that says to a person, "You can learn here and it will be fun." We had also been reviewing the information designs resulting from our experiment in student-controlled inquiry sequencing (Horn, 1964). I became again aware that a tremendous amount of learning took place when students and others selected avocations and, with little or no help from an instructor, became expert in certain skills and absorbed a lot of information. In a preliminary functional analysis of the interactions between instructors and students, I had observed that the instructor too often acted as a transmitter of information obtainable elsewhere. Not only could the students read the same material approximately three times as fast as the instructor could say it but, if the instructor could spend that time discussing with students their individual learning problems, the gross effectiveness and efficiency of the teaching-learning situation could be increased substantially. These concerns suggested the possibility of building a learning information environment to incorporate these features of the teaching-learning situation. Of the twenty portable learning stations, sixteen were devoted to a particular aspect of the programmed instruction content, four were empty. The topics of the sixteen learning stations—each of which was furnished with five to twenty hours of materials—were: Instructional Systems, Task Analysis, Objectives, Writing Sequences, Writing Frames, Developmental Testing, Field Testing, Audiovisual Components I and II, Research, How to Keep Up to Date, Use in Schools, Use in Industry, Analysis and Evaluation, Behavior Study, Sequence Analysis, and Editing.

LEARNING STATIONS

The learning stations were set up in one half of the room; the other half contained tables and a circle of comfortable lounge chairs.

The stations were made of thirty-by-forty-inch matting board, the kind used in picture framing. Each piece was scored with a razor blade or knife so it could be folded in two, making dimensions of twenty by thirty inches. Masking tape held this fold together at the corners and the five pieces for each station were put together end to end with masking tape on both sides. The pictures, articles, or magazines selected were glued to the matting board. For the titles on the learning stations, we used transfer letters available in most art stores. Every attempt was made, with the use of many museum exhibit and display techniques, to make the learning stations attractive. At each station we used a variety of notebooks and library file boxes containing file folders. Three stations held tape recorders for audio material. I tore out chapters and paragraphs from my own books and ruthlessly cut material in an attempt to make the contents relevant, excellent, and not redundant.

Since each of the twenty stations was devoted to a different aspect of the subject, the student had to make a conscious decision about what to study next. In fact, he had to get up and move to some other place to study it. This element of the design is important because one of the intentional effects of the course was the student's increased awareness that he was making learning decisions about time and sequence. Each station was fully stocked with material pertinent to one broad aspect of the subject. All material was in one place. Duplication was avoided. This gave the student who wanted, for example, to study the analysis and evaluation of programmed instruction a chance to sit in one place and see the reviews of published programs, various criteria for evaluating programmed instruction, and theoretical and practical articles on the notions of analysis and evaluation. Each station contained up-to-date material. Often it contained prepublication drafts and small circulation technical reports of research completed or in progress. This material provided something of a surprise to many graduate students who were often dependent only on published materials which frequently reach press several years after the work has been done. Many of the stations provided feedback to the students in the form of self-tests and programmed instruction sequences.

One of the basic concerns in constructing these stations was to give students random access to the information they sought. A lecturer using printed materials generally imposes his own choice of order in presenting those materials to his students. If the material were arranged so that it was easily accessible, the individual student would determine a rational sequence of study. This was true of the macrosequence of broad paths of inquiry; the microsequence of printed paragraphs was not controlled. The students used the learning station environment voluntarily. No time or sequence constraints were imposed; there was no need to ask permission to come or go; there was no constraint to study when the student did not wish to. The course was not graded but self-evaluated. To provide the security and lack of tension that good learning requires, students were assured that their goals were of paramount importance and that they would receive only a pass or fail on their university reports.

Each learner had substantial control over his selection of goals, both short and long term. Students were told, at the beginning of the course, that they would be in complete charge of the learning process. They were free to change their objectives at any time. They were encouraged to be explicit about their objectives by writing them down on log sheets and were encouraged by the instructor to discuss goal setting. Each learner had substantial control over the time he spent on each topic. The only time constraints were the hours when the room was open. Students could stop, rest, relax, get a cup of coffee, talk with one another or with the instructor at any time they chose. While each learner had substantial control over the sequence of learning and could follow his own path of inquiry, he could ask the instructor for advice on recommended sequences. Because the materials were arranged in small, random access chunks, the student had a better chance to control the sequence than he normally had when sitting with a couple of books. Each learner had substantial control over the evaluation process. Since he had selected the goals, the learner could, if he wished, evaluate himself in terms of how well he had met these self-imposed goals. He could ask the instructor for an evaluation of his work or for an opinion on a particular topic.

The sequence of steps to be taken by the student could be decided by the instructor or by each student himself. These decisions might be based on the traditional variables to which educators pay attention, such as age, IQ, reading level, aptitude, and learning rates. However, I feel that these are not the relevant individual differences that the instructional designer must take into account for adults. When students are tested according to traditional variables, it is generally the instructor who decides what the student's learning design shall be. The important variables are the differences in learning goals, in background and experience, and in learning style preferences. When this less conventional set of variables is used for testing, it is the learner, who knows most about them, who makes the important decisions about learning designs. Pretesting as a way of allocating each student's curriculum appears to be expensive and time-consuming. The student can do the job more quickly and precisely.

OBJECTIVES AND GOALS

Learning consists of making responses: one reads, tries to do something, practices, reviews, organizes, analyzes, and so on. The responses that a student makes during a course can be analyzed into two broad categories: one pertaining to the attitudinal and interpersonal characteristics of his relationship with his learning environment; the other pertaining to the content of the course. For example, consider two persons studying the same subject. One has been given a research paper to read. The other has decided that he is interested in the research paper. Both have interacted with the same research paper, but one has followed directions, the other has made his own decision about learning. We can expand our field of vision from the reading of one research paper to all the responses a student makes in a course or, for that matter, in his entire schooling, and ask what proportion of the responses he makes can be considered as following directions and what proportion as setting his own goals and receiving the consequences of such practice. It is clear that a student needs to practice both. In our educational process we have overemphasized the practice in following directions. Too often our education system produces docile sheep whom we, as teachers, managers, or citizens, then regard as lacking in initiative, unable to be leaders, uncreative, and whom our sociologists, psychiatrists, and social critics find "full of feelings of helplessness—directionless, alienated."

The designer of instructional systems must consider these matters as he prepares the course. I made several analyses to guide my designs for the instruction and for my behavior during the workshops. First, I prepared an analysis of what was to be incorporated into the learning stations. This analysis was then translated into a set of possible objectives for the students to follow. The introduction to the list of objectives stated: "The title *Possible Objectives* is intended to suggest that not all of these objectives may be *your* goals. . . . One of the important things we do every day in our lives is to select goals for ourselves. The conduct of this course assumes that this goal-setting process will continue in the classroom. Thus, it is entirely up to you to decide what aspects of programmed instruction and instructional systems design you want to study during this course. These possible objectives are . . . merely to assist you in formulating your goals explicitly."

Second, I made an analysis of what learning decisions have to be made repeatedly in the course of an instructional period. I assumed that somebody has to make decisions about objectives, time, sequence, plans, resources, and what to do with the information provided. I also assumed that selecting goals for oneself cannot be taught when the instructor makes every major decision; that allocation of time and decisions about the sequence for learning cannot be taught through lectures and assignments by the instructor; and that the evaluation of complex issues cannot be learned if the instructor predigests the evaluation. My analysis of learning decisions began with the student seeking acceptable goals or objectives. The instructor can help the student draw out objectives from himself; he cannot accept objectives for the student. The information needed for formulating objectives comes chiefly from the student himself through the instructor's asking such questions as: what does this student want to be able to do? What must the student be able to do? What does the student think he can accomplish? What are the possible objectives?

The student must allocate his time among his several objectives within the course and may change the proportional allocation. The necessary information about how long it takes to do various things described at the learning stations can be obtained partly from the instructor, partly from the labels on the learning stations, and partly from the student himself. The student also decides upon the sequence of activities and may alter it at will. The instructor may recommend a sequence if asked or may indicate prerequisites where there is a best sequence. Where applicable, prerequisites are listed at learning stations. Decisions about skills and information provoke questions such as: Shall I just scan this? Shall I just read this information? Shall I try to remember this? Should I learn how to do this? Shall I make notes for reference? Shall I get an outside evaluation of my accomplishment? The decisions must almost always be the student's, though the instructor may be consulted. The suitability of the activities consequent to these decisions, too, can best be assessed by the student.

Third, I made an analysis to help guide the conduct of the course. This was a set of predictions of students' expectations for graduate courses at the college, how our course would contradict these expectations, and what behavior we could predict because of the contradictions. The analysis is displayed in Table 1. Notice that in the left-hand column the role expectations are designated as *initial state* and the right-hand column, *optimal state*. I expected some students to enter the course with optimal state expectations and others to achieve them in a few minutes. Some students would enter the course with strongly ingrained initial state expectations and move toward optimal state expectations and behavior only with great difficulty. This role-expectation analysis gave several insights into student behavior and how I might guide behavioral change in my interactions with the students. It enabled me to anticipate pleas of helplessness, requests for direction, demands for guidance and approval of goals, and to plan my responses to these reactions. Implicit in this analysis is the assumption that I would not reward docile dependence on the instructor for guidance and direction nor would I reward inadequate preparation before consultation with the instructor. By giving them attention and suggestions, I would reward students who asked intelligent questions, who had made prior decisions and wanted to discuss a course of study, who had done inquiry work at the stations.

INFORMATION AND IMPRESSIONS

Every teaching-learning situation, even the most conventional lecture, is an experiment. The hyothesis of any teaching-learning experiment is that an input of instruction will produce an output in terms of changes in students' behavior. However, it is not possible to assess everything one might wish in one course; my choice of variables was based on their relationship to the assumptions of the design. Thus, I attempted to answer questions about individual differences in background, interests, and learning styles of our students. I collected information on what they thought their learning goals would be and how these goals changed while they were in the learning station environment. In addition I obtained anecdotes about what the students felt about the learning experiences. Some summaries appear below.

Each person studying a subject has a particular point of view different from that of other persons studying the same subject, therefore different students will have different learning goals within the same subject. In most instructor-controlled courses, a student finds that some of his learning goals are met and some are not because the instructor controls the sequence and amount of time spent on each aspect of the subject. Having decided to turn over to the students the decisions on sequence and time, I wanted to find out exactly what goals they had. On the first morning of the course I collected data on the students' goals, using a form that asked the student to allocate the available fifty hours among twenty-three topics I suggested, and to write in other topics if necessary. There was no one topic in which all of the students were interested. But every one of the twenty-three received an allocation of time from at least one student. One item, How do you test a program?, interested nine of the students; the amount of

Role-Expectations of Student for Himself, Instructor, and Peers: Initial State

Instructor sets goals and proficiency level. Both I and the group will accept these goals and proficiency levels. He is not interested in my goals.

Instructor will determine each learning activity (duration, sequence, and type of participation). Both I and the group will do what is required and assigned. I will contribute what I can.

Instructor will be primary information transmitter. Group will act as information receivers. I will listen and take notes.

Instructor will be primary interpreter and evaluator of subject. Group may question his evaluation to some extent.

Instructor will give me some directions and advice on personal goals and learning problems and will cut me off when I have taken too much time. Group will tolerate occasional questions during discussion. I will make requests when I feel it appropriate, but there will not be time for much of this.

Instructor is not interested in my evaluations of the course and of his instruction. Group will generally not criticize the instructor—or compliment him. I will avoid making my feelings known.

Instructor does not care if members of the class help each other. Group is interested in themselves, not in helping. I do not expect to give or receive much help from other members of the class.

Instructor will discuss subject matter content questions when asked in class discussion. Group will tolerate questions even if they are not interested in them. I may ask questions on content and will tolerate other questions.

Instructor will answer any subject matter question I put to him personally.

Communication in Work Conference to Contradict These Role-Expectations

Instructor provides only a list of possible goals and indicates that learners must choose proficiency level. Only pass or fail grades will be given.

Instructor indicates that duration, sequences, and type of participation are up to the student. Learning stations provide resources.

Learning stations are primary information transmitters.

Instructor indicates that he expects each learner to evaluate and interpret subject matter for himself.

Instructor will indicate that all of his time will be available for personal consulting with individual students.

Instructor seeks student-evaluation of the course, of materials, and of himself.

Instructor will provide class with a profile of resources within the class so that help may be asked. Indicates general approval of helping each other.

Instructor indicates that he will answer content questions in the group setting only if all members are interested in the question and all have used the prerequisite learning stations.

Instructor indicates that he will answer only those questions which are not answered by the learning station materials.

78

CHANGING STUDENTS' ROLE-EXPECTATIONS

Student's Reaction to this Contradiction of his Expectations	Instructor's Response to Student's Reaction	Optimal State of Student's Role-Expectations for Course
Silent frustration. Request for direction. Pleas of helplessness. Demands for guidance, for approval of goals.	Points out resources for choice. Offers to help in evaluating goals.	I must make final decisions on my goals and level of proficiency. Instructor might help after I have done my job.
Vague, aimless wandering. Exploration. Curiosity.	Encouragement, counseling and help in identifying goals.	I must make my own choices on duration, sequence, and type of participation. Instructor may help me clarify my choices.
Requests information which is in learning station.	Learner told to consult appropriate station.	I must actively seek out information, decide what to learn, and where it is.
"Tell me what to think," requests. Dogmatic stances.	What do you think? How do you make an evaluation?	I am able to make my own interpretations and evaluations.
Apologetic requests. Anxiety over taking up too much of the instructor's time.	Consults. Gives advice on learning problems, feedback on how learner is progressing.	Instructor is a resource for advice on learning problems. I can get feedback. I have learned how to use this resource.
Suspicion, disbelief, some criticism.	Actively seeks evaluation, changes behavior and class structure on the basis of student's criticism.	I will make my feelings known to the instructor because he is interested in them and will change his behavior on the basis of what I say.
Tentative groups form. Suspicion, disbelief. Some help given and received.	Encourages groups to form and suggest specific forms of cooperation.	I expect to give and receive help from other members of the class.
Some student attempts to engage class in subject matter discussion.	Maintain stance. Gives answer if all are interested.	Instructor will not discuss subject matter content questions unless whole class desires it and all are prepared.
Frustration. Requests for help.	Maintain stance.	I can use the learning stations first, and use the time I have with the instructor better.

79

time they wanted spent on it varied from two to five hours. One student wanted to spend twenty hours examining the best programmed instruction published. One wanted to spend fourteen hours preparing transparencies and overlays. Four wanted to spend from fourteen to twenty-four hours writing their own programs. We can infer from these data some of the reasons we see so many bored faces in our classrooms. I suspect that in any course the results might be similar. The question that faces the instructor—the instructional systems designer— is how to arrange conditions and environment so that students can learn what they are interested in learning.

By the time students are adults their learning goals differ and so do their learning styles. While I was collecting the information on the learning goals of the students I also obtained data on how they would like to have the course arranged, and discovered that two students did not want to speak with the instructor at all. Others, upon learning that the instructor had a total of fifty hours to distribute among twenty students, wanted ten of those fifty hours for personal tutoring. Especially noticeable was the lack of interest students had in talking to one another; only three allotted any time to discussions with others; only two indicated a willingness to work on a group project.

STUDENT REACTION

The only assignment students were given during the course was to write an evaluation of the experience of using the learning stations. The following excerpts from the papers of five students have been chosen to give some of the flavor of the course as they experienced it.

Student A: "The instructor was very cordial but did not tell any student just where he would begin visiting the stations. This was strange, I guess, being used to the conventional type of classroom procedure on the first day of school. After a few minutes of exploring and observing, I soon decided each person began wherever he desired. I do feel that my major objectives were accomplished. In a few days I soon realized how much a person can learn through self-instruction."

Student B: "In the workshop I stumbled and groped. I knew I needed more background, I knew I wanted to write a program, but the first day I felt the instructor was groping, too. Since I had never attended a workshop before, I had no *mind-set* for procedure or expectation. I had only a desire to solve the need I felt for better materials. It took me a little while to adjust from a mind-set calling for a lecture type of class to the format of the workshop. The informality of 'what does the group want to do?' approach and the nervous mannerisms of the instructor caused an unpleasant reaction at first. I wanted direction. I wanted the security of a planned program—a plan I could recognize. Never one to give up easily, I joined the clamor for an overview lecture and then went to the writing sequence booth. My first visit to the sequence booth was frustrating and the overview lecture was a repetition of what I already knew (okay, so you were right about the *lecture mind-set*). I reread the objectives of the course, got lost in the *givens*, got confused in the sequences, and determined that 'I paid my money and, by golly, I'm going to get something more than frustration out of this workshop!' I began to read with a vengeance at each learning station . . ."

Student C: "My chief impression from the learning station sessions is one of awe. Knowing how much there is to know about programmed instruction is a lesson in itself. Had the class been faced with a stack of books and papers to inspect, the experience undoubtedly would have been quite different. The books would have looked like nothing more than books—a forest of verbiage to plow through—a literary obstacle to be hurdled, and the impression would have been the usual one experienced by over-assigned students: despair . . . not awe. But the logical presorting of ideas by topic converted the assignment into a challenge. Right there before his eyes, the student could view the whole field of knowledge, grasp the full scope of how much he could learn and, very helpfully to have this happen so early in the course, appreciate keenly that he could not humanly learn everything offered in each station and had to choose a specialty, ultimately, if not at once. Then, with a special objective selected, the challenge remained. The availability of the station material throughout the day represented a strong inducement to continue poring over the subject for hours. My only regret now is that I'll probably never again enjoy an opportunity to digest such a complete sampling . . ."

Student D: "I was completely frightened the first day of the course. The question sheets were so hurriedly passed out and collected and not explained thoroughly. I also had a feeling during the first few days that I had made a terrible mistake in taking the course because I suspected that all of the people in the class had more experience than I. I suppose that this was because we didn't have time to become well acquainted on the first day and were secluded behind a station the rest of the time. I have never been in a class where *action* research was going on. I feel that the instructors in the course are attempting to find better ways of teaching this course. I have claimed to be an advocate of this type of experimenting. However, I was astonished when I found myself whining to my husband and others that I wasn't getting any attention. I complained at various times that I didn't know what I was doing, that I didn't have enough of a background to be left on my own devices like this, and also complaining that I had not been forewarned that the class was going to be taught in this manner. This complaining seems peculiar because I was actually very happy each morning as I settled down to reading and taking notes as I saw fit. The complaining also seems peculiar because I never felt that I had completed what I had planned for the day."

Student E: "Interaction with the instructor was crucial to me when I was in the early phases of getting acquainted with the basic concepts in the field. This is the time when possible confusion, lack of background, or just plain not understanding an item can reduce motivation a great deal. Ready access to the instructor enabled me to maintain myself on a continuous reinforcement schedule, which, as Amsel says, is important in early learning stages. I could get a point cleared up or receive confirmation of a discrimination I had made and to this, I attribute my desire to go on and on . . . As I thought about the effect of the present learning station system, I attempted to phrase this question to myself: 'How is it different from an ordinary library? What's so different about it?' In order of discrimination, this is what came out: (1) It offers the basic concepts, research data, the research bibliography, etc., in readily available form. One would have to spend time searching in the stacks, walking to and from the library, waiting on reserved book lines, etc. To me ready access is a powerful reinforcer. (2) It enables a neophyte to form a set-of-field by simply viewing the various stations as a logical subsystem of the total system, which, even though imposed and, therefore, unreal to an extent, enables one to guide oneself through moving from simple whole to complex wholes . . . To try and say it another way: a learner comes with a unique combination of knowledge, response styles, propensities, interests, etc. Random-access in the learning station system would appear to make the person and the material an intrinsic programmed self-controlled system responding to (computer style) the information and the choosing of the next step as it seems most fitting at that time, at that level of sophistication."

My dominant reaction to the workshop experience was that I had worked at the top of my capacity every minute. By changing my role from that of lecturer, or primary information transmitter, to that of consultant, I felt that what I said to each individual who came over to me for a chat was relevant to his concerns at the moment. I was free from the anxiety I always feel in lecturing; namely, that half of the students either are not listening because they already know the subject, or that they are missing my carefully phrased discriminations. In the workshop situation with the learning stations, I felt that, when a student came to me with a problem or a question, I could put my full effort into helping him—without worrying that twenty or more students were sitting around wasting their time.

My second satisfaction was that I had made the best use of my limited time, money, and materials. On other occasions, I had spent most of my preparation time producing lectures or laboratory exercises that contained, as in all fields, the work of many researchers before me. Much of what I said in a lecture had been written down earlier by somebody else. In allocating my time before the workshop to selecting and organizing what had already been done in the field, I made a system that provided better access to more material for more students.

No longer an information transmitter, I could get a much better picture of how the individual students were doing. When they came to me with problems, questions, and requests for evaluation, I had time to find out precisely what their difficulties were and how I could help. The evaluation in depth of these personal encounters was far more helpful to the student than the usual evaluation of a symbol on a report card. Even though we had set up a pass-fail system for the course, I felt that, because of these meetings with the students, I could have given more precise grades than I could under conventional testing methods. These meetings with students also provided an insight into the defects of the instructional materials they were using. I can't imagine how I could have learned so much in so short a time by any other method. It is hard to imagine counting on a mere library list again to produce predictable behavior changes.

The biggest differences I noted among the students was in their ability to use me as a resource. Some were very skilled at it; others were poor. Some came with specific questions and had a clear idea of what they wanted me to do; others would come over, talk about themselves, and appear to be asking me to relieve some anxiety they had in making decisions. I felt that practice, regardless of the level of skill, in using some person as a learning resource was needed. I might mention that I had to learn to be a consultant in this kind of situation. During the first afternoon of the workshop, I sat waiting for students to come over and ask me questions. None did. I sat there with nothing to do. I felt strong impulses to go over to the learning station area and look over shoulders. There they were, studying hard, and I wanted to interrupt them. I wanted to know what they were doing. I felt that the workshop was out of my control. I resisted the impulse and found something to read, but not before pondering the thought that perhaps we instructors often overrate our own importance in the minute-to-minute control of student behavior. Nevertheless, I did not have to wait long before the stream of visitors started, and kept on uninterrupted, for the rest of the workshop.

Undoubtedly I would do it again. My dominant feeling, supplied by the learner protocols and my own observations, was that the learning station design, coupled with self-sequencing, did help students achieve their own objectives. Approximately 75 per cent of the students gave unsolicited statements to the effect that they would build such learning stations in their own classrooms. No investigation a year later was made to see if they carried out their intentions.

I have already mentioned that two classes used the learning stations. One class, according to the catalog, met for two weeks from 9:00 A.M. to 4:00 P.M. The other class started on the same day and was scheduled to meet for six weeks (from 8:00 A.M. to 9:00 A.M.). During the first two weeks of this latter course, students were told that they could use the learning stations as much as they wished. There was a total of nine required hours. A tally showed that these students actually used the learning stations an average of twenty-one hours during the two-week period. Their use ranged from twelve hours to forty hours. In other workshops that I have conducted, students would arrive in the morning and stand and talk for a long time before beginning work. One of the striking things about this workshop was the typical behavior of the students upon entering the room: they immediately began work, although half of the room had been furnished especially for informal conversation. I concluded that, if inquiry results in readily obtained answers, a high and steady rate of inquiry takes place. This is an interesting hypothesis for further research.

Based on my experiences with previous workshops of similar duration, I can say that I was impressed by the high quality of the programmed instruction units written in this setting as compared with previous settings, although fewer students actually chose to write sequences (in other courses, writing sequences had been required). Perhaps the lower quality in previous courses was a result of our requiring the writing before the learners felt ready; perhaps not. I do not know.

The possibility of creative behavior did not occur to me until it happened. At least two students came to me with innovative programmed instruction techniques during the course of the workshop. In no previous course had I encountered such innovation.

I will change a number of my operating procedures the next time I use the learning stations for a course. The lack of pretests and posttests would not prevent me from using the same design again, but it would definitely improve the overall design to include them. I would also devise self-tests for each of the learning stations. I used a few this time; next time I would want more. I would also change the printed sheet of possible objectives to enable neophytes to make better judgments about their time. I feel now that the student should have access to a chart listing objectives, minimum acceptable standards, and the time he could expect to spend in achieving the objectives. I would also like to relate the objectives to specific secondary objectives and suggested learning materials. There was little unanimity among the students when I asked what topics for learning stations they would suggest I add to the existing collection. I would definitely add one called the [Robert] Horn Station. Late in the second week, one student suggested it. He said he had noticed papers of mine scattered throughout the learning stations, but did not know whether he had read all of them. I recognized a very natural desire on the part of students to want to know, early in a course, about that stranger called the teacher. Finally, I would rent an office copier for students to copy pages of the materials. If there was one universal complaint, it was about the lack of such equipment. It is an interesting complaint: it means that we had generated a publishing need; it means that students are affluent enough to trade money for time in note-taking.

DEDUCTIONS AND IMPLICATIONS

It is not enough to put students, a teacher, and some books into a room and hope for the best. Nor is it enough, when trying out some innovation in instruction, to consider only one factor. Too often I read reports of experiments that pay attention to only one factor; they change the grading system or try to alter the norms or alter the objectives or change the information environment. Seldom do we find attention given simultaneously to all of these factors in an instructional systems design. In designing or evaluating any instructional system, one must examine such variables as: the characteristics of the students, their interests and goals as well as their background and abilities; the availability and design of the information environment; the ability of the instructor and the information environment to provide feedback to the students; the properties of the interpersonal associations among students and instructors; the behavioral outcomes of the instruction period; the allocation of decision-making responsibilities among students and faculty; the reward system for the students and for the instructor; the role-expectations of the instructor and the learners; the resources of time, material, space, and money. Change any one of these and you change important characteristics of the system.

The self-sequencing learning station design certainly cannot be applied in every course. Students also need some practice in following directions, listening to lectures and going to the library. However, I do feel that the ideas can be applied to the design of instructional resource centers in all of the grades, elementary school through professional training, as well as in adult education, management training, and skill centers for industry training departments. An interesting possibility for higher education is the permanent establishment, supported by an academic department, of a room like mine in which all introductory courses are taught. Different advanced courses could have different prerequisites, which could be acquired according to the student's choice in the learning environment. Few professors seem to like to teach introductory courses anyway. So, it would appear that the wedge for innovation might be there.

For me, the work with this system brought into focus several important areas for further study. One is the problem of designing information specifically for students who are engaged in the process of self-instruction, and who are in charge of their own goal-setting and decision-making. Another is the problem of teaching people to manage their own learning. Finally, the experience of trying to design a total system that was novel from start to finish has suggested that I explore other combinations of objectives, social systems, information environments, and decision-making allocations. There are many other such designs, some novel and some which have been tried out, which should be implemented more widely.

Norman Springer

A Teacher in
An Alien Field

When I undertook to teach Euclidean geometry—a subject foreign to my own training in English literature—my central concern was to demonstrate that it was possible to come to understand a subject by one's own effort, through study and discussion, without the help of a teacher who had the answers. That the sixteen freshmen who met me that first morning at the outset of our nine-month journey did not believe this was not surprising, since how anyone perceives education affects how he goes about achieving it. One's attitude may even decide whether or not one believes one can achieve it and, perhaps specially important at present, whether or not one even wants to achieve it. For most of my students, learning was essentially a matter of memorizing. Knowledge was equated with the possession of information or, if it were something else, it was a concern not of theirs but of those who had the time. Such a belief is prevalent for a number of reasons that are not new in principle but take on special force in our

VI

Saint Mary's College

time. By force I mean the widely noted effect of putting in the places of highest esteem the attainment of specialized knowledge as it is embodied in its high priests, the scientists, professionals, and experts. (Millionaires, too, are specialists of a kind.) This effect, attached to the dazzling achievement of contemporary technology, imposes on all of us with a variety of results, but works special results on students. At some stage of their development they may well believe that all the vast paraphernalia of power and pleasure exists through magic, invented by the lucky few who possess something out-of-this-world called genius. To believe this, or a variation of it, while going to school (which officially contradicts such a view), leads to a variety of crippling strategies for bridging what seems to be unbridgeable.

While the concept of school does imply the possibility of intellectual achievement, the emphasis on dazzling achievement, which has so absolute an effect on the world outside, is rigidly reflected

89

within the school itself. Within the school as without, the expert reigns: the teacher sees himself as one; he is paid to be one. He stands alone, at the head of his class, "telling," asking and answering questions, approving or disapproving of others' answers. Rarely does he examine seriously with his students the assumptions underlying his discipline; there is little or no time for this, he feels, if he is to prepare students properly for the major, that is, to prepare them for the demands of the graduate school. Most introductory courses are inevitably emasculated by the professional who finds them useful for their extraordinary power to cut time spent in considering fundamental questions in favor of time spent handing over, by lecturing, the necessary language and information in preparation for the specialty. And the student, who in the beginning is an especially accepting student, responds accordingly.

For example, in my specialty, the average student who decides to major in English literature expects whatever education he gets to come from the teacher who has, he supposes, accumulated a vast amount of information to be parceled out to him at regular intervals, all of it somehow related by the legend—Department of English. The earnest student believes implicitly that to understand the subject means to pass tests in it—that is, to be able to repeat the contents of assigned works, to be able to name the kinds of works they are, to be able to list the chronology of the authors, and to have some idea of their lives and period. For the student to begin to probe, to think consistently and extensively about literary form and the principles of judgment which lie beyond mere impressions, to raise questions about the basis of the classifications all are eager to use—to do any of these is to destroy the timetable and to court disaster. To raise such questions would inevitably drive one to matters which underlie any effort to understand, but are not always officially part of a discipline. What, for example, does one mean by principle? What does it mean to say that this is so, that this is not so? How do you know?

It is here, at the outset, that hard thought to discover the roots of the discipline ought to take place. Is it not only after one has thought about the rationale of the discipline, its tools, their powers and ambiguity, that one begins to understand the discipline as a structure based on foundations necessarily connected to things other than the structure? And is it not the struggle to discover this that makes it belong to the learner? Yet, in the main, classrooms are run on the

basis of presenting these structures as if they were merely packages
of accumulated information with a table of operations to be mastered.
When I state this I am quite aware of the cry, "We are not philosophers; there is just no time." While this is a normal reaction for those
of us trained in graduate schools, it is a view in great part responsible
for the failure of liberal education. It is a view which rejects curiosity
that is not departmental, nor split into the disciplines. It rejects a
curiosity that is open to all things and ready to be harnessed to the
pursuit of those questions asked by any human being who looks out
at the world and wants to know what and how things are. This, in the
pejorative terms of the specialists, is *not* a matter of learning a little
bit about a lot of things. Though it is common to recognize and re-
joice in this wonderment as it appears in the very young, it is frequently considered naive in undergraduates, let alone graduate students.

While the powers of technology and specialization have been
recognized, their debilitating effects have also been widely noted and
documented. The effects on students have been particularly disastrous.
One has only to consider the usual college graduates. Rarely are they
men and women with ranging critical intellects. At best, they are good
material for the graduate school; at worst, merely time-servers. Unde-
niably, there have been extraordinary teachers who have, within their
specialties, stirred their students to respond with wonderment and,
through inner direction, to pursue learning with great joy. Occasionally, this pursuit has produced not only remarkable achievement but
also wisdom, though perhaps this may be despite graduate schools and
even formal education. We do know that contemporary education can
take inherent, powerful curiosity and fulfill its demands quickly and
productively by channeling it in its own way. It is another matter to
consider the numerous students whose natural curiosity has been se-
verely curtailed by the demands of specialization. One can avoid the
issue by maintaining that only a few persons are capable of any sustained thought and accomplishment. I do not grant that this is necessarily true, for I maintain that serious, liberating education has not
been tried in any consistent and widespread manner. Until this kind
of education is pursued on a wider scale, it is impossible to say how
many are capable of profiting from it.

Speaking *On Liberal Education,* Jacob Klein, a former dean
of Saint John's College, Annapolis, described how experts develop:

In the perspective of a detached inquiry the meaning of a word usually loses its "natural" ambiguity, becomes more fixed, gains a definite significance determined by the scope of the attempted and sustained investigation, which investigation may lead to the establishment of a science, an art, a *techne*. The inquirer then turns, of necessity, into an "expert" who is able to pass his knowledge on to others, who is able, in other words, to become a teacher. It is thus that words do indeed become "technical" and transcend the habitual and familiar. Special terms, moreover, may be coined to satisfy more fully the understanding gained in the investigation. And yet, the "technical" use of words tends, in turn, to become accepted and to win a familiarity of its own. The passing on of sciences, arts, and skills, especially of intellectual ones, cannot quite avoid the danger of blurring the original understanding, on which the disciplines are based. The terms which embody that understanding, the indispensable terms of the art, of the *techne* in question, the "technical" terms, acquire gradually a life of their own, severed from the original insights. In the process of perpetuating the art those insights tend to approach the status of sediments, that is, of something understood derivatively and in a matter-of-course fashion. The technical terms begin to form a technical jargon spreading a thick veil over the primordial sources.[1]

When Klein speaks of "blurring the original understanding" and of "spreading a thick veil over the primordial sources," he does not mean to distinguish between ancient views, pejoratively called primitive by some and sophisticated, modern views. Rather he is making a distinction between primary, fundamental understanding and the derivative understanding reflected in jargon. In Klein's view, it follows that liberal education has "to counteract this process of sedimentation" and inspire in "the learner as well as the teacher the practice of philosophical reflection and the awareness of its guiding role." If Klein is right, and I think he is, the key to any possibility of change lies with the teacher. He must find a way to break out of the pattern that holds

[1] In *Proceedings of the Colloquium on the Liberal Arts Curriculum: Structure and Content,* Saint Mary's College, California, March 1965, Edward Sparrow (Ed.).

him and begin to cultivate whatever it is that will break him from the mold and force him into instability, into the position of learner while he occupies the seat of authority. In such a position, he will not be able to decamp and become simply a student, nor will he be merely a moderator, nor the one who asks the questions, though at any one time, he, as well as the students, may do any of these things. Whatever authority he has will be based on the fact that he "is older, more experienced, more aware of the kinds of ignorance he has as well as the kind and quality of his knowledge."[2] Once he is in this position, what takes place in the classroom may change startlingly.

UNRAVELING EUCLID

But, if one is a teacher of English literature, why go into Euclid's geometry? Because I discovered what many men in the past have known, that the study of Euclid was one extraordinary way of examining, from the ground up, much that goes into understanding any extended order of knowledge, a way of dynamiting the roots of a host of the most casually held all-encompassing assumptions.

Euclid starts with entities—point, line, circle—that have a kind of existence not difficult to assent to. Euclid's geometry is a subject, which in contrast to others, allows an unusually clear view of its language and operations because it does not depend on physical objects. It is a subject which addresses itself to describing and demonstrating what it understands to be true, not to what is merely a matter of consistency or opinion. All the terms, which I use so easily, quickly came under our scrutiny to be wondered at: from the ground up, understanding, extended order of knowledge, roots, all-encompassing assumptions, existence, geometry, subject, describe, demonstrate, true, consistency, opinion.

When my colleagues asked if I would be willing to lead a class in Euclid for the academic year, I found the proposal frightening, first because I knew nothing about the subject (in high school I had only just passed it), second, because I was sorely tempted.[3] For an

[2] In *The Integrated Liberal Arts Curriculum,* a brochure issued by Saint Mary's College, California, 1965.

[3] A small part of the total offering at Saint Mary's College, California, is a special program, The Integrated Liberal Arts Curriculum, modeled almost wholly after the Saint John's program at Annapolis and Santa Fe. The program consists of four years of integrated studies, leading to a Bachelor of Arts de-

English teacher who does not pride himself on any great versatility,
my ignorance seemed an insurmountable barrier. My colleagues reported that the mathematicians who had dealt with the course had
failed to arouse any probing interest or curiosity about geometry. It
had been like any high school course. Would I go in with the freshmen and break it open with them? All I needed was the ability to
look hard at what was in front of me. "You could do it with Hamlet,
couldn't you?" "You start at the very first line, 'Who's there' and follow wherever it leads. Do the same with Euclid: start with the first
definition, *a point is that which has no parts,* and follow that wherever
it leads. If you get stuck," they suggested, "look at those around the
seminar table to see how far any member of the group can take it.
Can further probing lead to any explanation? If that fails, the group
can formulate the issue, hold it in abeyance, and so go on to other
problems which may reflect back to the first question and make it
clearer. Or, you may find an opposite effect—the issue may become
even more obscure after the discussion and much larger than you
think. In an absolute impasse there will always be the expert to consult." (In actual practice, on the rare occasions when we asked for
help from a mathematician, we found ourselves thrown back on our
own resources, puzzling, when he had concluded his explanation and
departed, over what had been said.) I was tempted to try to lead the
Euclid seminar because I had always believed in interdisciplinary pursuits but had only confronted those most obviously touching English.
Alongside my courses in English, I had been leading a seminar in the
Great Books—philosophy, history, and Greek epics and drama in
translation. Moreover, I was somewhat less than a free agent for I

gree, in which the student is required to reflect on language, mathematics and
music, the laboratory study of material conditions that surround him, and to
read intelligently some of the works of the greatest thinkers and writers. The
books range from Homer's *Iliad* to Einstein's *Relativity*. At Saint John's College,
which is nondenominational, the program involves the entire student body; at
Saint Mary's only sixty students, of eight hundred and fifty, follow it. Since
1962 there has been an exchange of the instructors between Saint John's and
Saint Mary's. A few instructors teach in both the Integrated Curriculum and in
their special fields. Part of the strategy of the program is to convince some
teachers to confront one field in which they are not trained, and, in time, to
consider other parts of the curriculum. An English teacher might be asked to
teach Euclid for several years; a mathematician might be asked to teach the
Great Books seminar and the language tutorial.

had myself insisted that any educated man, especially a teacher, given some time, ought to be able to begin to come to terms with whatever was put in front of him, though with no pretense of being an expert. Always embarrassed by the way I was cut off from the sciences and mathematics (I had not seriously considered them since high school) I felt that my own education was quite inadequate. General education falls short because the notion of generality is undercut by most of its advocates; science and mathematics are simply not in their ken. The failure is recognized when students are asked to fulfill distribution requirements by taking courses for nonmajors from specialists with little interest in general education.

I shall not forget the first time I went to the blackboard to do the first proposition. I was alone in a classroom with two colleagues. They had asked me to study the proposition and expected me to demonstrate it at the board without the text, that is, to prove that what I, not Euclid, was trying to say was so; *to describe an equilateral triangle on a given finite straight line.* I was puzzled, for it seemed necessary merely to transcribe Euclid, a simple matter of memorization. I was puzzled only until I tried to explain what I was doing and why I was doing it.

To those who blanch at the mention of mathematics, any effort to discuss it may be repugnant. To those with some confidence in the processes of geometry, the whole operation may seem infinitely naive. But it is important that I describe, in some detail, a process I found so rewarding. For, through the effort to control such detail, the process came directly to conclusions to which I was forced to assent. To be able to say this was no mean achievement. Part of the delight was being able to say yes, with so much conviction—after all, the ingrained cliché is the one about the more you know the less you know, which seems to leave more and more open to question. The humility that grows from this cliché does away with assertions that what one says is true; to be an honest man, let alone to look like one, it is wiser to assert that one may be wrong. But, to understand and demonstrate that first proposition, I could not say I was wrong. Or, to put it more acceptably for a moment, the demonstration of the first proposition ended with a conclusion less open to undermining than others, and for reasons less obscure than most. I was fascinated by what I meant by less open and by being able to say yes with so much conviction.

Part of the problem may be that my training allowed me to derive satisfaction only from manipulating what seemed to be eminently complex. To move from a simple principle to a necessary conclusion often smacks of gross simplification.

At the blackboard I struggled, red-faced, to explain how I thought the first proposition was to be demonstrated. I believed (a belief which had saved me a lot of work) that there were those who could do mathematics and those, like myself, who could not. When I nervously paused to consider what made the demonstration possible, it slowly came to me that, inherent in the definition of a circle, was the possibility of making the equal-sided triangle. The possibility was electrifying because at first I saw only a series of steps to be listed in my head and to be used to hasten to a conclusion; the moment I saw, built into the definition of circle (*A circle is a plane figure contained by one line, which is called the circumference, and is such that all straight lines drawn from a certain point within the figure to the circumference are equal to one another*), equal lines, each step became part of a powerful process pushing me to a necessary conclusion, the process inseparable from that conclusion. Once grant me the right to draw a line, I can use that line, see it if I so desire, as the radius of two separate circles which overlap. Consider it: draw the line AB;

A ————B

then, using the line AB as radius, draw the boundary of a circle with A as center; then, using the same line AB as radius, draw the boundary

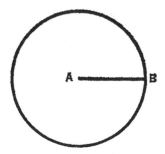

of another circle, this time with B as center which touches, or cuts, the first circle at another point we can call C;

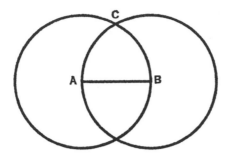

then join A to C, which is another radius in the circle, and B to C, which is another radius in the second circle.

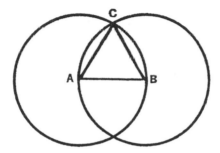

This gives us the triangle ACB, of which we can see that all sides are equal. Radius AB equals CB for the same reason. So, since AB is common to both circles, lines AC and CB are equal to each other, naturally—that is, because of the *common notion* (a phrase worthy of great consideration): *things equal to the same thing are equal to each other*.

Today, this demonstration seems as beautiful as when I first discovered it. Once accept the definition of circle, with its potential *always* to make equal lines of any size, then an explosive power becomes apparent; that is, there is present a potential similar to chemical action, always ready to spring at the motion of an idea, like Japanese flowers of wood-shavings, which, once in water, unfold into most unexpected blossoms. That Euclid, and his predecessors, and I saw this, separate and nameable, made it a significant matter—not a question of the past or present, but a matter of something there and so, for any man at any time to discover.

When, with a flush of pride, I finished explaining the proposition, I felt I had, by myself, mined and pulled to the surface something embedded in me and yet irrevocably connected to the world outside. I understood the proposition: saw how it worked and where and what it came from; further, I had a tumultuous intimation that I had caught a glimpse of an immense implication that I could not yet articulate. It seemed significant to be able to circumscribe space in this way, to consider, for instance, the sun as a center and to think of equal lines radiating from it to an imaginary boundary. (Later, after spring vacation, in the first year's work, there would be a leap to the stars; we would be engaged in observing the heavens by doing what Ptolemy did, Ptolemy whose universe rotated about the earth, whose system can still be used reliably to navigate the globe, who claimed that, with geometry and with what his eyes saw, he could explain the movement in the heavens. And we would ask then: if this is so, what does it mean to say something is true by appearance?)

We were thoroughly perplexed in the early classes (we met an hour a day, five days a week), when all sixteen of us around a table faced the first proposition. Some were puzzled by what they considered trivia: to them this was only geometry and transparently clear; others were puzzled from the outset by the definitions stated so simply, but obscure the moment one probed their sources. I was faced with two other problems: how to convince the students that I was as ignorant as I seemed, and how to convince them that our effort was actually to discover, together, what was before us and how best to proceed. As we plunged into the rush of questions, which appeared at every step of the way, we soon recognized that such difficulties were a primary part of the enterprise. Most of us came to see perplexity as fuel for our persistent pursuit. Stopped dead by one question, we tried to rephrase it, or let it hang fire, for we always discovered a host of new tangential questions we could pursue and possibly use as a way back to the original question, which was likely to have been transformed by the time we returned to it. After such activity, it was impossible for me to look like one who posed his own questions from a stronghold of withheld answers; ignorance was the only stance possible. As I did at first, they wondered whether there was anything to discuss. Could not this proposition be memorized and transferred from the page to the board? Was even this necessary, since everybody had the text? What was in front of them was there to be dealt with. Language was not something to be examined but something to start from, a means one used to get to what was most important, the matter, which was somewhere ahead. For them, one did not pause at words, such as describe, an, on, given, let, which appeared in the first sentence of the first proposition: *To describe an equilateral triangle on a given finite straight line.*

Let AB be the given straight line: it is required to describe an equilateral triangle on AB.

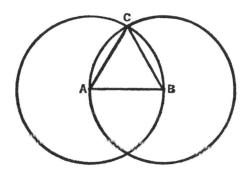

The first man at the board went through the proposition almost word for word with no interruption. Then there was silence. Why *describe?* Why *let?* Later on in the proposition the circles are said to cut one another at C. What is meant by *cut?* How can lines, which are without breadth, do so? (Part of the growing excitement was the discovery that there were occasions to pause, and that the pause could get longer as one examined the occasions.) If equilateral had already been identified in the definitions (of three-sided figures Euclid had said, *An equilateral triangle is that which has three equal sides*), why have the first demonstration a construction of what we already know? Why not just draw it? Perhaps, we asked, we might get some insight by considering the word *describe,* which the translater uses instead of the word *draw,* which we expected. We did not yet know the Greek word. *Describe* meant more in this context than *set forth in words,* our common view of it. More so than *draw,* we thought, the word underlined the existence of a concrete object to look at in the mind, one which we could make available for our joint contemplation by our ability to construct a rough copy of it through language and diagram. The right to do this, to *describe* one line equal to another came from the power given in the definition of circle and in postulate No. 3: *Let it be granted that a circle may be described from any center*

at any distance from that center. We could have used a compass and a ruler, but then we would have been thrown from a dependence on the definition of circle to a dependence on ruler and compass which, while making lines appear accurate and thus more pleasing to the eye, would still be only approximate. For example, the nearest tenth of a millimeter that one can note with an instrument is only a reminder that something is left over, immeasurable in terms of the instrument. The precision of the drawing, then, is not the issue if one knows that, in any circle, the lines stand for the perfectly equal lines from center to circumference. That perfect circle we hold in mind is there to remind us of measure, that standard by which we know the difference between equal lines and those we draw.

There was a significant difference, then, between what we said about the object and the object itself. This made us especially shy about using the words perfect circle, because we recognized our limitations. Yet we found ourselves able to say, with undeniable confidence, that this was true: those lines stand for radii and they are perfectly equal. Some of us caught a glimpse of at least three implications in such confidence: there was a relation, between the object circle and what we said about it, that was closer than the relation between the object circle and the ruled and compassed lines representing i , that some things did hold ground, were not a matter of opinion; perhaps most significant, that, if we truly understood anything, it might be as demonstrable as that first proposition. How did we mean this? Were not geometrical proofs different from other proofs? Or were they? What was demonstration? If it meant proof of the absolutely so, how could one explain the undemonstrable on which it was based? For some, absolutely so had always meant that nothing was to be granted; everything could be a matter of question. In order to proceed, it was necessary to grant the definitions, and the postulates as well, since they specifically asked, among other things, for the right— *Let it be granted*—to draw a line from one point to another; for the right to describe a circle *from any center at any distance from the center.*

As the class thought about it, this too seemed too obvious to discuss. To get anything done, one starts somewhere. To pick away at such transparent matters, is circular and useless. As we made that first motion, it was what appeared most obvious that most perplexed us. In any pursuit, it was impossible to escape an opening, which is usually understood and unstated: "Let me use these words to begin with, so that I can get to what I want to say." That one asks for permission, implies a large area of what is common. The way we thought about our starting point might reveal how we could come to know any other thing, not just Euclid. And we tried. My exhilarating experience came from the growing recognition that there was time, long stretches of it, which allowed us to pause, to circle, to probe for more. For some time the students did not believe this. For them there were only short lengths of time to be passed and piled up. My job was to let them convince themselves otherwise by pausing, retracing their steps, wondering, reformulating, listening, digressing. By doing this themselves, they might discover that the proper expenditure of time had nothing to do with classrooms, periods, semesters; that learning had everything to do with ruminating around the table, with allowing oneself to unfold without hurry, with opening oneself to the perplexities, with confronting them without fear.

I reproduce a small part of what we considered to indicate how demanding and richly suggestive the process was; and to indicate how, by holding hard to what Euclid was doing, one could find vast areas to explore, which, in the reverberations set off, cut across a profusion of other considerations, which had nothing directly to do with Euclid. For instance, what were we committing ourselves to when we accepted the definition of circle? Why accept it in the first place? This led us to the notion of definition itself. At first Euclid sets out some thirty definitions, as well as some postulates and common notions. What were these definitions identifying? Were they merely arbitrary, pulled out of a hat and made up out of whole cloth? Or were they descriptions of something that actually existed outside the mind? What distinguished the definitions from the postulates and common notions? What did it mean to say, as the first definition did, *A point is that which has no parts?* Where did it come from? Could we proceed with any confidence without investigating every single source? That the definition appears with the inherent expectation that it will be understood, points to an overwhelming context, an entire order of users, reflected by a grammar and a language. Every one of the eight words in the definition could be examined; that would force us back to the roots of language underlying geometry. (In the language tutorial of the Saint John's College program, students were investigating ancient Greek, as well as Euclid. What is language? What is a gram-

mar?) For us in the Euclid tutorial, the most immediate problem was
how far we could proceed in uncovering the sources of geometry. Reflecting on Euclid forced us to reflect on language and grammar also;
that is, was *A point is that which had no parts* a meaningless statement? How can any existent thing have no parts? What did one mean
by existent? Did one mean only physical objects? If so, were we saying
that what we could not touch had no being? (In a Catholic school,
this was a useful complication; at least some of the students had encountered in theology something as startling: One who was without
parts.) Was not endless regression necessary since everything is based
on undemonstrated statements? Did not this mean that nothing was
really so, but only assumed to be so? Or, if this endless regression
seemed necessary, would not that be because one never found an assumption that was self-evident, evident of itself, without needing anything else to justify it? Was there anything, like the self-evident, which
could, in any way, be as powerful as demonstration, by which was
meant science? After all, students could see unimpeachable signs of
precision at work in the clear evidence of technological progress; to
them science meant the precise; the precise meant the true. (They
had started life believing in the self-evident, but their formal education had almost worn away this belief, and they had replaced it by
belief in the rational, which they took to mean belief in what could
be demonstrated. To be able to do this meant to be educated, a state
to which the scientist, they thought, came closest.)

We could say this much about the definition of point: what
we put on the page was not point, for it could be divided, it had
parts. Could we imagine, that is, have in mind a point without parts?
Only if we could imagine it without body; this was difficult for we
were accustomed to considering it as a spot in place. But why not
consider it that way? If we did, how could we make any sense of no
parts? Consider the second definition: *A line is breadthless length;*
and the third definition: *The extremities of a line are points.* The second definition helps us to see that a line in a diagram cannot be a geo-
metric line as defined by the second definition, since the drawn line
has length and breadth; it is a representation of line, certainly not the
same as the one we have in mind. What do we lose then, if anything?
Breadth is surely a major addition, but how does this affect our understanding? We see the distinction between the diagram on the
blackboard, when the lines have breadth and length, and the defini-

tion which speaks of breadthless length only, which is like the distinction made between the point with parts and no parts. But what difference does it make? The third definition might help, at least for a time, for it identifies two points (*The extremities of a line are points.*) as extremities. (Are they always to be considered only as extremities?) Here they are, here they exist and, when a finite line appears, they are an inherent feature of such a line. Yet, the language raises difficulties. The third definition clearly makes point, as extremity, a part of the definition itself. But, we asked, does it also imply that point is a part of a finite line? Such an implication does not necessarily follow. Could point be a part of something else and yet not be divisible itself? (Later we would discover that for Euclid, units, which are parts of a number, are not divisible.) To speak of the part of a straight line as being always divisible, we would need an insight besides that provided by the definition. That insight, along with the first definition, would suggest that points cannot be parts of a line. Again, language in itself cannot help us.

CHANGING STUDENTS

It is important to say that I am not simply dealing with a method of teaching. I am posing, through my discussion of Euclid, the central question: how do you know what is so and what is not so?—a question inseparable from finding language to formulate what you know. The procedure I describe is not accidental, but is unavoidable, if attaining knowledge has to do with reaching common understanding (distinct from the unique and the merely private), which in turn cannot be separate from formulation. The problem of formulation, inescapably bound to geometry, is also bound to my work in literary criticism and the problems of teaching English. As necessary to the study of literary criticism as to the study of geometry, is an understanding of the nature of principles and the uses and limits of definition, hypothesis, demonstration, and evidence. Consider the perplexities the undergraduate faces when he chooses to study literary objects, self-contained structures made of words—phenomena not to be observed like inanimate structures, or biological objects, not like historical accounts based on artifacts and eyewitness reports also made of words, not like geometry controlled by the strictures of definitions and diagrams referring to defined objects in the imagination which they represent. One way of viewing literary study is to see it as concerned with describing and evaluating works understood as concrete artistic wholes in words, and controlled by emotional effects which dictate internal requirements—beginnings, middles, endings, the order of parts and whole, and the decisions involved in discovering appropriate diction for the construction of this whole. Questions one might consider include: What kind of an object is *Hamlet?* Being made of words and not wood, how can it be said to have existence? Why were these words, in this order, chosen by Shakespeare for Scene 1, rather than some others? What form does the play take which causes people to call it tragic? Does form mean the same as kind? Is the play a good one? What do we mean by a good work, a bad work? Or, to consider a different kind of question: How does *Hamlet* reveal its author as an Elizabethan? What was the state of the materials (sources, speech, literary and dramatic tradition)' Shakespeare had at hand when he wrote the play? By what means could one judge his works as progressively better than those written before him? What does one mean, in literary history, by progress? Can one begin to speak about it without considering the nature of history? The complexities inherent in literary study, not unlike those in other studies, require a mind ready to acquire the large apparatus necessary to handle a vast tradition and a host of vocabularies. A student entering such a study needs, to be prepared to become one who not only knows how to be openly puzzled, practiced in speculation, but one who has reflected specifically on the nature of language and formulation. Geometry is, I suggest, especially useful to this reflection for, among other reasons, its groundwork can be looked at much more directly than that of literature. The rigorous work of learning how to be reflective makes it possible to enter a new field of study with a developed critical intelligence ready to undertake and understand substantially more than can the usual novice entering the sacrosanct realms of the experts.

The obvious inability of most students to deal with ideas and their consequences causes most teachers to respond in a variety of unprofitable ways: some water down courses and resign themselves to the expected results; some, in horror of lowering standards, present high-powered lectures aimed at the few; some increase the length of the reading lists, thus filling the course with matter, but assuring little or no confrontation with principle and theory. Whatever the response, teachers on the whole force most students to resort to memorizing and jargonizing. Some students convince themselves that they know the subject; others despair of knowing anything about the subject even while they pass their tests and get their degrees. A few will go on to become competent, occasionally brilliant (the very nature of professionalism makes this possible), with little idea of the roots of their work and with a lopsided view of their enterprise. There will be those who will be driven, despite their training, or because of an unusual teacher, to make the extended effort to know what they are doing, or at least to come to understand the quality of their ignorance and power.

I am quite aware that there are teachers who, whenever possible, try to produce a direct confrontation with material through the continuous give and take of serious discussion in the classroom. (After such continuous activity, an occasional formal lecture, or any extensive statement written or spoken and open for examination, can be rich in its effect.) These teachers understand the need for students to become engaged with the material; they know that the puzzling and loving pursuit, which comes from the direct confrontation with one's subject, is the only way one comes to some legitimate understanding of it. But I suggest that such battles are generally losing battles, because, in the first place, so few of these classes have any way of making the long and hard struggle with fundamentals go far beyond the strictures of the disciplines. The graduate schools, through all of us trained by them, have absolute control of what is taught, how it is taught, and the complete organization of the curriculum. Courses are designed to delimit the subject and prepare for later work in the field; they are constructed on a timetable which by its nature must cut deeply into any extended work on the bases of the discipline. It is a losing battle, in the second place, because whatever effort we do make, to engage the students slowly and painstakingly, is essentially an isolated effort, although we may like to think differently. No coordinated and ordered, long-term, school-wide attack takes place.

A student does get engaged in his own education when he starts where men naturally start: as one man, one pair of eyes looking out at the world, unified and not departmentalized, not disavowing the connectedness of things. (Whatever men have actually learned in or out of school, they have learned in this way.) Though it is possible to pursue this connectedness in a number of fruitful ways, there is a special value in confronting Euclid because he depends on fewer hierarchies than most; because he can be seen to straddle the ground between the disciplines, touching, in surprising ways, various fields generally assumed to be quite distinct. The separation of the sciences from the arts is not an issue. What can make Euclid immediately exciting for undergraduates is that it is concerned with the question of demonstration and of how you know that anything is true. For them, the question of education lies just here. Is everything relative, only a matter of men's saying it? Or is it true? Is it possible to use such a word? If one can know truths, is science the only place we can get any verification? For many students, torn between what seems so obvious and their awakening thought that perhaps everything is relative, the opportunity to deal straightforwardly with the question of demonstration, that is, of proof, can be rewarding because it can be raised for an extended time, and at the beginning, when their respect for college education is still high.

Most men grapple with the issues we raised. What is true? How do I know? And if it is true, how do I proceed? If I proceed in this way, how does it affect the way I previously proceeded? As I proceed, how does this change further what I thought? If what I thought has changed, how am I to change if I am to act as I think? If I act on what I think is so, how am I to act rightly in accordance with it? Such a natural connection between what we think is so and how we act is always present. It is the most immediate cause for the common demand for contemporaneity, which, for most students and teachers, means relevance; the demand to deal with the real world, not with the ancients, the dead philosophers, the old books and the dead issues; the demand to deal with the world of Salinger, Mailer, Camus, Marx, Marcuse, Vatican II, with making a living and having a family, with revolution, poverty, black power, with whatever is considered here and now. The demand, when formulated this way, places a special premium on the specialist, for he is the one who makes it his duty to accumulate the latest information. He seems like the doctor, and is almost as necessary, who, in order to save lives, simply must keep up with the latest. If we understand relevance in this way we will proceed in the schools in the usual debilitating way with new material as the only indication of change. The very slogan relevance contributes to the onward dash to get more and more of what is now. Education under this slogan remains a matter of accumulation, and learning how best to get material organized and tabulated. Teachers and students will always be behind and in constant fear that something will be left out; even the most trivial item may turn out to be part of a new hypothesis which could change all that preceded it.

There must be another way to conceive of relevance, for what we were doing in that Euclid class was clearly not a matter of dead issues and ancient books. While we were always considering what it means to say that such and such was true, we were also reminded that language lay at the center of the enterprise, and Euclid could not proceed without it—a somewhat unexpected reminder for most students. Our work with him had to allow for the continual separation between word, or sign, and the object in our imagination and for the way in which such a momentous (relevant, contemporary) separation affects every attempt to say what we understand. Our task was to break the language, detached from its sources and sealed off on the page, out of its insulation; to establish the natural ambiguity of the word and to maintain a living edge of awareness between what one said and the object about which one said it, moment by moment, class by class. There was no other way to do this but by working with other individuals engaged in the same effort of confronting a common subject, who were willing to listen and see, to speak and be silent, and by determinating what does this mean; what am I saying now; does he understand; how much have I not stated; can I state it; do I understand him; how can I help him make what he wants to say clearer; does he mean that; is it related to what was already said; has he changed the question; what are we speaking about? We cannot do this without one another. The living face, the eyes and voice are there, ready, at the slightest sign, to modulate, to qualify, to pause; the mind is there, ready to reverse itself or to affirm. While an expert is especially adept at spotting digression and stopping it the instant it arises, digression itself can become a dramatic source of discovery. Our power in class was just that awkwardness which led us to traverse a path and come to a dead stop only when we had struck a barrier. In this way, we were pressed to turn ourselves about, and, thus constrained, to reach back, in any way we could, to what we had departed from. In one sense, learning to know what our subject was and was not could be seen as our continual discovery of the difference between a digression and its opposite.

In a richly provocative lecture, Eva Brann speaks of the distinction between formulation of problems and real questions: "A genuine question does not demand an answer in its own terms or on its own level, but seeks its desire wherever it may hope to find it, remaining open to any intimation its object might give. Nor will it rest satisfied by a construct or a fiction fabricated only to set it at rest, for it wants only what is in itself worth having. Problems are ultimately exercises, mere means, but questions are the serious and final human business . . . The most sophisticated machine *can never ask a question.* For it can never feel the desire to know, which is the heart of a question . . . everything that is presented to me *about* learning in observation or in books, is external and insufficient; I want to know *for myself,* and yet, in the *common language* of human beings, what makes the thing what it is. I am not looking for a preconceived x, unknown for the moment but so involved with and defined by the problem itself that I need only to rearrange the terms cleverly enough to get a solution, but I want something beyond these, namely the reason why the thing is what it is, and I want this reason to be freely communicable. Every "academic" search, particularly the kind nowadays called "research," moves strictly within the set terms of its discipline, and is therefore usually of interest only to the expert specialist, while many others can live without it: the quest of a question alone is after that without which we can hardly be said to *live* our lives, at least as human beings. "The Student's Problem. A Lecture on the Liberal Arts," Saint John's College, Annapolis, Maryland (October, 1967).

The class became a kind of foundry in which the job was to forge a common object that we could hold onto as long as possible in order to contemplate it. Part of the battle was how to stay on or near the fragile line between what we see and hear of the object and what we understand and say about it to one another. As we worked together, the necessary community grew, and the learner grew in the midst of it; because he watched and was part of the process, he began to sense, simultaneously, that he could learn and that there was something of great value to learn. No manner or number of speeches worked. Having begun to sniff it out himself, he experienced, perhaps more and more often, the head joy of seeing for a moment what he had not imagined before. In my mind, the whole academic year was an occasion to find out how best to make those who worked with me fall in love with learning; everything was bent to that end: how best I could draw the students out so they would speak directly to one another, to draw one another out, at times to do nothing but help another student by questioning and listening, perhaps by formulating, for him, what the other student wanted to say so that the first student might probe even further (especially difficult since the usual classroom is geared to private performance of student and teacher in answering questions); how I could encourage a student to stop the group and insist on pushing forward an issue that he did not understand, or to feel free to halt the discussion and ask another student, "Where are we?" and "How did you get there?"

What happened in class had everything to do with how I, personally, thought about and worked on Euclid. By this I do not mean how well I knew the answers and could explain them, but rather how I opened up the questions for my own private examination and dealt with them, and then, how I entered the classroom, unresolved if necessary; how my own day-to-day struggle with the material alongside others, who were also in the struggle, was reflected. Their search and puzzlement were related to how I searched and was puzzled—a matter controlled, as it was for everybody in the class, by how I knew and how I did not know. Certainly my tone of voice revealed both my serious puzzlement (unavoidable in taking on an entirely new subject) and my willingness to listen to others who were equally puzzled. My being honestly without answers, in the midst of a group of young men who already knew that I was a teacher, was electrifying. It had never happened to them before, and it compelled them, sooner or later, to recognize, or at least to consider, that what happened was up to them, that perhaps they could work their own way out, that it might even be respectable to do so. Through this they might come to see what they had never before believed for one moment (no short period is going to demonstrate this) that they did not need a teacher in the accepted sense. For me, the special problem was to find my way between appearing to be one of the boys (which can be lethal to the whole process, for it is never true) and continuing in the usual role of authority. The special potency here was in the unique and unavoidable tension between my official status and my position among the students, at the center of the pursuit: that is, listening to what was said, helping others clarify their thoughts; and, simultaneously, stumbling, like the others, into discoveries or serious error. I was a learner, responsible for my own education, yet, in a special way, at the same time responsible for the students'. The responsibility made for a flexibility and intensity, a sense of pacing inherent in the use of digression and pause. The atmosphere which developed, controlled by the geometry we discovered through the one immovable object, Euclid, encouraged the blossoming of a rich perplexity within a context of mutually discovered possibilities. Though it was painful for the student not to demand instant answers, what made the class work, in part, was the concrete implication that there was something out there which we were reaching for—an end more significant than the process and the exercise. During each class hour we probed and, by the end of the hour, we might arrive where we had not expected to be. Individual class sessions were not self-contained units, but steps on a path opening out toward more insight—through the astounding Book V on proportion, Book VII on number, and the final Book XIII on the five solids. The steps which, though consolidated as we went along, changed in their significance the more we understood, so that, by the end of the investigation, the whole which we contemplated in wonder, affected the parts along the way in a manner impossible to have foreseen at the outset. With Euclid, we now saw the edifice entire—many-sided, giving upon unexpected prospects, and suggesting neighboring demesnes yet unseen.

CHANGING TEACHERS

Though I would not have taught my course at Saint Mary's College without the existence of the Saint John's program and the Integrated Liberal Arts Curriculum, it is quite possible to start such a program. One needs approximately fifteen students, preferably freshmen of varying interests and abilities, and a teacher especially interested in the problems of learning, who is willing to break out of the preoccupations of his own field for at least one academic year. A single course investigating Euclid given by a non-mathematician might, as an experimental section of a general humanities requirement, have an electrifying effect. Though, as I have suggested, Euclid has especially powerful qualities which cut across the usual departmentalization, a non-specialist might devote a course to an investigation of measurement in the physics laboratory (an excellent syllabus for such a course already exists), or investigate, beginning with the fundamentals, any one of the disciplines with which he is unfamiliar. This will put the teacher into the painful position of learner all over again, but with the new problem of teaching while facing a massive series of perplexing questions he may have by-passed or may never have confronted seriously. Such a course can have an incalculable, liberating effect on his own intellect and will, affect the way he thinks about his specialization, and affect, as well, his thinking about teaching and what he does day-by-day in the classroom.

John D. W. Andrews

Encounter in
Freshman Writing

I wanted to teach writing to college freshmen in a way that would help them make the medium an effective extension of themselves, and not merely an external, mechanical skill as so often happens. I also wanted to find out how much could be done within the conventional context: a class of twenty that was typical of the freshman English seminars at my university.[1] I believe that the first small class a student encounters has much more impact than is provided by the subject matter alone; it is an important first experience in college learning, and therefore a unique opportunity for a university to provide its students with good models of this process. I wanted to find some new and better ways of making freshman English function this way.

[1] I wish to thank Taylor Stoehr, formerly director of the freshman English program at Buffalo, for the opportunity to try my ideas as part of a program that is highly innovative in its own right.

112

VII

State University of
New York at Buffalo

I brought to the problem an atypical set of qualifications: a long career as an occasional writer of poetry and fiction, and a good deal of experience with the communication problems of small groups, in and out of classrooms, acquired as a leader of Encounter Groups, and in other ways. My trade is social psychology, not literature, and partly for this reason I approached the problem of learning to write as a problem of communication. I attempted to help students explore the impact of their writing on other members of the group so that this impact could not only be understood but felt. This approach to writing makes sense. Language is learned in an intensely interpersonal and emotion-laden context; thought, personal expression, and communication are thoroughly intertwined from early childhood (Flavell, 1963; Kris, 1952; Mead, 1956), and, from these roots, writing develops. A group exploration of writing is not merely an experience somehow tacked on to an essentially individual process; it is the evocation of an

113

important formative process, and should be a good vehicle for developing the capacity to use language. Intense group contact provides the opportunity to learn about the personal messages one sends through tone, word sound, imagery, rhythm, metaphor, and so on. These personal messages probably have much to do with what is rich, individual, and satisfying in really good writing. Writing should be taught in an open, honest group situation because, for most people, it is intimately bound up with the self-image, self-esteem, and self-presentation. This means that writing will usually be surrounded by many of the anxieties about rejection and devaluation that surround any important self-perception. Defensive maneuvers will be used to resist the immediacy of the situation in which people are responding to one another, a reaction that probably causes failure in many classes and writing workshops. But this situation has potential for many kinds of growth. If people can be helped to trust and to take the risk of dealing with one another and with one another's writing directly, the group can bring to life the connections between self and writing that enable the individual to make the medium genuinely his own.

This approach challenges several widely held attitudes about writing. The first is that writing is a craft and that acquiring certain, objectively defined skills is a first, basic learning objective. The second is that, "Since writing is essentially a solitary and personal affair, the classroom approach tends—at least in some ways—to subvert the aims of the course." The third is the argument that making a writer more aware of his audience is dangerous, perhaps even a form of prostitution, and is likely to distort his natural development. Without responding in detail, I will state my working principle that to help students gain command of the emotional impact their writing has on others is valuable in itself. I hope that this mastery will help awaken latent word skill that students are not using, and that it will make writers less, not more, vulnerable to the passing whims of the public.

GOALS FOR THE COURSE

In the course, by using particular learning processes and promoting particular relationships between the instructor and the students and among the students themselves, I hoped to foster changes in the individuals.

The course should help students to become more aware of their own and of others' feelings, expressed in writing and in other ways. It should help students enter open relationships with others, within the class group and elsewhere. The course should enable students to master effective writing, and use it freely and naturally to express feelings and ideas that are important to them. This mastery must include, but go beyond technical skill.

To attain such personal goals, the student must be willing to expose himself to response from other people. For many students, simply writing about important feelings or experiences is a beginning. To read one's writing in the class is also an important step, and a difficult one for many; it is especially anxiety-provoking when one actively volunteers, rather than waiting to be picked, since this will heighten commitment to the outcome. The course will be effective if it can foster this sort of risk-taking. Individual risk-taking is only part of the process, however. For learning and communication to take place, others must respond, as directly as possible, with their feelings, attitudes, and judgments. To do this is also risky, since it can produce hurt feelings, anger, and self-doubt, but these must be dealt with if individual self-exposure to feedback is to have meaning. Helping students cope with the tensions of this process is an important aim of the course.

Leadership and responsibility for course movement provide structures for role-relationships and decision-making, and provide learning in themselves as well as setting a necessary context for attaining the objectives described above. They concern the mutual expectations between instructor and students, and between student and student, and I believe that success or failure on this level often determines what can be accomplished in other areas of a course.

In my view the instructor has a very complex leadership role to play in a class of this sort. Since the course demands a great deal of effort and willingness to confront one's own and others' feelings, and sometimes requires one to say difficult things about others' writing, there is a great need for leadership that is unwavering in its commitment to working through such encounters. For the course to succeed, it is vital, for example, that the instructor be sensitive to those moments when a student is holding back a comment because he fears to hurt the writer or fears to look foolish himself. If the instructor can help break the barrier at such points, the class will be able to move toward more open communication. The instructor's leadership activities need to be balanced against the value of student initiative. If, for example, he frequently calls on students to speak, or selects the writing to be discussed in class, he may win some acquiescence but defeat the aim of fostering emotional involvement and spontaneity; by taking over too much responsibility for the risks involved, he may seriously limit the opportunities for personal commitment on the part of students.

Students should be in charge of how and when they participate in discussions or presentations of writing. A student who feels he has no real right to say no if asked to comment will have difficulty in saying a genuine yes on other occasions. Especially in a course that attempts, as this one does, to foster emotional self-disclosure, students need to feel they can protect themselves without deception or withdrawal; self-disclosure is genuine only when actively chosen, and for this reason involvement in the course depends on students having a true choice about it. Success of the course also requires another sort of student involvement: a concern for one another's learning. When, for example, students encourage one another to talk, the increasing support and trust should help everyone to be more open.

TECHNIQUES USED

I have given this course twice, in somewhat different forms (to be referred to as Course I and Course II). Both lasted one semester, and were part of the freshman English program at the State University of New York at Buffalo. This is a required course, with considerable variety in how the individual sections are taught. In principle, freshmen can choose what they want, for example, analytic writing, polemics, and so on. In practice the choice is often made vaguely, hastily, or on the basis of scheduling. Few of my students had any conception of the course they had signed up for. In one sense this was a drawback, since I had none of the advantages of student self-selection or special commitment to the idea; in another sense, it helped in evaluation since the results can be more easily applied to any group of freshmen selected randomly. Like all sections in this program, the course was graded on a pass-fail basis and met for three one-hour sessions per week.

In introducing the course, I made clear my expectation that people would get personally involved, and that my goal was to help them use writing for their own self-expression, regardless of form. I stated that I would expect one piece of writing a week (a rule that was usually, but not strictly kept), and that this would not be one assignment to be submitted in a bundle at the end of the semester. I also told the students that all who participated in the course would pass, since I expected that such participation would generate worthwhile learning whatever their level of competence. I indicated that class sessions would be devoted basically to getting to know and react to one another, mainly, but not only, through writing. Time in class was used primarily for reading aloud and responding to the writing. Often I provided a particular structure to the session to help foster communication. I did not plan much ahead of time how to use a meeting but did have repertoire of approaches, which gradually became familiar to the group and which I could draw upon.

In many ways, reading and commentary in a large group were the most difficult to handle because the size of the audience intimidated people and because there was uncertainty about what was appropriate to say, and to whom. Another unfortunate effect was that people were less likely to talk to one another and more likely to talk into the air. When the students were working in pairs or trios, I would move from group to group, or talk to individuals about their writing, or would appoint one member of each small group to help, not by commenting directly on the writing, but by drawing people out when difficulties arose and by keeping things on the track. This assistant role is difficult to learn, and, several times, to make it work, I demonstrated before the whole group the kind of behavior I sought. These sessions helped to create a more intimate and manageable situation, where the conversation was directed to someone and so allowed people to get acquainted. They were also useful in distributing responsibility for response and evaluation, since students were listening and talking to students and were not awaiting the final word from the professor. During *fishbowl* or observation sessions, part of the group carried on a discussion while the rest were observers, concerned not only with what was being discussed but also with how people communicated. In one version, I asked half the group—those who had just finished acting as critics in one-to-one meetings—to meet in the center of the room to talk about criticizing; this helped to elucidate the concerns, such as fear of hurting, fear of misunderstanding, fear of seeming presumptuous, fear of being wrong, that were acting as barriers to judging the writing. In another version, when the entire group was openly worrying about how to respond to writing, I asked the inner group of seven people to carry on a miniature session. This allowed the outside observers to comment on what was said and left unsaid, to challenge silent members, and to notice the range of possible responses to a piece of writing. This helped solve our problem about how to respond; according to students' reports, it also increased their feeling of commitment to the goals of the course and to one another.

In the role-playing sessions, a piece of writing, often a character sketch or story, was used as a source of roles for students to enact in the group. The actors followed, not a script, but their own instincts from the starting point thus putting themselves into the situation. How a person chose to interpret a role was a way for us to discover more about the diversity of meaning that could be drawn out of a piece of writing by individuals with different personal outlooks and ways of experiencing life. When we were most successful, even the writer saw meanings that he had not intended but that were actually important themes in his own life.

The need for sessions during which only negative comments were permitted arose when students began to complain that everyone was holding back criticisms. One of my responses to this was temporarily to rule out nice comments. This simplified the situation for students, since being negative was no longer an individual choice, and did lead to some increased bluntness. However, it is a restrictive device and I felt comfortable using it only as a response to clearly expressed dissatisfaction from the students.

In the group fantasy sessions, two or more people would speak aloud, as if describing a dream sequence, but allowing themselves to be influenced by and incorporating the fantasy of the others. My intent in doing this was to help people communicate more directly and to make words and imagery more interpersonally relevant, in the hope of affecting students' writing. The first effect was accomplished, but I doubt whether the connection between the spoken fantasies and writing was ever usefully grasped by the students. Possibly a more frequent use of this approach would have helped them do so.

After a reading, a second person would respond to comments and questions as if he had written the piece. The aim of this was to make visible one individual's interpretation of what was at the root of another's work. Usually the difference was substantial, and this led to new discussions and comparisons between what was intended and what was actually conveyed.

I want to emphasize strongly that the techniques described above do not make the course. They are aids only; their success depends on when, where, and how they are introduced to a class. They can be used only on instructor's initiative; at first, most of the techniques are strange to students and can produce dependency and confusion as easily as freedom. Issues of timing and context, crucial in determining the effect, are best discussed with reference to concrete examples.

CRITICAL INCIDENTS

I have chosen some critical incidents to show how various situations arose and were handled by me and by others during the course. They should be thought of as critical rather than as representative incidents for several reasons. First since they are used as illustrations, they were usually chosen for their richness, clarity, and dramatic impact. Naturally not all that happened had these characteristics, and those events that were confused, unfulfilled, or just banal are probably underrepresented. Also, while both successes and failures are included, the sampling is probably not representative either. There are some situations that are so formless that they are not worth discussing, and their failure lies precisely in their lack of clarity. Such situations are not well represented. However, the sample need not be representative since the material is intended not to prove anything, but to indicate the structure of my own thinking and the sorts of events that I used, during and after the course, as guideposts to tell me how I was doing and where I was going. Incidents from Course I and Course II are grouped together, but there is no significance in their order.

In one session I introduced a group fantasy in which I set the scene (climbing a mountain and finding a cave) and asked each person to close his eyes and imagine what he saw happening next. Afterward, I asked anyone who felt inclined to tell what he had seen. After several responses, I began to feel annoyed with one student, a chronic sourpuss who at that moment appeared to be asleep, and asked him pointblank what he had imagined. He mumbled something about "nothin'—I went down the mountain and took a swim." Unwilling to let go, I took this as part of the fantasy and said, "I think I'll join you on the beach." He replied that he was walking down the beach away from me because he wanted to be alone, and this led us into a fantasy-argument that ended with his running away from camp and giving a fifteen-minute fantasy-monologue about his trip back home. At the end he acknowledged that "that was good." I felt closer to him and it seemed clear that he too had been involved. Yet he did not return to class for several weeks. Some time later he wrote a painful paper on his unhappiness at college, and then disappeared again for a long time.

This incident illustrates both the successes and the problems I experienced in Course I. I was effective in drawing this student into much greater self-disclosure and into a closer relationship with me; but I had gained this through a great deal of pressure, which was not consistent with the role I had defined for myself as instructor. This pressure may account for his subsequent disappearance, since it would be one way of reducing a threat of exposure he felt unable to control in my presence. In short, the immediate gain was overshadowed by a long-range problem.

One session, beginning with a debate over criticism and the anxieties it causes, led a student to comment, "Well, I know I'm no good—I just can't write." I took up the challenge, and asked him to read and let us decide for ourselves. He did; he had written an account of getting stuck in the snow with his car and not being able to get out. Afterward the comment was made that the piece was not smooth like a football announcer's style, and lacked suspense, dramatic effect, and so on. Yet I felt that, mediocre as this writing was, it had an effect of its own—a pessimistic disgust that was conveyed by such anticlimactic lines as: "I roared down one hill to get momentum, and I knew I wouldn't make it. I started up the other hill, and I didn't." I pointed this out and added that it seemed to be part of his own style, as reflected also in the pessimism with which he had presented the piece to us in the first place. He agreed that pessimism was familiar to him, and this led us into a general discussion of writing to express yourself as opposed to writing according to some abstract model of what is good.

This situation illustrates one way of handling uninspired writing while avoiding the awkward step of dismissing it as trivial at a stage when this might have inhibited everyone. Instead of evaluating, I dealt with the personal context of the writing, particularly with the relation of its anticlimactic quality to the writer's pessimistic interpersonal style. To me, this connection supports the notion that emotional rhythms do govern writing even when this effect is not self-consciously sought. The feedback this student received may help him use his style with more deliberate choice in his future writing.

After about ten sessions in Course I, attendance began to decline. I asked whether students thought that it was a reaction to what was going on. I got blank stares, assurances that attendance "wasn't so bad," and the like. This was no real response to my efforts, I felt, and became angry, saying that life was too short for such apathy. This produced the reaction that "we weren't taught to think for ourselves," and other similar pleas. Without learning much from this attempt, I concluded that students were getting bored and began to introduce more stimulus: group fantasy, role-playing, and other exercises.

I am not, even now, fully certain what caused the drop in attendance, whether outside events, boredom, fear of being exposed, or something else. I believe now, though, that to ask students for reasons at this stage was not an effective way of sharing responsibility for the evaluation and direction of the course. For students to participate, or perhaps even to know what was bothering them, was almost certainly more than they were prepared to cope with; and, as my approach was often punitive, whatever self-doubts contributed to keeping them quiet could only be magnified. Even the attempt to discuss the issue may have intensified the impasse for, if my demanding too much disclosure too soon was, as I believe, creating stubborn resistance in them, my asking for feedback and participation could only be regarded as one more demand to be fought in the same way. Such situations are among the most difficult I encounter in classrooms, and once they occur there seems to be no really good solution to them. In Course II, however, I managed to find some ways of avoiding them entirely.

One day about midway in the course, five students arrived and we drifted into a discussion of the group's progress. One girl said she disliked my probing, searching questioning when an issue came up; she felt intruded upon. I replied that it was my way of trying to deal with the inertia of the class, and this led us into a full and involved discussion of the problem of participation. Discouraged with the active approach, which was obviously not producing participation, I decided on a radical switch for the next session: I came into the class and said nothing. After a period of fidgeting and giggling and trying to start up little conversations, several students became annoyed and one walked out. There was some discussion of silence and how people felt in it, and then one young man, talkative yet somehow shy too, said "Why should we communicate? I'd rather write for myself." Several others indignantly challenged him, and there developed a brisk discussion of social relatedness, which lasted the rest of the hour.

This incident demonstrates some of the extreme oscillations of behavior one finds when a basic problem, in this case that of mutual responsibility between instructor and students, remains essentially unsolved. The failures of one extreme (my probing, demanding approach) press one, with great force, to the opposite extreme (total silence). It may even be that, once caught in the bind, this is the best course to take. Because of my action some strong reactions were expressed, and if nothing else this was a step toward improving the honesty of relationships. Even better, the silence led some students to explore intently their reasons for communicating at all. Nevertheless, I am not satisfied with this approach, because its effectiveness depends too much on its being a sudden, dramatic move on the instructor's part. Although I was quite silent and nondirective during the discussion, this negative act provided for the students an external stimulus which cannot, in the long run, be a substitute for their own initiative.

About midway through the course, I introduced role-playing as a way of exploring the implications and possible interpretations of a written character sketch. This met with a string of objections from the class, including doubts about whether they could act, whether one could correctly sustain a consistent role, whether a character really exists beyond what the writer has presented. We fought these through by trying them out at my insistence, over a period of four or five class hours, to a point where some understanding and assent had been won. Then we began working on a short sketch about Dave, a student who sat in the cafeteria spouting political nihilism and exuding sourness and discouragement toward friends who showed any interest. We enacted various ways to wake Dave up; he was totally impervious to political arguments for activism, but somewhat more responsive to personal interest from a girl. Some versions of Dave were surly and uncommunicative, while other versions expressed to friends the sad, lost thoughts which the sketch presented as internal monologue. We learned about the character as it was presented in the sketch and as it was refracted through the personal constructs of various readers.

I consider this an effective segment of the course, for several reasons. I succeeded in exerting leadership usefully by insisting that we stick with an approach, articulate people's difficulties with it, and work through to some answers, positive or negative, individual or shared. I tried, with some success, to introduce a time perspective that would allow us to cope more easily with people's anxiety during the exploration of this new medium. Many students did make closer connections between the written material and their own feelings and perceptions about people. I value particularly our having understood, at least partly, the rich variety of interpretations that can grow out of a work. Students were able to see that these interpretations are bound up with each interpreter's feelings and ways of looking at the world.

Broadly speaking, the goals and teaching approaches in Course I and Course II were similar. The one major difference was that, after teaching Course I, I had a better sense of students' needs and their limits of tolerance for self-disclosure, and was able to pace my expectations more closely with their capacities and avoid some of the unproductive extremes that occurred in Course I.

In an early meeting of Course II, I asked the students to participate in a plan for the hour that began with fifteen minutes of paired discussion, with one student acting as critic for the other; subsequently, the critics met in the center of the group and discussed how the role felt to them. Problems they mentioned include fear to hurt the writer by criticism, feelings of inadequacy in the role of judge, dislike of picky grammatical comments. I had intended, then, to reverse the situation and ask the critics to have their work read, but one girl from the critic group said that her partner's poem was so good we should all hear it. He was willing, and read us a long, complex poem full of disjointed, tumultuous and often frightening imagery. Response was strong: some liked the imagery; others found it frightening but still liked it; others were somewhat repelled. There was some comment on the obscurity of the poem, but my impression is that those who were most confused by it simply remained silent.

This incident shows increasing student involvement in dealing with the problems of self-disclosure. The plan was intended to help students articulate some of the barriers to forthright criticism through an arrangement that would get at the issue without singling anyone out too much. But the group raised my bet in a gratifying way: the girl who spoke up risked making her own judgment public, but provided assurance and support to help the writer read his poem. My

gradual introduction of more and more self-expression during the previous sessions had helped the class build up to this session; but this
was, on its own terms, an important step toward shared reponsibility
for moving the group along.

One of the students was a woman of about thirty, whose initial
writing was a satirical critique of television commercials which to me
seemed shallow. In one class she discussed poverty in a way that made
me ask, "Are you talking about yourself?" She said she was. In a long
discussion after class, I urged her to write more from her own experiences. She was hesitant and felt it would be very hard; I said I understood that but hoped she would try anyhow. Her first attempt, which
she read to the class, was a long prose description of her parents' life
in the 1930's. Intended to be explanatory, it sounded more like an indictment of today's indulged youth and provoked an intense argument
in class. At the end I pointed out how polarized our discussion had
become because of the critical tone of the essay. Again I suggested
that she write from her own experience; she responded that she did
not want people to pity her, but was willing to try, at least for me
to read, and produced an evocative description of her own youth.

My private work with this student involved a long and difficult
process of helping her arrive at a direct personal expression of her
own experience. Before she could write in this way, we had to deal
with her stereotypes about correct but empty writing, the television
piece; her judgmental, defensive stance in the discussion of the thirties
(a tone she seemed unaware of until she saw the group's reaction);
her anxiety about being pitied if she wrote of her own troubled childhood. Probably, she was able to work through these barriers partly
because she did not give up easily, partly because she received useful
support and direct feedback from me and others.

After the whole group had had a number of reading sessions
together, I asked how people felt about volunteering for this. We had
never lacked for volunteers, but usually they were the same few people. A number of people said that it was not a comfortable situation
but, to make the course work, had to be accepted. I then said, "Well,
since we're agreed in principle, now who'd like to volunteer?" As
usual, people were awkward; one individual "volunteered" someone
else; another, turning to a silent faction, asked, "How come we never
hear from those people?"; and a third said, "It would be much easier
if you just pulled names out of a hat." I asked her how she felt about

reading. She replied, "Oh I will if you want me to." Excited, I said that what I did not want was that sort of half-hearted agreement and that that was why I would never pull names out of a hat; that I did not want mechanical students in here and that I felt that, if we were going to have anything worthwhile, we each had to choose whether to read or not. After some discussion, we had a genuine volunteer.

Volunteering often stands for commitment and responsibility for furthering group goals. Because I had asked the initial question, people had to worry about the problem of participation. Some responded with concern for nonparticipants; others tried to regress to the authoritarian method of having the teacher call on students. Had I asked the question at a less opportune time (earlier in the course, before we had had some success), I suspect that I might have drawn nothing but blank stares, which happened in Course I. As it was, I felt that I had an opportunity to make explicit my own values in explaining why I would not take over and draw names from a hat. With this explanation, I staked out an area of student autonomy, which I would not encroach on.

About two-thirds of the way through the second course, various frustrations and confusions led us to an explicit discussion of how we should be using response and feedback. We wrestled with this problem for an entire session, discovering how varied were people's preferences. In the next session, one of the more articulate and involved students began discussing what group response meant to him. First he said he wrote for himself and would not change anything on the basis of a class comment; he was accused of being a snob. Then he said criticism was irrelevant since it was what he felt that mattered, and promptly the authenticity of the feelings he had expressed in a poem was challenged. Another student said, "Yes, but what if your metaphors just don't make it?" and, "I just can't get at you through your writing." Even though we arrived at no explicit decisions about how to proceed, this day was a high point of intensity and challenge between writer and audience. In such sessions, we were all wrestling with group responsibility for decisions that the class had no time to make. The discussion was often frustrating and people felt they were getting nowhere. The intensity reached in the second of these sessions did not recur spontaneously, for I had organized ways of using feedback, for example, by setting aside fifteen minutes when only negative comments would be permitted. In retrospect, I wonder if continued struggle might have sustained the high point we did reach, or if people might simply have given up. I do not know, but maybe I will experiment a little more boldly next time.

During the last weeks, many of the students read "before and after" pieces: something written at the beginning of the course and something written at the end. One student, whose poetry was, at the beginning, rich in imagery, evocative and frightening but scarcely understandable, moved progressively to writing that kept some of these qualities but was much less mysterious and showed, much more directly, where he was emotionally. This was the group's judgment, and mine, and the group felt more able to relate to the later writing. I have very mixed feelings about the situation. I am pleased that the writer now feels more able to contact people with his writing—an understandable outcome of writing in a group that stresses communication. However, there was a mysterious fascination about those early images that had a different immediacy. Although the later work did communicate better, and seemed better controlled, it may have become geared to the understanding of this particular group of people; the writer was, therefore, constricted by his audience. Another audience might have had a different effect; in some ways he might be better off writing alone for himself. At the very least his writing is changed because of the group experience. In evaluating this, we touch on the issues of style and value in art that are vital but that will remain to be explored.

EVALUATION

A questionnaire was given at the close of the semester to students in Course II and to five other freshman English classes taught by graduate students. These other classes, to be referred to as control courses, shared with Course II an emphasis on personally expressive student writing, but were quite different in format, instructor's style, and so on. Thus the comparison is between different approaches to approximately similar objectives. The objection may be raised here that the comparison is not useful, since the other instructors were considerably less experienced than I was and that this alone might account for differences in success. Whatever antecedent causes one assigns, however, the central problem remains that of understanding how the instructor's behavior in the classroom affected the learning process in the different courses. For this purpose I believe the control groups used were appropriate.

The questionnaire consisted of forty-five statements that might describe how a class functions as a social unit; a few of these statements are reproduced in the Appendix. These items were to be rated in two ways: first, according to how the students saw their class; and second, according to how they would like the class to be. They were also asked to rate their satisfaction with the class as a learning experience and with their own contribution and performance.

The questionnaire contained two measures of overall satisfaction with the class as a learning experience: the direct ratings of satisfaction, and the sum of discrepancies between perceived and desired conditions on the individual descriptive items. These measures are positively intercorrelated ($r = +.57$), indicating that both probably reflect the same set of attitudes toward the experience. Course II was given a mean rating of 4.50 on a scale ranging from 1 to 5. This mean rating exceeded the mean rating of every control class to a statistically significant degree ($P < .01$ by t tests). The second important criterion of success is how closely the conditions in the course match the ideal group-climate described in the section on goals. To answer this, I composed a subscale of the questionnaire (called the Climate Scale) consisting of 16 items related to four major areas of the course. Each item could be scored zero to three; out of a possible score of 48, Course II was rated at 35.4. The nearest mean among the control classes was 26.0. The differences between Course II and all the control classes were statistically significant ($P < .0001$ by t tests).

More than the others, Course II was perceived as a place where people talked about themselves and each other in important ways and where personal relationships were formed. Students indicated they felt highly involved in what went on and had considerable autonomy. The instructor was seen as playing a democratic, facilitative role.

In addition to the two measures of satisfaction, I constructed a second scale consisting of items that refer to how student apathy is handled (the Apathy Scale). Eight of these items concern instructor's behavior, so that the focus of the scale is on how the instructor handles the problem of participation. When my rankings of ideal instructor's behavior, described in the section on goals, are compared with the reality perceived by students, Course II appears quite successful: the Spearman rank-order correlation is +.74, which is statistically significant at $P < .05$. By contrast, the correlations of my ideal rating with conditions in other courses were .33, .29, .13, 00, and −.28, and were not statistically significant.

The above data help to evaluate the course, as perceived by the students, in terms of *my* goals. It is also necessary to know how closely the reality students perceived matched *their own* values. To do this, I ranked the items in the climate and apathy scales once according to the mean *perceived* rating, and once according to the mean *desired* rating in each class; the correlation between these two sets of rankings in a class gives a measure of how closely the perceived reality corresponded to the ideal. On the Climate Scale, this correlation in Course II is +.65 ($P < .05$), and, in the control courses, are +.60 ($P < .05$), +.46, +.37, +.24, and +.02. On the Apathy Scale, the correlation in Course II is nearly perfect: +.96 ($P < .05$), and in the control courses is much lower: +.58, +.52, +.51, +.30, and −.06. These data indicate consistently that Course II succeeded in meeting its stated objectives with respect to learning climate and also satisfied the students.

It is also important to compare each instructor's goals with the conditions perceived by the students in his course. To do this we rank the instructor's desired ratings and the mean *perceived* ratings of his students, and obtain a correlation between the two. On the Climate Scale, the correlation in Course II is +.63 ($P < .05$); in the control courses, are +.37, +.29, −.07, and −.47; for the Apathy Scale, the correlation in Course II is +.63, and in the control courses are +.00, +.08, +.04, and −.09. Thus Course II also met the instructor's own goals better than the control courses did.

It is also important to ask how similar were the goals of all parties involved: myself, the other instructors, and the students. We must know whether we were applying one common standard or several different standards in evaluating the courses. The evidence indicates that there was a single, widely shared set of preferences as to how these classes should function. To begin with, the students' preference-rankings from the different sections of the course are all highly intercorrelated both for the Climate Scale (median rho = +.90) and for the Apathy Scale (median rho = +.87). A similar pattern holds, though less strongly, for the instructors' preference-rankings, the median correlations being +.40 and +.57. When the instructors' and the students' preference-rankings are pooled and compared, the resulting correlation is +.50. Within courses, also, there is congruence between the *desired* ratings of instructors and students: on the Apathy Scale, the correlations are .67 (Course II), .87, .75, .69, .66, and .30; on the Climate Scale, .89 (Course II), .93, .86, .81, .80, and .75. It seems clear that we were comparing courses for which both instructors and students had similar objectives and that Course II was, from all points of view, the most effective in reaching those goals. Since the preferences of students and instructors were so similar and since there is no reason to suppose that the class groups were different to begin with, it seems likely that the instructor's style of leadership is a critical variable in determining success or failure. Data from the Apathy Scale measurements indicate that instructors in the control courses differ in terms of active structuring versus passive permissiveness; they tended to be ranked high on all of the items at one or the other end of this polarity. By contrast, the instructor's style in the experimental course, neutral on this continuum, was highly distinctive in another way: high-ranked items described positively-toned characteristics that placed trust in students, while low-ranked items described either traditional, autocratic behavior, or a kind of negative goading; both of which might be expected to inhibit students.

In short, it seems that the control instructors organized their behavior around a construct of activity versus passivity, without discriminating between effective and destructive aspects of either approach. In Course II, the valuable aspects of both activity and passivity were combined (the two items ranked highest were "When people are hesitant to talk, the instructor waits and lets the class struggle until it comes up with something to do" and "When people are hesitant to talk the instructor tries to put them at ease and helps them to express themselves"), while the negative features were successfully avoided. It is interesting to note also that extremes of directiveness and passivity, combined often with a critical tone, were characteristic of my own behavior in Course I, which was in my opinion no more successful than the control courses. Apparently my mistakes in Course I were rather similar to those the control instructors made.

The writing produced by students in Course II was evaluated by a member of the English Department faculty who was familiar with freshman writing and with the course goals of personal expression and integrated command of writing. He evaluated two pieces of writing from each student—the first of the course and a later product —against the norm from his prior experience. He did not have time to make similar ratings of writing from the control courses. His judgment was that Course II began below the average of where students typically begin this kind of course in writing and ended at about the average of where students typically end. This means that the amount of improvement was above average—a reasonable, though not striking, confirmation of Course II's effectiveness.

Course I and Course II were in some ways similar and, in others, different. The aims were much the same, in my mind, and, I believe, as presented to the two classes, and so was the repertoire of classroom techniques on which I drew. In both courses I intended to set up a learning cycle involving self-disclosure and feedback, but the way this worked out differed sharply in each course. In Course I, there was little self-disclosure, except on my initiative, and I provided more response and feedback than was healthy for active student participation. Course II proceeded more organically: the issue of self-risk arose gradually at first, and it was only when a number of students had resolved this by taking initiatives that the need for group-response was genuinely felt and could be fulfilled.

The difference in practice was caused, primarily I think, by differences in the leadership I provided in each course. In Course I, looking for ways to stimulate the class, I oscillated from one extreme of activity to another. I did not find a pace that was comfortable and usable by the students. Students, especially freshmen, come to classes full of self-doubt and the need for self-protection. They are—often with good reason—like wild animals entering an unfamiliar part of the jungle; they must sniff the air, listen for small sounds, generally test the situation before they can relax enough to take in any nourishment. When the duration of this scanning process exceeds the instructor's ability to tolerate uncertainty, there will be trouble. Almost certainly, this happened in Course I and in the control courses. Since the scanning is mostly covert, the instructor may come to believe that nothing is happening, that the students are a collection of empty-headed dolts. Or he may begin to rummage around among his own self-doubts, and conclude that he is failing to make things interesting enough. When this happens, the instructor may react in a number of ways. He may criticize the class for being dull; barrage them with activities or challenges in the hope of stirring up some life; abandon hope of participation and begin lecturing; let them stew in their own juice of inactivity; or command responses in a heavy-handed manner. These are dangerous things to do because they obscure the original situation while setting up vicious cycles that further intensify the complexity and tension of the classroom situation at precisely the moment when students and instructor are struggling to master the existing conditions. This intensifies the anxiety and self-doubt that produced the inactivity in the first place, and ultimately students and instructors can come to believe that neither is interested or even very much alive. This then becomes the myth that underlies the unsatisfying routines or struggles of so many class meetings.

The attitude that helped me most in Course II was the simple belief that, given a chance, most students would want to become excited, take a few risks, and become better acquainted. Thus I assumed, when things were slow, that people needed more time to explore and settle their anxieties and not that either I or they were at fault. I had an equilibrium that enabled me to move with the mood of a situation, to sense what was needed from me, to be more spontaneous myself, and to avoid overwhelming anyone. In these terms, and in the light of students' ratings, I view Course II as successful, whereas Course I was not.

More could have been done. Some students were never involved, many responses were superficial, and not all students improved their writing as much as I had hoped. My approach sacrificed some rigor and toughness in the discussion of writing. The students apparently agreed, for they indicated that we had all held back too many of our negative comments. In many ways, an uncritical atmosphere is essential if people are to become free enough to explore themselves and one another. However, the criticisms are still there, and often are legitimate; we should not fool ourselves that they can be eliminated. The course ended at a stage along the way; with more time and effort I would want us to be both tougher and more trusting with one another; toughness and trust are inseparable.

APPENDIX: CLASS DESCRIPTION SHEET

Instructions. . . . Following each statement are two blanks; in the first, place a number, according to the code described below, that indicates how well the statement describes your section. In the second blank place a number to indicate *how you would like things to be in your section.*

Rating Code:

0—Rarely or never happens

1—Occasionally happens

2—Often happens

3—Very often happens

Item	The class as you see it	The class as you want it to be
3. People discuss their feelings about each other or each others' writing.	....	....
8. People say what they like and dislike in students' writing.	....	....
12. I feel apathetic or bored.	....	....
13. When people are hesitant to talk, other students try to encourage them.	....	....
14. In discussion or in their writing, people talk about things that are very important to them.	....	....
20. I want the experience of having my ideas or writing discussed.	....	....
21. The instructor asks the class for suggestions about what to do.	....	....
22. People evaluate students' writing in terms of how good or bad it is.	....	....
27. Friendships develop among members of the class.	....	....
29. People are able to choose when and how much they will participate or reveal themselves in discussions.	....	....
30. I feel free to participate in discussions.	....	....
31. People hold back their negative comments about students' writings.	....	....

33. The instructor strongly controls the direction and content of the discussion. ....

35. Most people participate freely in the discussion. ....

37. When people are hesitant to talk, the instructor tries to put them at ease and helps them to express themselves. ....

Philip J. Runkel

The Campus
As a Laboratory

Learning is a process of changing one's mode of adaptation as the patterns in the environment change. Most college students adapt very well.[1] The first principle I used in designing my course in social psychology is that students do not have to be made to learn; they are adapting (learning) during every waking moment. The other chief principle upon which my design rests is that human beings are always seeking freedom—whenever they do not need to be seeking food and shelter. When we say a human is free, one essential thing we mean is that he is usually forming his own new ways of relating to his environment by exploring it from his own starting point. He is not free when he must accept a mode of behavior, from some person in power, without ascertaining on his own judgment how well that mode of be-

[1] I am indebted to the University of Oregon for special funds with which to assess outcome, and to Daniel Langmeyer, Mary Newcomb, Theodore Newcomb, and Oron South for especially helpful criticisms of the manuscript.

134

VIII

University
of Oregon

havior fits his world as he knows it. Conversely, if a human is always seeking to learn, he is always seeking freedom, willy-nilly. In schools, as elsewhere in life, students give most of their attention to learning how to adapt to other humans—to teachers and to fellow students. Here, as elsewhere, what offers freedom offers learning. I am arguing the ancient principle of academic freedom, but for students as well as for teachers.

Imagine, having signed up for the sophomore course in social psychology, that we walk into a room where there are sixty, or one hundred, or even two hundred other students who are moderately curious about what is going to happen. At the first meeting of the course, the teacher explains that social psychology has to do with the interaction between people—the ways that people go about working with one another, dealing with one another, loving one another, ignoring one another. He says that one of the important communities of people within which we find ourselves is the campus community, that we find ourselves in interaction with teachers, with our fellow students, and with other people belonging to this campus. Therefore, if we want to see the processes of social interaction at first hand, we have only to look around us. The teacher tells us that he is going to ask us to use the university campus, and the people on it, as a laboratory. He asks us to observe some social processes that are taking place within this laboratory; he asks us to make the observations systematically and to write a report on what we have seen. In particular, he says, he wants us to look at conditions and processes of social interaction that affect the teaching and learning that take place on this campus. The teacher explains that the job of making observations and reporting on them takes a good deal of time and is a larger task than any one person can do effectively during eleven weeks. Therefore, he asks us to work in groups where we can divide up the job. He is leaving to us the task of forming groups in which we care to work and the task of finding the particular projects we want to carry out in this attempt to study social interactions on the campus that affect teaching and learning. He tells us that the whole job for the term is to decide upon a project, to collect and interpret the data, and to write the report. There will be no examinations, no assigned readings, no formal lectures. The teacher explains further that there will be certain aids available to us. We will find that we have resources within ourselves that will enable us to help one another in projects. To work effectively in groups requires certain interpersonal skills, and he will give practice in some of these skills as the days go by. He gives us a bibliography listing readings on the technicalities of collecting data, and on roles and other matters relevant to human coordination. He has arranged for us to be in contact with people who have already been through this kind of course; namely, some of the students who took this course last year. He asks these people to stand up, and we see a dozen people scattered throughout the room rise. The teacher tells us that these students will act as consultants during this year's course. They are not going to serve as assistant teachers in any traditional way; they are not here to teach us how to talk about social psychology. Rather, they will help us with our projects and with any other perplexity we want to ask them about.

As the teacher, one demand I feel heavy upon me on the first day of a course is to move the attention of the students beyond my preferences and the rewards and punishments at my command. It is not sufficient to tell the students that they should look beyond the teacher and seek rewards of their own shaping in the tasks to be done. The best technique I have found is to say something on the first day that shows that my own attention has gone beyond the matter of rewards and punishments. I have chosen to describe to the students the relations between faculty and students that make me ashamed. The chief points of my introductory lecture, highly compressed, are: "We tell you that you are unimportant; what you deserve from a professor is often only 1/200 or 1/500 of three hours a week of this time. So unimportant is the matter of how much attention you get that we do not even bother to assess whether our attention to you is producing any results. You are uninformed or unintelligent: we do not ask you to contribute your knowledge of the world, or of your own needs, to the pool of resources at the university. We do not arrange communication channels so that you can do so. We tell you that men should be well rounded when obviously we do not think we should be. We tell you that we will free you from our ministrations in upper division and graduate school when obviously we have set aside the bulk of our salary money so that we can pay more attention to the upper division and the graduate students. You are untrustworthy: only the faculty can be trusted to decide whether you do or do not know something, when you are ready for a new idea, when you should come to class, how long it should take you to learn something, whether your achievements are admirable, and so on. But in any case, you are not individuals; you are a mass of something to be processed."

A second demand I feel is that of making a bridge to the world beyond the classroom. There is no doubt that the questions of what might be learned at a university, and of how it might be learned, are burning questions for many students. There is no doubt, either, that relations between students and faculty provoke great frustration and yearning for a great many students. Both these pressing problems, of what to learn, and of student-faculty relations, are interlaced with conflict, between persons and inside persons. Consequently, reactions to these features of campus life can be strongly motivating.

An important criterion for progress in investigating actual conditions on an actual campus is provided by the exterior facts themselves. People do not need to be told whether their work group has agreed upon a plan, whether the several members of the group are doing what they agreed to do, whether the data the group had planned to collect have indeed been collected. Much of the information necessary for a work group to obtain is impossible for the teacher to provide. The members of the work group must obtain this information from their own activity or from one another and only they are qualified to make many of the decisions called for along the way. A realm of learning that deals with exterior facts observable by both students and teacher has certain useful consequences. First, the conduct of the task itself enables students to gauge their own progress when they most need to have this information. A teacher cannot possibly furnish judgments about progress as often or as well-timed. Second, the task gives an orientation for conferences between students and teacher that encourages the conferences to be task-oriented and reality-oriented rather than teacher-oriented. Third, the contact with the exterior reality helps keep the teacher honest. I cannot easily delude myself that I know the best answer merely because I can talk the professional lingo if I know that my advice will be tested in the field. Fourth, when an outside reality constitutes the means by which students can judge much of their own performance as learners, their power is increased in relation to that of the teacher, and this, in turn, enables them to communicate more freely and openly with the teacher. Finally, though the teacher may be an expert on the abstract principles of social psychology, his students know, better than he does, what actual processes are taking place within their work groups. The group members themselves must become experts about one another and their interrelations if they are to do their project competently. They are the only ones with whom they can check to ascertain their success in learning about one another. This fact helps a great deal in enabling the students to learn the proper role of the resource person who is their teacher.

My goals for the students are not that they should acquire the knowledge that is now mine; not that they should read what I have read; not that they should be able to say what I can say. Therefore, I administer no examinations and I assign or require no readings. The only formal requirement is the report on the project. My goals for the students are that they should see new happenings in the world about them; should bring new skills to bear on their interaction with that world; should add new criteria to their judgments of their own potentialities in that world. Even the report on the project must be adapted more to the demands of that outer world than to my convenience, so I have made it clear that the report is due when the requirements of the project permit it to be completed. Many reports come in after the official close of the term.

Compared with traditional methods, my design for learning greatly increases the amount of immediate feedback the student can get, from portions of the environment important to him, about his progress and the quality of his work. The design makes use of the principle of pacing or readiness, enabling the student to begin by engaging himself with the social processes most visible to him. It maximizes the initiative of the student in using the teacher as a resource and minimizes the degree to which the teacher can impress his own ways of doing things upon the students. It uses the principle of cognitive balance or consonance, giving the student experiences that involve his ego and for which he must seek satisfying explanations, driven not by the external threat of the grade, but by his own values and learnings.

Drawing upon the fact that the students have enrolled in the university and in this course and have thereby implicitly promised to accept at least a certain amount of restriction from me, I do draw a boundary around a certain area of free movement. A firm part of the boundary is my insistence that the projects of the students deal centrally with observable facts in the environment, not with statements in books or lectures. Another is that I require that the narrative of the projects and their results be reported to me in written form. Ideally, I would prefer the reports to be circulated to everyone in the class, but I have not been able to do this with the money and machinery at my disposal. However, the students have been made aware, to some extent, of what was going on in other work groups during the term through oral and written progress reports occasionally made in class. The last part of this boundary is that the project must be limited to the financial resources available. Some of these resources have been provided by the students themselves; some—a hundred dollars or so— by agencies within the university. Once or twice the financial limitations have hurt the possibilities for very worthwhile projects; but this has happened only rarely.

Some of the techniques I found helpful in putting the principles of my design into effect provide the students with tools for their research on the campus; others enable them to make the transition from a traditional teacher-student relationship to the new situation into which I have put them.

Getting facts in any quantity by observation requires more manpower than one student can spare during a typical term. Consequently, I insist that students form themselves into work teams of no fewer than four persons. Students come to the course already enrolled in one of a number of sections, about fifteen to twenty students per section. These sections meet four times a week, separately and without me twice, and together, as a total class, with me twice. At the beginning of the term, the first task within a section of fifteen or twenty students is to generate ideas for possible projects and then to separate into smaller work groups, each group undertaking a project. I find that groups consisting of four to six or seven students can learn to work together and produce a worthwhile project in the space of an academic quarter or a little more.

If a work group is to produce an adequate project, the members must learn to work together effectively. This fact provides most of the motivation and much of the material, the empirical facts, through which the students learn the subject matter of social psychology during the term. Also, it motivates them both to observe the social processes in which they are participating and to turn to readings or to class discussions to find better ways of explaining to themselves what they feel to be happening. Because students will need to work together and do not usually have the requisite skills for doing so productively, I have taken time to conduct special exercises at the meetings of the total class to teach the students some communicative skills. These exercises include listening (that is, checking one's understanding of another's intended meaning), describing behavior objectively, checking perception of the emotions of others, and helping a pair of others to communicate with each other. The students quickly find that making observations and recording data are not the simple processes they imagine at the outset. They quickly ask for information about how to write questionnaires and interviews, how to design samples, how to think about the ways that data are connected to conclusions. Typically at this point, they ask for advice and assign one or more of the members within a work group to study these matters.

The transition from the standard teacher-dominated lecture to a learning situation characterized by a high degree of free choice about cognitive content and its scheduling is an experience new and frightening to most students; the ambiguity is great. Ambiguity about sources of reward and punishment increases anxiety; anxiety, in turn, reduces the range and scope of attention, and tends to focus the narrowed range of attention upon those elements of the environment that the individual perceives as most relevant to the immediate task. In the college classroom, almost every student perceives the teacher and the rewards and punishments he controls as most relevant to the immediate task. Consequently, I prefer teaching that requires a very low level of anxiety rather than a high level. To reduce anxiety, one must reduce ambiguity and threat, and enable students to feel confident that they can determine reliably the sources and conditions of reward and punishment.

No experiment should be judged as a success or a failure in the first year. It is almost inevitable that anyone violating the traditional methods will find, during his first trial, that he has misestimated some ambiguities and has stirred up serious fears within some of his students. The experimenting teacher should, therefore, give himself at least a second year, with a revised design, before reaching a confident conclusion about the results of his particular experiment.

When encountering any course that weakens the traditional dominance of the teacher, most students call the new situation unstructured; they mistake a different social structure for a lack of structure. Similarly, some students take the lack of a uniform reading or writing requirement to be equivalent to no requirement at all. Both these misapprehensions lead to a certain amount of pain, but both become less frequent as a course acquires a reputation and students enroll with some notion of what to expect. I provide instructions, as explicit as I can make them, about the project report, though they are limited to the form and organization of the report. In general, the outline of the report is very much like that used in scientific reports in professional journals. Finally, the outline calls for a narrative of the life of the work group that produced the report; and any principle of interpersonal interaction mentioned must be accompanied by a citation to some literature. Throughout the course, I have tried to make it next to impossible for a student to follow directions without learning something useful about human interaction. The requirement of a citation to literature, if a psychological principle is enunciated, is an example of this technique. The project reports from the course taught in 1967–68 reveal that then, every group but one (a group that en-countered no serious interpersonal difficulties within itself) had appar-ently turned to books to help them understand some experiences they had undergone, and did, in my judgment, reach a very useful level of understanding as a result.

Probably the most effective way of reducing the anxiety stu-dents have in an experimental class is to give them evidence that other students have surmounted this challenge in the past. It is not enough for the teacher to claim that this evidence exists—students are suspi-cious of claims that teachers make about their courses—the evidence must come from some other source. In the second year of a course, it is easy to provide this kind of evidence. Before beginning the course in the winter of 1967–68, I invited some members of the previous year's class to act as consultants to the new class. For this help, the student consultants received academic credit in Reading and Confer-ence, or in Research. Such students can provide inestimable help be-cause they are a positive reference group for those who have not yet taken the course; they are a much more important and persuasive reference group than the faculty.

THE COURSE IN 1966–67

As far as I am sure about my own inner processes, the im-mediate causes of my design for the course in introductory social psy-chology taught during the winter of 1966–67 were two weeks of train-ing in human relations under the auspices of the National Training Laboratories, a demonstration of teaching in a problem-solving style given by Herbert Thelen in Chicago in November 1966, and an ar-ticle by Roger Harrison and Richard L. Hopkins (1967).

I had two paid assistants and a class of about two hundred students. I knew I wanted to divide the class into ten sections of about twenty students each. Through the concern and generosity of my col-league, Fred Fosmire, I was able to recruit about ten graduate stu-dents who wanted to try their skills, two or three hours a week, in helping groups to work. Happily, news of the experiment spread and other students from the psychology, sociology, and education depart-ments came to sign up as consultants just for the fun of it. I began the term with two paid assistants and eighteen unpaid—all graduate students. Robert Talbott, one of the graduate assistants, described the opening of the term:

We were told that it was going to be an innovation in education on the campus, but no one, including Runkel, knew just how it was going to be run. While I somehow got the job, I really didn't know anything about what was going to happen except for the following: (1) the class would permit the student a wide latitude of inquiry, (2) there would be no tests, lectures (in the usual sense), or assigned texts, (3) the students were to work with each other, in groups, and develop research projects, and (4) the students would learn from "doing." I still think that Runkel didn't know much more than this himself at the beginning. However, he had some novel ideas, I liked the money, and ever since my life has been changed because of this class. . . . In a sense it was very unfair. That is, none of the students who sat in that large room the first day had any idea of what they were in for when Runkel strode in much like any other "prof." However, from the first very casual words he spoke, the students became aware that this was to be a very unusual course. Speaking to them, he said something very much like this: "Traditionally, people in this course have received assigned readings, lectures, and tests. However, rather than giving you my view of the world and the way it is organized, there is another approach to learning, which you will all engage in. Instead of tests, you will turn in at the end of the term a research paper concerned with conditions which help and hinder learning on this campus." The reaction of the class was mixed. Some of the students were quiet, others talked among themselves, and some few raised their hands to ask questions. To one question Runkel responded, "Yes, there are some very good books in social psychology which you can read. However, none deals with the conditions here and now on this campus." Then Runkel told them that the education they would receive would be largely their own doing. He said that the research projects would be the products of groups of students which would form out of large discussion sections.

With this class of two hundred students, I sought to communicate skills through leaders appointed for the ten sections. At the second meeting, I arbitrarily designated three people from each section as leaders. At each Tuesday meeting of the entire class, I gathered the thirty leaders at center front and dealt with them as if they were a class in themselves. I carried them through the lesson for the day and asked them to do likewise at the next meetings of their sections. The rest of the class was invited to attend the Tuesday session and even to ask questions, but they were not included in the active discussion. On the first three or four Thursdays, we had feedback from sections: a leader from each section, in turn, reporting orally. The entire class was invited to attend and join in discussing the work with leaders, assistants, and me. After the first couple of meetings, the students conducted these meetings largely on their own, while my assistants and I sat with the audience. I was amazed and delighted with the courtesy and order maintained in these discussions; the students displayed both a concern for the rights of others and an insistence on productivity to which I was not accustomed in my meetings with faculty. About the Thursday meetings, Talbott wrote:

> For the first few trials, these reports were very formal; the leaders would typically read off the things that had been discussed and then sit down. Something very much like the following was usual at the beginning: "In our groups we discussed the things that Dr. Runkel had spoken of last Tuesday, but we came to no agreement about it. Instead we undertook the job of deciding on research projects and three groups proposed. . . ." This sort of presentation reflected the training that these students had prior to the course. That is, the idea that others would be interested in the interpersonal difficulties encountered was the farthest thing from their minds. Early on, Runkel interrupted a leader in the middle of his speech and asked, "Do you suppose that is what the class is interested in knowing? Try asking them what they would like to know." This intervention changed the complexion of a good part of subsequent Thursday sessions, for it became immediately evident that people wanted to know how others were interacting and what problems had arisen in the groups. Questions of the following sort were immediately put to the leader: Do the people in your discussion group talk more to one another now? Are the members of your discussion groups offering resistance to the authoritarian efforts of your leaders?

Do you find that the leaders have an extra work load? Did
you have trouble getting members to split into buzz groups?
Up to this point most of the interpersonal work that had gone
on was seen as private knowledge belonging to the various
sections separately. . . . After this . . . each leader was expected to address himself to both the content of the discussion
section meetings and the process as well. Thursday was sometimes a trial to the leaders. They appeared before the whole
class and their reports were subject to the scrutiny of members
of their sections that were present. It sometimes happened
that a leader conveyed an impression of a meeting different
from that held by a member; more than once a voice came
from the audience saying something like this: "That's not the
way it happened at all. What really happened was . . ."
These occasions led easily into demonstrations of the dynamics
of perception and their effects on group life.

I gave very few preplanned lectures—one on the first day and,
in response to requests from students, three or four at the end of the
term. On the matter of lectures, Talbott wrote:

[When a lecture was given,] it was done so that the
message was relevant to the needs of the class. For instance,
at one point certain conditions in the sections became evident
to the staff and among these was the very important fact that
the leaders were not conveying to the rest of the students all
the information that was being given them. Runkel responded
with the following sequence of events during a session with the
leaders. First, the class was told that "hypotheses" were attempts to represent certain aspects of the state of nature, and
that these attempts must be checked for their validity. Runkel
then stated that he entertained certain hypotheses about the
state of communications that existed between the leaders and
the groups. These were: (1) Some sections don't have the
message that a project is required. (2) Some leaders think
that what I do in class on Tuesdays must be replicated closely
during section meetings. (3) Some projects may not be dealing with the "here and now." (4) Some of the papers distributed to leaders have not been passed on to non-leaders.

Runkel then drew two paradigms of communication networks on the board. One was an "in-series" hierarchical model which relied upon certain key people to ensure that a message is transmitted. Opposed to this was a model in which multiple channels were available over which information could be transmitted. He said that to the extent that this former model happened to fit the class at that time, it was possible to say that some messages were not getting across to at least some people because of distortion or a failure of the relays (leaders). The leaders were then requested to discuss among themselves (1) whether the facts in their hands substantiated these hypotheses, and (2) if they did, what actions they would think appropriate.

Some few sessions in the later portion of the course were devoted almost exclusively to lecturing . . . one lecture, dealing with Sherif's work on superordinate goals, drew much interest if the number of questions coming from the audience is any criterion, but it was difficult to assess how much this sort of activity on Runkel's part affected the thinking of the students. It certainly could have been immediately useful to them since they were all members of groups which had at various times felt some hostility toward others—some sense of "us versus them." Yet the only basis this writer could use to judge effectiveness of the lecture was listening to the conversations afterward. I did not detect at that time any "Ah, ha!" remark.

On the whole, it seemed that lectures of this more formal type did not have as much effect on the class as did those which were concerned with things with which the class was immediately concerned and found useful. The example given above, which dealt with "hypotheses," had an immediate impact on the leaders. After Runkel finished he asked them to form buzz groups and discuss what had been presented to them. They were so concerned with this speech that they did not want to report back to Runkel when he asked them to do so after about twenty minutes; instead, they wanted more time to "hash it over."

I agree that the brief "lecturettes" inserted at points where some stress indicated that a lecture could serve an immediate need seemed much more effective than the later, preplanned lectures. Although many students found the more formal lectures interesting, the response to the more task-oriented brief lectures went beyond mere interest to application to life in and out of class.

I had intended the consultants to help smooth the struggles of the students in their planning sections and work groups, to help the students catch onto interpersonal skills, and generally to ease anxiety when it became hurtfully high. In 1966–67, the scheme did not work out as successfully as I had hoped. I turn again to Talbott for his view:

> Role clarity from the standpoint of the groups was something else again. To them the consultants were strange phenomena that had to be tested, and complaints came to the staff over the whole term, though with less intensity in the later weeks. The following is a list of some of the grievances aired by the students: The consultant talks most of the period. We were trying to "plop" him but he wouldn't be plopped. We had decided on a project, and had started to design it, but the consultant held us back.
>
> Contributing to the confusion was the fact that these consultants were graduate students and therefore knowledgeable in the students' eyes. They were not easily identified by the students either as peers or as teachers. One girl stood up, very perplexed, in a Thursday session and asked, "What do we do when the consultant says one thing and we think another? After all, they have read so many books." To this Runkel replied, "Well, in some cases it is proper to defer to 'book learning,' but groups present many novel events, and you have as much right to see these novel events in your way as he has to see them in his way."
>
> What I saw and heard convinced me that the use of consultants was a wise decision. It is true that at times the consultants stepped into the middle of group activity when they should have stayed out, but more times than not these actions, at least in retrospect, focused the attention of the group on some important issue. On the occasions when I saw consultants in action they generally seemed to make the ap-

propriate interventions and eventually many of the group members themselves began to model the same behaviors. That is, maintenance and task activities became important to some of the students themselves.

At the beginning of the course, we designated three leaders per section without regard to the qualifications of those we chose—we walked down the aisle and handed cards to students as the urge struck us. I instructed the students to look upon these leaders as temporary and as replaceable at their pleasure. Nevertheless, I was surprised at the power these leaders took upon themselves and were granted by the members in the sections. Surprisingly often, leaders became tyrants who could be overthrown only by enlisting the help of the section consultant. Some of the leaders were skillful and helpful, but others rode roughshod over proposals contrary to their preconceptions, pretended to be divinely-chosen emissaries, and kept useful information secret. In my opinion, the struggles with the leaders produced a great amount of useful learning about selves and about group dynamics, but these same struggles slowed work on the projects. This, in turn, weakened the confidence that some of the task-oriented students placed in the value of the course.

The planning sections, of about twenty persons each, served their purposes very well. They seemed the right size for exploratory groups from which project groups could develop. They were comfortable for preliminary discussions—large enough so that no one needed to feel in the spotlight if he were not ready; small enough so that a conversational form could be used. The following picture of a planning section, written by a student as part of a project report, is typical:

> Well, our discussion group met every week. We began to discuss the same things over and over again. As the [meetings] went on, our group became more and more frustrated. You could see it in the way people acted, things they said. Someone always brought up grading at least once. People in our group wanted things mapped out for them in black and white. I wanted something concrete. This shows what I said before, about how most of us have been taught for many years by things being decided for us, which I feel makes a person very dependent, and thus unable to function well in making real

decisions. . . . Then it hit. We finally decided what we as a group were supposed to be doing. We were supposed to be learning our own reactions and the reactions of others in our group. In other words, how we worked within our group and working with other people . . . what we gained from others. . . . Giving us this topic of learning conditions, was just a topic to work at, to obtain these goals of learning by working with others.

From the beginning, I knew that grading would be a problem. When the term opened, I still had not decided how to solve it. I knew I could not read and comment on forty project reports during examination week, nor could I know which members of a project team contributed more than others. I put a great deal of thought into this problem and discussed it with my assistants and with the students. Finally, about the third week of the course, I told the students that the only solution I could see was that they must grade themselves. Every project group would give me a list showing the grade for each person. I would hand in that grade, no matter what it was. Then I would read the reports at my leisure. Like the problem of leadership, the grading process also occasioned much learning. But again, I felt that the learning was bought at too high a cost. As part of a final report, one student described the typical conflict:

I felt very uneasy about the whole topic because I have never been asked to grade my peers and have never had them grade me. But then I did not feel we should take the responsibility lightly, since the outcome is important to each of us. I was also disturbed about the blunt statement of how each member could sure use an A. Not saying they deserved it, just that they could use one. This bothered me because I feel if a student decided he or she needs a certain grade they will then set up a grading system that will give them that grade.

In the end, the grades the students awarded one another came to about two-thirds As, one-third Bs, and only one lonely C. After the term finished in the middle of March, I began reading the thirty-six reports (about a third came in during the next term and one in late June). Upon finishing each report, I wrote a letter to the members of the project group, telling them what in the report had made me happy and unhappy, and telling them what grade I would have given the report had I been grading it. My distribution of grades was lower than theirs: thirty-five As, thirty-eight Bs, twenty-eight Cs, thirteen Ds, eight Fs and seventy-five needing more work.

Many of the students indicated their eagerness to continue this kind of work. During the summer I sent a letter to about fifty of the students to whom I would have awarded an A or a B, asking if they wished to serve as consultants the following year. Twenty-two volunteered and, of the sixteen who still served as consultants during the winter term, 1967–68, four became deeply involved in a research report (Runkel, Lawrence, Oldfield, Rider, and Clark, in press) on the development of the project groups during that second year, and carried that work through to its conclusion (four of them without pay or credit) in the fall of 1968. During the winter term of 1967–68, the sixteen consultants received academic credit either for Reading and Conference or for Research.

In the previous year, 1965–66, I had taught the course much more traditionally, with regular lectures, weekly quizzes, term papers, and the like, though there were some unusual features in the course. At the end of that course, and at the end of the 1966–67 course, I distributed questionnaires to the students asking their opinions about the course. Some questions were the same on both sheets. The first question was, "Do you feel that you learned anything of value in this course?" In 1965–66, 44 per cent chose the happiest alternative offered; namely, "Yes, quite a lot." In 1966–67, this percentage rose to 56 per cent. The second question was, "If you learned something of value in this course, does any particular thing stand out in your mind?" The percentage who chose the answer, "Yes, something does stand out for me" (and in most instances wrote out an explanation), rose from 55 the previous year to 90 in 1966–67. The complaints made in the earlier year seemed generally to have a rejecting tone, with a flavor of, "I'm glad I'm done with that." In 1966–67, however, the complaints seemed to come chiefly from people who liked the course and wanted to tell me how it could be made even better.

As it happened, a group of students conducted a Course-Reaction Survey in the winter of 1966–67. Compared with the university average, my students rated their course somewhat inferior in organization, profitable and worth while class meetings, clearly defined objectives, and the teacher's being prepared for class. Rated about the same as the university average were the number of hours per week spent studying for the course and the good use made of examples and illustrations. Rated somewhat or markedly more favorably than the university average were the levels of general satisfaction and level of work stimulated; the clear interpretation of abstract ideas and theories; the teacher's having made the course stimulating, been clear in his explanations, and inspired confidence in his knowledge of the subject. Rated strongly or even remarkably more favorably than average were the teacher's communicating enthusiasm, encouraging independent thinking, giving personal help, taking personal interest, and respecting the questions and opinions of students.

THE COURSE IN 1967–68

The second time I gave the course, enrollment was limited. I had no paid or graduate assistants, but did have sixteen undergraduate consultants to work with the fifty-eight students enrolled in the course. Although I have no formal data, I am convinced that the undergraduates were more effective consultants than the graduate students had been the previous year, for two reasons: the undergraduates, having been through the course, did not have to try to anticipate events from my verbal and faulty guesses, and they were a more persuasive reference group for the students. Another change that year was that I scheduled the students to two meetings per week of their planning sections, instead of the one meeting per week held the previous year. The two meetings per week (on Tuesdays and Thursdays) of the entire class stayed the same. Each meeting, as in the previous year, lasted an hour and a half.

For the second year's course I had much more written matter ready. For example, a three-page descriptive synopsis told the students about the planning sections, the project groups, the use of consultants, and the requirements, which were stated thus: "Putting all this together, it means that you will produce the following things during the term: From an arbitrary collection of fifteen to twenty people in a planning section, you will produce a small project group, which is coordinated and productive. From your own experiences and from the guiding ideas in books, you will produce a description of some information worth getting, and a plan for getting it. From the results of the work of your project group, you will produce a report displaying the new information and assessing its usefulness." As well as the usual lists of bibliographies, term schedules, room numbers for planning sections, and assignment of chairmen, I had ready self-instruction sheets for four or five communication skills. (For these I am indebted to John Wallen and Rosalie Howard.) From time to time I also made available reprints of articles from journals.

A helpful structural alteration was a scheme for automatically deposing the leaders in the planning sections. I handed out sheets on which everyone was assigned a number, and leaders were assigned by person-number. Two leaders (in case one was sick) were assigned to each meeting and nobody acted as leader for more than two meetings. Because there were only three planning sections and because about forty to forty-five usually attended the sessions of the entire class, I worked with the whole class instead of working only with representatives from sections. Often I would carry on a demonstration with a dozen students sitting in a ring inside the rest of the class and then rotate the groups. The projects of 1967–68 turned out to be of much higher quality, on the average, than those of 1966–67. Near the end of the term I composed a newsletter describing all the projects; it went to all students and to a number of colleagues in the Psychology Department. This year I did not ask the students to grade themselves; I awarded grades to all projects. As a part of its final report, I asked each project team to tell me how they wanted the grade for the report to be distributed among the individuals.

Toward the end of the 1967–68 winter term, I again asked for volunteers for consultantships in 1968–69. As I write, I have begun the 1968–69 term with 16 consultants. One consultant started work even before the term opened, condensing a technical article for use by the new class.

In a dissertation conducted by Daniel Langmeyer (1968), the effectiveness of students from my classes, when working in groups on two standard tasks, was compared with the effectiveness of groups of other sorts. Langmeyer used three different kinds of groups. In one series of groups, all three members of each group were college students who had no previous training in group process. All three were strangers and none was given any legitimate status as a leader. In the second series of groups, drawn from my class in social psychology, one member of each group was one of the consultants who had been helping the other two members in a section of my course. In the third series of groups, drawn from the faculties of a number of public schools in a suburb of a large West Coast city, each group consisted of the principal and two teachers from the same school. Langmeyer's conclusion was that the groups from my class were superior to the other two types of groups in terms of giving leadership to the most competent member, foregoing individual gratifications so as to accomplish a common goal, allowing reduction in the autonomy and power of individual members, agreeing on a definition of the problem, and monitoring (recognizing and making known) ineffective and obstructive behavior.

The university-wide Course-Reaction Survey was conducted again in 1967–68. On a measure of course quality compounded from a number of items in that survey, about 75 per cent of my students rated my course higher than students rated courses in the university on the average that term. On the item, "encourages independent thinking," 96 per cent of my students rated the course higher than the university mean. On an indicator compounded of an item about availability of personal help and one about taking a personal interest in the class, 97 per cent of my students rated the course higher than average. At the same time, most of my students rated the course a little more difficult than the average course.

In the booklet (Browning and Tyson, 1968) reporting the results of the survey, my course was described as follows:

RUNKEL'S REFRESHING WRINKLE

[In this course,] no reading material is assigned. No exams are given. An independent research project is required.

Perhaps mystified, often excited, always stimulated, the class in general finds Dr. Runkel refreshing. Small group interpersonal-relations meetings have drawn raves, while the loosely structured, informal lectures are highly praised for the emphasis on freedom of thought and liberal self-expression. The small-group discussions, while described as "pure hell" and "very frustrating," are fervently cited, in the same breath, as "invaluable" and "extremely worthwhile" in learning to communicate and adjust in social situations. The main criticism seems to be that there is insufficient time to follow discussions farther.

Many commend Runkel on his openness to suggestion and his willingness to answer questions or clarify particularly

sticky points. There is great admiration and respect for Dr.
Runkel personally and many think that "his style of teaching
should be studied as a good example by other instructors."
One student, reflecting the general attitude of overwhelming
approval of anything Dr. Runkel says or does, adds somewhat
hesitantly, "Phil Runkel ought to stop pacing—although it's
probably useful."

Forty-three out of forty-four [respondents] recommend
this course! [to other students].

As this is being written, the winter term has opened for a third
round of the course. This time, there are about one hundred and
twenty students enrolled. My one paid assistant (who will share the
actual teaching) was one of the consultants in 1966–67. She and my
sixteen consultants are as eager as I to get to the stage where the project groups begin understanding their dynamics as human groups with
a worthwhile job to do. We are asking ourselves whether it can be
made a better course than last year's.

William R. Torbert
J. Richard Hackman

Taking the Fun Out of
Outfoxing the System

If the Paul Goodmans, the free universities, and the demands for
more intellectual freedom for students influenced us, we were not
aware of it when we started. Instead, our decision to try an experimental course grew more from our disaffection with traditional procedures than from any vision of a new approach to education. Our
charge was a common one: to help some sixty Yale undergraduates
learn something about the psychology of administration in one semester's time. Our initial reaction was as common: frustration that the
classic format of large college classes—lectures, punctuated now and
then by examinations—provides little opportunity for students to become meaningfully involved in a course. From the conversation which
began then and continued over the next several weeks, we derived
three insights which guided our attempt to restructure the course.

The first insight was that the usual dichotomy between large,
impersonal classes and small, intimate classes is probably a false dis-

156

IX

Yale University

tinction, though one that pervades discussions of educational reform —usually in the hope that smaller classes will result in more contact between students and faculty. It is commonly assumed that good discussions cannot take place with too many people present. But our experience was that discussions in small seminars often are just as dry, academic, and non-involving as those in larger groups. When asked why such discussions do not work, students often cite size as a factor: it seems that there are sometimes too many people present for a good discussion even in five-man seminars. We concluded that size itself probably is not the most important reason for the lack of meaningful interaction and involvement in large classes. More likely culprits, we felt, are the generally accepted rules of conduct, which specify what is and what is not appropriate behavior in the classroom. These rules place a high premium on grades and social approval—resulting in the fierce (but always genteel) competition so often observed among stu-

157

dents. They condemn any indication of personal or academic weakness, thus leading students to place first priority on defending their own ideas and behavior instead of on engaging in honest, mutually helpful activities. They dictate that personalities and emotions are out of bounds in academic discussions, thus denying students the opportunity to deal with the very problems which may be inhibiting successful classroom discussions. We felt that if we could find a way to organize our class so that these interpersonal issues could be addressed and dealt with effectively, the problem of size might disappear entirely.

Our second insight was that the content of our course could be used as a means of addressing just these issues. Among the topics often included in a course on the psychology of administration are leadership, communication, decision-making, motivation, and attitude-change. These phenomena—although usually ignored by students and faculty alike—are present in every classroom, and affect what takes place there. We resolved to use the research findings and scholarly literature available on these topics to help our students (and ourselves) understand the day-to-day operation of our own course. We expected that, by examining with the students the ways in which problems in the psychology of administration were affecting our class, we would be better able to confront and overcome the interpersonal issues which usually detract from the effectiveness of large classes. Another important payoff seemed likely to result from attention to process issues. As students actually experienced problems of leadership, communication, and so on, we hoped that the problem areas themselves would become more meaningful and important to them. This, we felt, could make their learning the course content much easier. Thus, our goal as instructors was to generate a spiral of increased awareness and understanding: we wanted to use classroom process as an important resource for learning the content of the course, while at the same time drawing on the scholarly content of the field to increase our competence in dealing with issues of process.

Finally, we came to feel an increasing reluctance to accept the dichotomies between academic and applied matters and between learning values and learning content. In the classroom, problems of values are handled ordinarily by conscientious attempts on the part of instructors to be vigorously objective, neutral, and value-free. Yet as we began to discuss issues of content—what we would teach, how it would be taught, and why it was worth teaching—it became clear that value choices were implicit in almost every decision we made about objective knowledge. We decided that it would be incongruent with reality and an active disservice to our students to refuse to make explicit the value problems which are inherent in our field of study and in our attempts to teach it.

The dichotomy between academic and applied affairs is usually avoided fairly easily by both eggheads and men of affairs: they avoid the problem simply by avoiding one another, and resorting instead to labels such as philistine or irrelevant, stupid or abstract, corrupt or cold. Even in courses such as ours, where the two worlds agree to meet, instructors frequently find themselves vacillating between presenting real-life case studies and presenting more general, abstract, and theoretical material. And, while students often are asked to get their hands dirty in a fieldwork course or a side job, these activities are rarely integrated with the academic curriculum. We concluded that we could not call a course in the psychology of administration successful unless we had at least attempted such an integration.

Traditional classroom procedures, which place the instructor on an elevated podium and large numbers of students in chairs bolted to the floor, clearly would not be conducive to achieving our goals. Therefore, we decided that much of the educational activity in the course would take place in small work groups of about eight members. These groups would be formed on the basis of common interests in particular content areas, and they would have tasks requiring close cooperation. The groups would develop and deliver to the class a presentation of material in their content areas—and be charged with making the presentations as innovative and involving as possible. They would design and carry out research projects relevant to their areas, and would use these projects to tie together theoretical and real-world concerns. Finally, they would be intimately involved in the evaluation of their own work, continuously, we hoped, throughout the semester. So that experiences and problems could be shared between groups and between the groups and ourselves, a steering committee would be formed, consisting of one member of each of the groups and ourselves. Thus, we would have a three-tiered organization (work groups, steering committee, and instructors) with all the problems of a real-life organization—which, of course, we would be.

Permeating the entire course would be a climate of openness

and collaboration. We wanted an organization in which students and instructors would feel just as free to talk about how the course was progressing as about intellectual or content issues. We wanted the students to have as much opportunity to make decisions about what we would do in the course and how we would do it as we ourselves would have. We wanted involvement and responsibility, and we thought we had designed an organization that would give us just what we wanted.

But what, we finally asked ourselves, would we do if the students resisted our dream-plans? Our organization was obviously both too intricate and too well designed to be tampered with by a collection of students who knew little about either education or the psychology of administration. Then emerged the overwhelming discrepancy between what we were saying our values were and what we were actually doing. On the one hand, we were planning to tell the students that we wanted them to collaborate with us as equals in an educational experiment in which both they and we could learn; on the other, we planned to tell them exactly how this collaborative venture was going to operate. And we were worrying that they might resist. Eventually—after a good deal of frustration and a few thoughts of retreat—the same values which made our inconsistencies so uncomfortable dictated a strategy for their resolution. Rather than planning the best course possible and then carrying it out as an accomplished plan, we would have to be genuinely open to influence by our students—to the extent that we would be willing to abandon our initial plans entirely if need be. Our values were forcing us to relinquish exclusive ownership of our ideas and control over what happened to them. With some uneasiness, we began to loosen our grip on the course.

We eventually concluded that we would present our thinking to the students on the first day of class, along with a written proposal based on it. We would discuss with them as openly as we could the risks and values of our views, ask them to reflect on what was happening and write down their reactions, amendments, and counterproposals— and only then decide, as a group, whether our course should be experimental or traditional. Thus, our task for the first class meeting became one of helping the students to gain a sense of what had occurred between ourselves in the preceding weeks, so that they would become able to join in the decision-making effectively from then on.

We decided that this might be done efficiently by actually retracing in conversation the developmental history of the course. So, after briefly introducing ourselves, we role-played the way we happened to come upon the idea of an experimental course. We discussed the possibilities and problems of the course, and the differences which remained between us. Then we said, in effect, "This is where we are right now; would you like to join us?" They did, eagerly and vigorously. The discussion passed rather quickly from technical questions ("How will such and such be done?") to more central issues ("Do you think the work groups will really work if everybody knows that you are not going to assign their grades?"), and finally to attempts to express a sense of the direction of the experiment as a whole and the personal risks and possibilities which it implied. We experienced shock and exhilaration as we saw for the first time our abstract ideas, theories, and plans take shape in the real world. It looked as if the experiment was working.

In their subsequent written reactions, a great many students appeared to be personally caught up in their appraisals of the proposal—whether they were emphasizing potential benefits: "I am certainly willing to give it the old college try. I haven't really been moved in three dull years at Yale and it would be nice to know that the academic side of Yale wasn't totally wasted on me," or whether they were more keenly aware of the threats: "I feel that it is extremely unfair to use students as experimental subjects at the possible expense of their academic averages, or at the risk of their other courses suffering due to a disproportionate amount of work (however unintended) in Psychology 33a. And since any modified version of the original proposal would still be an experiment with similar hazards involved, I must cast my vote strongly for the traditional, but proven, lecture method of presentation."

Most students were eager to try the experimental course. Those reservations that were expressed tended to focus on three specific, important aspects of the proposed course.

First, questions were raised about the possible costs of using classroom process as an input to learning. Several students worried that by spending time examining process we would necessarily spend less time on the scholarly content—a trade-off that many would be hesitant to accept. One student put it this way: "I would like to see lectures form the basis of the course, because the knowledge which is a base for further studies in administrative sciences and which the instructors have gained already, is to me more valuable and more central to the course than the group knowledge acquired."

The second aspect to attract considerable comment was the plan for work groups. Several students were concerned that problems of coordination and conflicting personalities might prevent the groups from functioning effectively. These problems were highlighted in the reactions of one student, who came up with some revealing recommendations to insure the success of the groups: "(1) Impose more order lest the groups waste (and I *do* think *waste,* since it is not end-directed behavior) much time in organizing to do their tasks. Set up a leadership structure which groups can change upon demonstrated desirability. (2) *Spell out* topics for classroom presentation from which groups can choose any fair means of choosing, since consensus is hardly foreseeable in most groups. (3) Set up procedures acceptable (to you) for deciding upon and allocating responsibility in group projects. All this must be most explicit."

The third aspect to cause concern was evaluation in general, and grading in particular. Considerable anxiety and distrust were evidenced about our proposal to share with students responsibility for determining final grades. After the novelty of the proposal had worn off, one student wrote: "Initially, excitement and unguarded acceptance were my reactions; the excitement I still feel for the course, but now my acceptance is guarded, essentially on one count. Student performance evaluation is my only worry. At the risk of appearing overly concerned with marks that are sent to the registrar, I do find myself a somewhat molded child of Yale's grading and recognition system. Viewing the proposal from that mold, my enthusiasm becomes tempered. The more that I think about it, the less I can accept the ability of the student groups to appraise the quality of their presentation and project."

Students were especially anxious about the form that participation in grading would take: did not the instructors' experience make them more objective? Would not some students be hurt if they were told by their peers why they were not evaluated favorably? Would not some students simply take the highest grade possible or downgrade others in order to look good by comparison? What would the instructors do if all members of a group did not do the work in the course—fail them? Surely the instructors were going to retain some kind of veto on so obviously critical a part of the course as the assignment of grades.

Our reaction to the issue was that evaluation could be the first item on the agenda for the steering committee and that if the students were willing to proceed with the experiment on that basis, so were we. They were: after considerable discussion, the class voted almost unanimously for a slightly modified version of the original proposal.

So, in a glow of consensus and enthusiasm, the experiment began. To provide a common background and language for the class to build upon, we were to give a series of content presentations during the first quarter of the semester. We worked hard preparing the lectures, organizing huge resource reading lists for the groups, bustling around making sure nothing was going wrong. Things did seem to be progressing smoothly. Our lectures, while not particularly innovative, were well attended. Apparently contrary to many students' fears, the work groups were not reporting significant problems in getting organized and underway. The steering committee was hard at work devising a procedure for evaluating student performance—although progress on this problem was hard to discern.

We attributed the confusion and uneasiness that surrounded our discussions of grading to the students' anxiety about being evaluated. But we did not come to understand the full extent of that anxiety until, late in the term, we were told about the secret agenda which the students had brought to one of the steering committee meetings.

Early in the semester, Yale College changed from a numerical grading system to a system of four categories: honors, high pass, pass, fail. The students on the steering committee found opportunity in this change: they conspired to railroad the instructors into accepting a grade of "high pass" for all students in the course, in effect solving the evaluation problem by doing away with evaluation. Any resistance to the proposal by us was to be repudiated as a betrayal of our announced decision to share responsibility; the students apparently surmised that they would have us caught in the net of our own stated values. The plan was unintentionally disrupted, however, when we agreed to consider a common grade as a possible solution—but argued against it on the basis that it eliminated the challenge of learning from honest, collaborative evaluation. Some students reported, in relating the incident to us later, that it was at this point that they really began to believe that we were serious about what we had been saying. Our im-

passe on the evaluation issue finally broke when the work group studying motivation proposed to study motivation, including student reactions to evaluation, in the course itself. This proposal made possible
and, in fact, encouraged the development and use of a variety of
evaluation procedures.

It was agreed that the midterm examination would cover only
the introductory, content lectures. Each student would write for one
hour on a choice of questions, hand his examination to another student for twenty minutes of written criticism, and then assign himself
a grade with written justification in the final ten minutes. We would
collect, read, and comment on each examination, and add our view
of the grade earned. The student could then compare his own perceptions of his performance with both those of his classmate and those
of the instructors. How this evaluative information would be used was
left to the work groups themselves. The eight groups settled on a
variety of procedures, ranging from one group which assigned all responsibility for evaluation to the instructors, to one which reverted to
assigning each student a common grade at the outset. While the various schemes were anything but uniform across groups, they seemed
likely to encourage students to exchange their ideas and experiences
about evaluation, and we were happy with them.

With the plans for evaluation taken care of, the class settled
into something of a routine. The eight work groups were presumably
preparing for their classroom presentations, and our lectures continued
to be unexceptional. Everyone was looking forward to the first class
period after the midterm, when the first work group would make its
presentation. The topic was to be Leadership.

The classroom was nearly full for the presentation—the best
attendance since the early days of the semester. Members of the leadership group were scurrying around the front of the room making last-
minute preparations. The first member of the group went to the lectern, made some comments about the topic in general, and announced
that since there was so much material available, the group had decided that the maximum amount of information could be gotten
across if each group member gave a short lecture on a subtopic in
the area. And so the parade began. Student after student read his
notes in a competent, machine-gun fashion. A tremendous amount of
information was dispensed. Pages and pages of notes were taken.

When the class ended, the students left dazed, disappointed, and hostile.

The reason for the hostility was revealed at the next meeting of the steering committee. The students felt that the leadership group had reneged on its mandate to be innovative and to excite the rest of the class about the content area. Instead, the group had out-professored the professors. Everyone agreed that in the future more creativity should be used in designing the presentations.

The next two groups did try to be more creative. One used a tape-recorded speech by Winston Churchill to demonstrate a technique of attitude change; the other used elaborate colored-chalk diagrams to illustrate aspects of organizational structure. But the basic format was unchanged: scholarly literature was reviewed and summarized in a series of short lectures by group members. The instructors had planned to use the class session following each group presentation to fill in any gaps in the literature left by the groups. Since the literature was being reviewed so comprehensively by the groups, there were few gaps to fill. Instead, we were able to use our classes for relatively leisurely reviews of particular issues, theories, or practices in the content areas.

Students soon became disillusioned about the course as a whole. When there had been rough spots earlier in the semester, we all had our anticipation of the really experimental part of the course to help pull us along. Now the experimental part of the course was here, and we were seeing how invalid our earlier expectations had been. The growing discontent and apathy, coupled with the knowledge that grades no longer depended on the students' coming to class, led to a sharp drop in attendance. The course clearly was getting out of hand. What had gone wrong?

We could not bring ourselves to blame the students. Yale undergraduates are as bright and as creative as any in the country. If the course was failing, it seemed likely that much of the fault must lie with its structure—or with our way of implementing it. Finally, we were jolted into realizing something that, in retrospect, seems so obvious. Once again what we were claiming to value simply did not fit with what we were doing. We were saying: "Be creative. Innovate. Don't be constrained by the usual lecture format. Get the class to *experience* what you have to say; make it exciting, involving." And all the while, whenever one of us was at the lectern, the traditional lecture-discussion format prevailed. We were asking the students to do something we could not or would not do; we were providing them with verbal instructions, but no model. And we had the gall to be disappointed that they had not succeeded where we had failed.

Posthaste we abandoned our assumptions about what activities are and are not appropriate for college classrooms, and came up with what one student later characterized as a series of "academic happenings." At the next class meeting (when we were to respond to the student presentation on organizational structure) we sent groups of students out of the classroom to interview various administrators, including a priest, the chairman of a university department, and a supervisor of secretarial services. We armed the students with questions about how different ways of designing organizations affect people's actions within them. On returning to the classroom, students compared notes and attempted to integrate the information they had collected.

Another week we imported a number of trained observers to consult with the work groups. The groups spent the class period focusing on members' problems in working together rather than on their actual tasks. Another time we asked the students to monitor various aspects of a live conversation between a boss and a subordinate (actually, one of us and his secretary). These data were then used to try to understand better the literature on communication in organizations. As we had hoped, the students also began to loosen up in their presentations. One group asked the class to indicate on a questionnaire what kind of work group they would compose in order to make a certain decision. These choices then were discussed in relation to the literature on group effectiveness. Another group had one of its members assume the role of a staff-researcher in an organization. He attempted to sell some line managers (the class) on the usefulness of a new approach to client relationships. The group then used this episode to discuss problems of organizational change. A third group, focusing on decision-making, played parts of tape-recorded interviews they had conducted with stock brokers regarding how decisions are made under conditions of high uncertainty.

Some students began to regain their earlier involvement and enthusiasm. One traced the history of his reactions to the course as follows:

I was skeptical from the very beginning about the chances for success in a venture of this sort, but started out resolved to make the most of it. But later I joined the great mass and turned the course into a gut. In the last two weeks I have come to regret that turn of events, and in the course of working on the group project have finally set to work and am getting something out of the course. It is late in the term for such a change; I must honestly admit that I have missed a hell of a lot. In the last two weeks, however, I have gained a perception of excitement and interest that was missing the whole rest of the term. . . . The students who took the gut route will probably regret it just as I did, and that in itself is of the utmost importance in the educational process.

Other students reported similar reactions. The course had seemed massive and difficult to move; suddenly it seemed to move itself. Disenchantment and apathy seemed to have become transformed into initiative and responsibility. We talked with students and tried to analyze what was going on to try to learn the reasons for the striking change. To our surprise and fascination, it appeared that the reasons were quite different for various students. Aspects of the course that effectively "turned on" some students "turned off" others; and many students apparently still had not been reached at all.

For some the innovative use of class time caused the change. One student reported:

. . . two experiences in the course point the way, though. One was with the outside observer in the group. Being observed by someone sensitive to the real issues going on was somehow intensely involving. The other was the conversation between Dick and Wendy [the secretary] when I was listening as intently as I had ever listened, and hearing and seeing new things that I would never have noticed before. Somehow the educational process needs to be structured so that it is as involving as it can be, so that it reaches out and asks the student for help in finding answers, in achieving understanding, insight.

Another did not find the experimental classes helpful: ". . . the key factor in a presentation became how differently it was done rather than what it said. Just seeing a presentation and getting a reading list gives you no place to start to organize thoughts on a particular subject." Some students saw the system of evaluation and the process of grade-assignment as causing the change:

> When the grading system went out my idea of becoming a successful grade-grubber went with it. I began to *have* to think about whether I was being a successful student—and to realize that the responsibility for this lay solely with myself. Your course was one of the primary instruments of discovery. And I think it was invaluable to me, in letting me discover things about myself as a student and person. In ten or twenty years I'll remember almost nothing from the dozen or so psychology courses I've taken. But I'll always remember the course that let me—even forced me—to see myself, student and person, the good and the bad.

The evaluation process appeared to have a particularly strong impact on members of two of the work groups. These groups distinguished themselves by being the only ones unable to agree upon and successfully complete term projects by the end of the semester. Members of both groups felt the bitterness of the failure, tried to cope with it, and in the coping seemed to learn something significant. The topic of one of these groups was Organizational Change. After several aborted attempts to begin a term project—and with the end of the semester only a few weeks away—members of the group invited the instructors to a meeting to "talk about the project." At that time the instructors were to be subjected to subtle attempts to change their attitudes about the course itself, and their plans for the course in future years. Thus, an actual change project would have been carried out, and the requirements met. So, in ignorance of their plans, we accepted an invitation to a group meeting. We listened for an hour or so to what seemed to be some general discussion about the course, and finally suggested that perhaps we could take up whatever agenda had prompted the group members to invite us. It took quite a bit of explaining before we understood that in fact the agenda had just been completed, and that the nature of that agenda was the execution of the group's term project. When we finally recovered our "cool," we helped the group do a post-mortem on the session. Together we identified several major problems: (1) we had already been predisposed to listen to what they had to say—thus, their assumption that our listening indicated the success of the procedures was not very convincing; (2) there had been no particular preplanned strategy for change; and (3) the project had been so hastily and incompletely planned that not even all of the group members present were aware that "this was it."

Some of the group members came to suspect (although they previously had been unaware of it) that an important motive for making such a desperate attempt at a project might have been to assuage their feelings of guilt about the group's obvious failure. The group decided that it had been fooling itself as much as it had been trying to fool us with the project, and set out to undertake a more ambitious effort to effect a change within Yale College—even though the plans would extend beyond the end of the semester and they would not get credit for it from us. This attempt also did not reach fruition. But many of the students did apparently achieve a better capability to deal with failure, and at the final evaluation session which was held later, the members agreed that they had failed on the project and deserved to be evaluated as failing.

The other group which had not completed a project also was initially unable to accept and deal with its failure, but attempted to cope with the difficulty in a different way. The group held an evaluation session, without the instructors, at which strong pressures developed for a grade of high pass for all members. If the decision had been unanimous, that would have been the final grade submitted to the registrar, since this group had decided earlier that it would determine the marks for each member. Two members, however, resisted the pressure: one stoutly maintained that he deserved no more than a pass, if that; one, the steering committee representative, felt that he might have earned honors. Attempts to override these objections failed, and the group members asked one of us to meet with them to help resolve their difficulty in reaching a consensus.

In the ensuing discussion, there was little examination of the basis for deciding on a common grade of high pass, virtually no mention of the fact that a project had not been completed, and a great deal of defensiveness expressed about the proposed common grade. The instructor's attempts to explore the reasoning behind the evaluation met with attacks on grading in general and assertions that the group had learned much which could not be measured. Eventually, the group began to realize that it was demanding conformity on this issue despite the lack of unanimity precisely because the members were highly uncertain and anxious about how well they had done. With this insight, the demand for conformity diminished, and there was a period of mutual exploration of the members' real—and predominantly negative—feelings about the group's performance as a work team. Later, members of the group evaluated themselves individually, and talked together at some length about their views. Many of the group members ultimately did award themselves high passes (partly on the basis of these final discussions, which some saw as a major breakthrough from which significant learning had taken place), and others placed themselves in the pass category. The pressures for uniformity had vanished.

These examples suggest the complexity of criteria for evaluating student performance in the course, and the level of anxiety surrounding the issue. The early anxieties of the students about evaluation were, it appears, generally well founded; however, they also could be worked through, with learning as a frequent outcome.

There seemed to be one additional aspect of the course which, for some students, led to a revitalization toward the end of the semester. This was a change in the standard rules of procedure or norms according to which groups worked. Many of the groups began the semester by operating according to a set of strong—but assumed and implicit—procedural norms. Probably the most powerful, the most antieducational, and the least noticeable of these was that the group should not openly discuss its own procedure—the motives and goals of its members, and their problems in working together to accomplish the task. A second commonly accepted norm prescribed that competent group behavior required competition among members and intellectualization of issues rather than genuinely collaborative, exploring, and personally revealing behavior; behaviors which might suggest low competence or any weakness, intellectual or personal, were actively suppressed. These two norms in effect placed all the factors which affected the creativity and productivity of the group outside the bounds of permissible group discussion. As individuals and groups broke through these previously unseen rules and strategies (and not all groups did), they often experienced the same exhilaration and sense of discovery that characterized other students' reactions to the experimental classes or to the process of evaluation. For example: "After a great deal of frustration with group meetings, I began to ask myself questions about group behavior and norms. By asking these questions, by viewing myself critically in group situations, and by accepting comments made by others, I really began to learn about myself and how I behave in group situations. It is one of the most meaningful experiences I've had during three years at Yale."

When this kind of breakthrough did not occur, the group experience was, more often than not, disappointing: "I was very disappointed with our group, and, not being a great crusader, made no effort to do anything about it. My failing, no excuses offered. The group meetings were a farce; the group project was not taken nearly so seriously as it ought to have been. The attitude of 'let's prepare the damn outline and get it over with' predominated."

While this student was willing to take responsibility for the failure of his group, so must we. We had expected that the excitement of working together on an academic project, coupled with our announced availability as consultants if problems should arise, would ensure the success of most groups. This was, it now appears, unrealistic. The same prohibitions against discussion of group problems that limited the effectiveness of some groups also prevented them from asking us for help. The result was, for some students, a feeling that we had abandoned them: "The groups were left on their own too much. Because of the aimlessness of the group I found I had nowhere to channel my desire to do work in the field. As a result my enthusiasm dissipated in this vacuum." Another put it this way:

> The whole thing is really quite frightening, for we are expected to get together with strangers and dredge some knowledge out of a vacuum and present it to the class. We would hopefully discover for ourselves how we could work most efficiently. But because we started from almost complete ignorance and without much sense of direction, we felt that an advisor might have been assigned to the group in its early stages, or that an instructor might have sat in on some group meetings, although we realize that he was always there for the asking.

As students summarized their overall feelings about the course and their learning at the end of the semester, some suggested that the lack of direction for the groups, highlighted by the student cited above, might be characteristic of the course as a whole:

> This course has obviously been one of experimentation, but the essence of an experiment is control over the experiment itself and that is where this course has failed. Furthermore, an experiment such as this must deal with reality, and here it has also failed. In an experiment such as this it is of paramount importance to recognize the hard core reality that a situation was created which easily could be taken advantage of.

On the other hand, many students were able to take advantage of the freedom provided by the experiment in a way which allowed them to try out a new kind of learning. One student, while admitting that he had not picked up much content, considered it a fair price to pay for gaining awareness:

> I don't think I got very much content out of this course. The presentations were, on the whole, not very challenging or exciting, and after the first three or four I didn't feel like I was missing very much by not going to class. Where the course was a success for me was in producing a new awareness of myself and my relations with others, and how little I really knew or noticed what was going on. My feeling is that I achieved only the barest beginnings in this respect, but enough to make me want to go on and explore more. . . . Throughout the semester, though, it seems to have been the discussions of the difficulties and failures of the course which have been most successful in breaking through to some awareness of what was happening beneath, above, or beyond the content, the specific tasks, which enables one to predict more reliably or envision more completely the consequences of any action, any change.

The confusing factor again and again seemed to be that suddenly, somehow, students' feelings and images of themselves had become entangled in what, until then, had been a mechanical, objective, externalized process.

I felt so guilty [about not working in the course], that I even tried to do a little independent reading. I failed miserably. Thus, everything seemed to point to the fact that I had deluded myself about my motivation; it was just a manifestation of my pseudo-intellect. Everything (my lack of traditional study, the implicit communications of the instructors, etc.)' seemed to say this. After a thorough (I think) reexamination of my position though, here's what I have to say in reply: I don't care what you say (or what I say). I am motivated in this subject—I spend more time thinking about it, and applying it to my everyday life than any other subject.

Such intermingling of the self, the emotions, and the intellect led to questions—hard questions, about what education is really for, and about what criteria really ought to be used to assess the success of a course and a student's performance in it.

Could negative feelings, such as being shaken, bored, or uncomfortable, be counted as positively valuable? "I have felt uncomfortable throughout the course—bored at times, annoyed at times. I feel shaken, and I also feel that the course has been the most valuable course I've taken here at Yale. But I'm not sure that I can describe or point specifically to what I've learned from the course." Could pleasurable effort really count as work? "The course is a gut. Those who don't want to work, don't have to. Those who do want to work find it easy and pleasurable."

What could be a measure of performance when one's level of aspiration begins to shoot so high that there is no possibility of success? "I suppose I should start by saying that I feel somewhat guilty about my performance in this course; not because of the lack of effort I have put into it, but rather because I have made so little of something that I am very much interested in and have a strong desire to learn about. It is an inwardly derived feeling, which because I must account for it myself is all the harder to take."

Could one call himself successful in the course if he came to see his failures more clearly—and if he came to doubt his potency to effect changes in the "real world" in the bargain?

In a way I am bitterly disappointed because what happened has been so much less than what I told myself I was going to do, that I feel I have not lived up to my promises. I wanted to try the change, but having to operate in the university system with four other goaded, tested courses kept me from reaching out and experimenting. I dislike yet value this course for this very reason, because it has shown me how very powerful the system is within which I am operating. Value because it is new knowledge; dislike because I shun the feelings of powerlessness, of weakness that I feel in the face of such a system, of the great difficulty of changing even the Yale University set-up that students might be more free. How much less chance, I find myself feeling, is there for a liberal philosophy hoping to have an effect on the events of the world, or on the U.S. Government.

Other students reinforced this last writer's view that large educational systems, such as Yale, are powerful and inertia-ridden. The larger system was seen as communicating potent expectations and pressures for high levels of intellectual performance; grades were seen as the lever by which the system enforced these prescriptions by controlling the options open to students in the future. One may respond to these pressures, or may try to beat the system; but he certainly ought to think twice about tampering with his future by experimenting within it. One student commented on how alien such experimentation was to him:

To my mind, the major reason for this lack of experimentation is that we (the students) are totally unaccustomed to experimentation in learning. It is important to note that we have been dealing with conventional techniques for thirteen years or more. It is hard to suddenly drop the guidelines set *for us* by these techniques and strike out on our own. I personally have not outgrown the spoonfeeding type of learning yet, which to be sure is unfortunate, but inescapable at this time.

Another described how the system may prevent involvement: "Whenever I thought of working for the internal rewards in this course, there was always something to do for an external reward that seemed more immediate. Occasionally I even had the feeling that I would like to do something for this course but I was afraid I would get very involved and neglect the other courses so I just did not start anything for this course." A third student described the cynicism which students use to defend themselves from involvement in a system that appears to punish involvement:

> . . . in this system a 75 on thirty minutes' work is far better than a 90 earned by five hours' work, even though the difference of four and one-half hours was spent in totally useless activity. Therefore, most Yale students devote their rare intelligence to defeating the system rather than achieving within it. The majority in Ad. Sci. Psych. 33a then looked on the course as an opportunity to get something for nothing, which is the overall tragedy of academics at Yale.

It has frequently been suggested that juvenile delinquents and minority group children often find that the safest ways of becoming involved are in beating the system. The foregoing comments, as well as the following one, suggest that university students play much the same game for much the same reasons, except that, on the whole, they are probably less overtly disrespectful and more successful.

> The view of learning as a means rather than an end pervades the campus much more than instructors of any course seem to realize. And asking a student to become interested in a course is actually an insult to his ability to beat the system—to get a grade in a course without actually learning anything from it. By not *requiring* anything [in this course], the instructors took the fun out of trying to outfox the system. There were two basic types of response to this. One was the one the instructors wanted—interested students willing to gamble to see what they actually *could* learn if they tried; and those who treated the course in the same manner they treated all their others—something to be gotten through with as little effort as possible. What could have been done to alter this situation I do not know. But if I can come up with any solution I will be glad to suggest it because this course has given me a much different outlook on studying and learning in general, and I think that most everyone could have benefited from a similar

experience if only they had not been so closed to the opportunity.

As teachers, we find ourselves as overwhelmed by the apparent contradictions in trying to assess the success of the course as the students did when they tried to evaluate their individual performances. Thus, perhaps the best way to summarize our feelings is simply to discuss the learning we, the instructors, experienced in the course, and the conclusions we reached as a result of it.

Clearly we were too optimistic at the beginning of the course about the ability of our students to respond to the wide-open opportunity for self-directed learning we tried to provide. Yale undergraduates—and probably most other college students in the country —generally are not ready to use intellectual freedom effectively in an environment which demands self-control. The difference between many students' initial reactions to our proposal and their often bleak assessments of their performance at the end of the semester suggests that this discovery was just as much a surprise to them as it was to us. Perhaps we should not have been so surprised. For most of their lives, college students have been in schools which rely on external incentives —grades, praise, even punishment—to provide the motivation for academic achievement. In retrospect, we can think of no reason why students reared in such organizations should have developed the capability to respond to a course in which the rewards for performance had to be almost entirely internal. Just because students say they want intellectual freedom and self-direction—and just because we say we want to give it to them—is no reason to presume either that they know how to use it once they get it, or that we know how to teach its use.

We learned that we did not and do not have a sound educational strategy for helping students develop the capability for self-directed learning. What we did, in effect, was encourage the students to jump into the water, and then provide encouragement by calling out "Swim! Swim!" from the shore. The effect was a period of considerable turmoil, out of which significant learning emerged for some students. One of us feels that such turmoil—accompanied by constant self-examination and evaluation—is the only presently viable way for an individual to develop meaningful self-direction in education. He believes that the wisdom which would be necessary to help students move gradually from external direction to internal direction currently is not available. The other writer is more optimistic. He feels that it may be possible now to develop and apply procedures for weaning a student away from dependence on external incentives and standards in learning situations—perhaps by providing students with a series of educational tasks which demand (and reward) increasing levels of personal responsibility and control.

Despite our procedural fumbling—or perhaps in part because of it—some students clearly were significantly affected by the course. As a result of the course, some began to take on full responsibility for their own lives, and came to repudiate things "out there" and beyond control as the causes of joy and suffering and learning. This move, spoken about by philosophers, theologians, and Jungian psychologists, appeared to occur to some extent for some of our students. With an increasing awareness of the effects which the larger system was having on them came a denial of the legitimacy of such control, suggested by phrases such as "Nevertheless, I must account for it myself," or "The responsibility for my failure lay solely with me." The impact which such a change can have on one's life was revealed by one student who came to one of us almost in tears near the end of the semester. "For three years," he said, "I've been blaming Yale for my lack of involvement and commitment and my poor performance. Now I realize that that has been a cop-out, that it was *me* who accepted the way I was being controlled by the system and the other students, and that I really didn't have the courage to risk fighting it." It is hard for us to imagine how even the most skeptical of our colleagues and students could deny that this represents learning of the first magnitude.

We found that our greatest impact on the students came not so much from what we said or from what we asked them to do as from the way we ourselves behaved. We had expected that by eliminating our control of grades we would reduce the influence we would have on student behavior. If anything, the reverse was true. With grade-enforced rules no longer relevant, the students apparently began to look to us as models of appropriate academic behavior. When we used classroom time for lecturing, they did the same; when we became innovative in our presentations, so did they; when we began to look at the process of the course as a source of data for learning about administration, they began to look at process in their work groups to try to make them more effective. Although we observed the modeling effect with considerable interest throughout the course, we did not use it as a resource for learning nearly as much as we might have. Numerous educational strategists have suggested the potency of modeling in learning situations. If students see new behaviors and new approaches to education working for others, they can try them on themselves relatively easily; if new or desired behaviors are both unknown to them and hidden from them (as when we were merely telling the students to make their presentations innovative), one can hardly expect much really new ground to be broken. What was most shocking to us was how blind we were to the impact which our behavior was having on the students as the course progressed.

Finally, we came to agree with the students that our course was significantly counter to the Yale educational system, and that for this reason it suffered to some degree. Throughout the course, we tried to emphasize simultaneous analysis and awareness at two levels: both behavior and values, both information and evaluation, both content and process. In this sense, the course may have been a more encompassing, self-conscious social system than the university as a whole: the course encouraged high involvement and high awareness simultaneously, while the students' (and our) view of the university is that it operates so as to encourage neither.

From such a perspective, it is tempting to conclude that all the failures of the course can be subsumed under its successes, because we were developing a system which had the self-consciousness and responsibility to identify its failures and work through them; students could and did leave the system—both behaviorally and psychologically —if they found it not to their liking, and could do so without fear of punishment; and many of the failures of the course appeared to be direct consequences of the unintended and implicit, but nonetheless potent, hostility of the larger system to active educational experimentation. The implication of this view is that the remedy for the failures of the course lies not in any fundamental changes in the course but rather in doing more of the same. This conclusion was drawn by one of the students:

> . . . a thought I just had which may give you a little moral
> support, or whatever, is that the one thing that is hurting you
> more than anything else is that you are carrying on an experimental class while the rest of Yale is not, thus the temptation to let 33a hold the proverbial bag. I wish only that all

my courses were held in this way and sincerely believe that to the extent that it is failing—to that extent (or more) should you try even harder next time.

The conclusion is not so inescapable for the instructors. It seems clear that the course missed about one-third of its students almost completely. Can we be so crass that we virtually ignore those individuals who cannot or do not respond to what we offer? Do we not have an obligation to help those students who are not ready to accept opportunities for self-directed and self-rewarded learning as well as those who are? Should we tell them more forcefully and less trustfully at the outset that the course we teach is less likely to meet their present needs than most of the other courses available? Or perhaps it is impossible to reach such students as long as we remain in a system which offers potent rewards for conformity to external learning requirements. Rather than offer more experimental courses, perhaps we should be devoting our energies toward making direct changes in the larger system so that it encourages more experimentation.

Whatever our next step may be in the practice of teaching, we are also led to speculate on the possible theoretical connections among some of these learnings. These speculations are touched off by three memories. One memory is of the instructors' shock when we recognized the incongruencies between our values and our behaviors, first in the transition between planning and implementing the course, and later when we had fallen into the lecture pattern while exhorting our students to try something new. These creative shocks had tremendous impact on the development of the course, and led us to adopt a much freer form of thinking together, almost free-associating in an effort to gain new perspectives on the tasks we were planning.

The other two memories are of student comments about failure. One related to the course: "It seems to have been the discussions of the difficulties and failures of the course which have been most successful in breaking through to some awareness of what was happening beneath, above, or beyond the content, the specific tasks, the specific goals." One related to the student himself: "In a way I am bitterly disappointed because what happened has been so much less than what I told myself I was going to do, that I feel I have not lived up to my promises."

While the shock of incongruency and failure may not be the best way to learn how to do things, it may be an inevitable part of learning who we are. One cannot say one has learned how to make a shoe until one has made it right—been successful. We overlook the fact that an important aspect of getting it right is learning to identify errors. Identifying errors is relatively easy in trying on a shoe. (Most of us can easily recognize when the shoe does not fit.) But what is an error in making ourselves? Is it an error even to say that we *make* ourselves? Is it perhaps more appropriate to say we *discover* ourselves? We are not sure. An easy way of avoiding this problem is to assume we know who we are, take on some role in front of others, and try to conceal our uncertainties. Being by and large unimaginative, we tend to dream up rather limited roles for ourselves; so limited, in fact, that we often find ourselves unable to relate to a given person or situation quite as we wanted. We can easily avoid seeing this shortcoming, too, by blaming external necessities for our problems. Gradually these roles and external necessities, rather than our search for some more genuine sense of identity and authenticity, come to direct our behavior. Different people may find this life either predominantly painful or predominantly pleasurable, but at least the pain can be blamed on someone else. As long as one lives in systems with lots of external controls, this explanation can be very plausible.

The effect which this process has on cutting us off from our inner lives and from one another's inner experience is shielded from our view by our way of cutting ourselves off: We simply lose awareness of our deeper thoughts, feelings, and sensations except on rare occasions, and then they can be dismissed as not making sense when compared with our daily way of life.

Our course shifted almost all the tangible responsibility for what happened to the shoulders of each student. As the quotations suggest, many students found it difficult to blame the environment for what happened to them because their own responsibility was so clear. Nor could the course easily be called a gut, since its requirements were not merely low but virtually and explicitly nonexistent except as the student saw fit to challenge himself. As the students began to assume responsibility for their own behavior, they began to see that they were not the independent, self-controlled, self-directed people they had pretended to themselves to be. In fact, they felt many external pressures, were unsure what they wanted to do, and found themselves not living up to their promises, just as we, the instructors, found it difficult to do what we said we wanted to do.

In this context, it is not difficult to understand why our course was less productively self-directive than deeply self-exploratory. None of us was in touch with a self that we would trust, or that had the ability, to direct us. Nor did we know how to learn, discover, become, or make such a self. Most courses provide axioms, methods, and careful definitions of the problems, asking us to learn by closing in on some solution. Suddenly we found ourselves in a situation in which such convergent, purely cognitive learning was manifestly inadequate. Instead, our learning required our opening to an enlarged awareness of our own and of one another's experiencing and only then beginning to discriminate the conditions of, and standards for, such enlarged awareness.

An openness to failure and the causes of failure seemed an important way in our course of enlarging our awareness. The exact dynamics of this openness to failure are not obvious, but the course illustrated several aspects of it. One aspect which seemed to minimize defensiveness at failure was that persons and groups initiated their own evaluations. This was not the case at the end of the semester when the instructors insisted that groups devise some form of evaluation, and it was necessary to overcome considerable defensiveness before our efforts produced greater awareness. A second aspect of openness to failure seemed to be a willingness to appropriate responsibility for one's part in causing the failure. Only in such cases did failure lead to greater awareness of one's relationship with things and people outside oneself. A third aspect of openness to failure seemed to be that failure came to cause suffering rather than pain—that is, failure would be felt personally as a lack of right relationship (to oneself, one's group, one's work, or one's teaching), which called for a new effort of understanding, rather than impersonally as a bothersome, external irritant which should be avoided if at all possible. Openness to failure may seem an unpleasant way to have to learn, and certainly it is not the only aspect of learning. But it may be a necessary aspect of learning and a particularly crucial one to recognize in the case of self-knowledge, since most social modes of presenting ourselves emphasize finished and polished self-possessedness.

Such theoretical and practical problems are, we feel, central both to classroom teaching and to large-scale educational planning. The concrete experience of our course helped us formulate them more clearly for ourselves; if through our writing about the course these issues have come alive for others, perhaps our conclusions can lead, not to an ending, but the beginning of new experiments.

Oron South

Creativity
for Engineers

Management of Creativity, ME-288 was, in 1968, an experiment in providing a planned environment to promote personal and professional growth among engineering students.[1] Thirty-seven students took part in the one-semester course, which met one night a week for three hours, at Vanderbilt University where I was a member of the Center for the Study of Engineering Management. The objective of the course—to put learning to use immediately in the service of personal and professional growth—required setting growth goals, planning to reach goals, trying different methods for goal achievement, evaluating progress, setting new goals, and replanning. Class sessions and assignments were both designed to support these objectives. I had taught ME-288 twice before, in each case using a text in addition to class exercises and outside readings. The classroom activities, based on

[1] I am indebted to Robert S. Rowe, Dean of the School of Engineering of Vanderbilt University, for his active support of this experiment.

Vanderbilt
University

laboratory training and on the writings of Arnold (1956), Gordon (1956), and Osborn (1953), were generally satisfactory but neither the texts nor the reading assignments produced the results I had hoped for. Students were unable to use concepts such as those of Maslow (1954), from their reading, for anything other than discussion, partly because their educational experience had stressed intellectual understanding rather than action. Moreover, my design did not present them with a coherent, congruent system. Their reading did not reinforce what was taking place in class and so they were often at a loss when they were asked to build on the concepts they found in their reading.

If we were to reach the goal of putting learning to use immediately—that is, of learning systematically from the environment, students would need to do specific things in this course, and my design would need to provide for this sort of learning. Each student would need to adjust to the idea of considering himself and others as environment in which learning depends on discovery and acceptance of the *I* who is initiating and responding; to develop a method for learning from himself and others; to develop an ability to see patterns in the environment and to see possibilities for changing them; to develop an activist approach to learning; to develop or borrow a storage system for organizing learning; to experiment with presenting himself and others with different environments to increase learning; to begin to restructure his own relationships to make the accomplishment of certain tasks easier or to increase learning possibilities.

As a guide and assistant to the student in helping him learn from his environment, I felt that I could be most useful if I were to show the student that I accepted his efforts to discover himself and others; to suggest methods for learning, such as systematic ways of observing and being aware; to present him with environments that contain different learning possibilities; to help him find ways to test the validity of his learning; and to suggest ways for organizing learning. From this perspective it seemed clear that I could safely rule out much reading material ordinarily used as not being helpful to the student who was beginning to try to learn systematically from his environment. My conviction, that reading that does not assist a student to see the reality assumed by a different orientation unless it suggests also directions for movement, was deepened in another class where I had assigned Rogers' *On Becoming a Person* (1961). From comments by students it seemed evident that they had been able to learn about themselves by examining their environment as Rogers had examined his; he gave them directions for looking. Literature of this sort is not readily available.

Earlier I had devised a reading test, to determine the extent to which students could derive implications about process from research findings, and had used it in a *T* group course. I found that students could summarize and understand well, but their notions about applications of what they read were vague and hazy; many could not see any possibility at all of applying what they read to organization. Taking into account the results of this reading test and of my analysis of learning structure, I finally put together a general design for ME-288. To encourage students to look at themselves and others as a source of learning, I would require a series of papers that would focus on the individual in the process of development, the individual's methods for learning about himself and others, and the individual's growth goals. I would use the class time to move from some structure to no structure, while trying to allow the students the maximum amount of choice and decision-making. I would try not to sanction or encourage any particular type of behavior on the part of the students. (For example, I did not wish to convey to those who had been in T groups that the T group type of behavior was wanted—nor did I wish to convey that it was not appropriate.) I hoped to convey, through my own behavior, that the choice was to be made by the individual, who was thus to be the authority for his own behavior. I wanted the students to accept the responsibility of taking risks.

Creativity can be thought of as an outgrowth of movement toward humanness and uniqueness: the individual increases his capacity to be creative as he becomes more human and as he develops his own uniqueness. To think of humanness in this fashion, one must reject the mechanistic and strictly biological models of human identity, and substitute for them a humanistic model, the conception of which must be grounded in a system that centers on human needs and human experience.

I gave the students a brief description of creativity in the general rationale for the course handed out at the first session. "There are at least two primary views one can take toward creativity. One is to consider that creativity should be directed toward producing a product. A course organized around this point of view would emphasize product creation. A second point of view is that which emphasizes the creative process in individuals and organizations. The difference between these two points of view may be thought of as the difference between an external and an internal approach to creativity . . . In the external approach men are conceived of as being in two classes so far as creativity is concerned. To increase creativity one studies those who are in the creative class of people, and attempts to find what distinguishes them from the noncreative . . . Then one can observe what creative people do and try to teach the noncreative the techniques developed by the creative. A course built on this viewpoint involves a considerable amount of reading to acquaint students with research findings, discussion of the findings, and practice in using techniques. Progress, then, is conceived of as learning more about the world external to the student. In the internal approach, men are not thought of as being divided into classes insofar as creative ability is concerned. Instead, the assumption is made that each individual has creative potential . . . In this course the focus is primarily on this second assumption, that is, that each person not only has creative potential but that this potential can be actualized by learning more about self and relational networks. We shall learn about the self by: 1) becoming more aware of experiences in different situations and learning to value (trust) that experience; 2) comparing our expectations of what we think we ought to feel, believe, and think with what we actually experience; 3) becoming more open to different kinds of experiencing—developing potential through risk taking; 4) experimenting with different forms of self expression."

By synthesizing concepts taken from Hocking (1966), Cassirer (1961), and Maslow (1962), reinforced by the work of Rogers (1961) and Gibb (Bradford, Gibb, and Benne, 1964), I was able to come up with guidelines for the course. I set out to provide a wide range of choices, presented so that the students will be aware constantly of the choices before them; to emphasize intentions, problem-solving, and decision-making; to have students work in groups to increase feeling of acceptance, and to let them select their groups; to provide for examination of the way in which groups are operating and, thereby, to facilitate change in group norms and standards, since a change in group standards of acceptance will permit individual change; to judge individual and group products in relation to potential, rather than as products; to accept students as persons, and groups as groups; to insure that my comments are relevant to what individuals are trying to do; and to provide ways for students to control their own behavior and choices and to influence my behavior.

I hypothesized that, if I succeeded in reaching my objectives, the students would develop a deeper sense of their own identity, they would be aware of themselves in different ways and would seek more satisfying ways of being and becoming; they would become more aware of the influence others have on them and the influence they have on others, and would feel how such influence limits or encourages self-actualization; the students would try, during the course, to move toward more acceptable self-realization as they discovered a lack of self-actualization.

In designing a course of this sort for engineers, one needs to keep in mind two things about the resources the students bring with them. All through their training, they work problems, do tasks, get on with the job, that is, they do not spend much time thinking about or looking at themselves in action; they are not process oriented. They have little experience in writing; most of them regard anything more than two pages as the equivalent of writing a book, as I have discovered from experience.

The seven papers required in the course formed the basis for the grade to be given. The relation of the papers to the goals of the course is apparent from their titles.

On Becoming Me—An account of your development as a person, to include some assessment of the influence of your parents or guardian on your values, problem-solving, decision-making, and preferred way of relating to others. What turns you on, and what turns you off.

Where I Am—Poem—Can be in rhyme or free verse. A description of how you see yourself as a person—how it is with you—your state of being.

My Learning Goals—A statement of the learning goals you have set for yourself, what they are and why you have set them. The paper should include statements about behaviors you hope to develop, new skills you hope to acquire, and how you are making use of resources inside and outside class. A description of how you expect to reach your goals, and what yardsticks you expect to use to measure goals.

The Climate in Class—A description of the climate as you have experienced it, and you observe it. This should include information about primary attitudes you see and the effect these attitudes have.

Principles of Observation—An analysis of how to observe, based on what you have done in class, and on outside reading.

Working with a Partner—A report on the process of interaction between you and another person where the intent is to try to let the other person know you and to try to know the other.

My Learning Goals—Final report on what you have tried to learn and assessment of success.

Students who can be secure only when they are following clearly outlined instructions could take comfort in the firm requirements for the papers. Each was to be of a minimum length of ten pages, typewritten, double spaced. To encourage quality, I announced penalties for sloppiness, misspelling, and lateness, and rewards for incorporating outside reading when appropriate. As an aid to structuring papers, I sometimes provided suggestions of content approaches.

"On Becoming Me": Suggestions and questions to stimulate thinking

1. Get with a group of three or four friends. Try to recall the earliest events you can remember in your life. In what ways are the events you recall different and similar to those of your friends? Does the pattern revealed suggest anything about later developments or habits?

3. What was your father's occupation? Were you raised as a typical child in this occupational group? (Consult a standard work in sociology if you want to do some outside reading.)

6. What was the belief system of your parents? What effect has this had on you?

7. What communication pattern did your parents use with you? Can you see effects of this on you?

8. What kind of pattern did your parents follow in expressing affection for you and for others? Did it have effects on you? In what ways?

10. In your memories of your childhood how did you see yourself? Do you still see yourself in the same way? If not, what was responsible for the change?

The emphasis on writing in this course reflected my conviction, and a general notion in the engineering school, that engineers need to learn how to write. I had other reasons, however, for requiring length and quality, reasons that relate to assumptions about learning and creativity. Doing the impossible can contribute to a sense of accomplishment and can raise the level of self-esteem. This might be especially important for students who find it difficult to participate freely in class activities. Also, I thought that papers would provide an opportunity for trying creative approaches. The effect of the writing assignment can be gained from the fact that fifteen students out of fifty-two gave up the course after the first session, some because they did not think they could keep up in other courses if they met my requirements, others because they had not expected to do so much work.

I was delighted with the unusual quality of the papers. As I read the papers, I came to feel that the students were trusting me with thoughts they had not, in many instances, been willing previously to voice to themselves. For example:

> In the past few days since that rather traumatic separation, I have come to several realizations concerning myself in relationship to others. Whether or not we can work out our problems by talking the whole relationship over—our attitudes, expectations, and personal needs—I hope from this experience I have gained insights which will prevent my making these same mistakes again.
>
> In any relationship, I must be myself but realize that I am not static and rigid . . . I must also, when dealing with others whose friendship and love mean a great deal to me, be able to communicate my feelings about myself in relation to them. A love relationship entails more than I thought and does not always present a picture of roses and soft music.

That excerpt is characteristic of many others in that the writer was dealing with life goals. When I wrote instructions for the paper on learning goals, I had in mind learning goals in the course; the students, almost without exception, interpreted them as life goals.

In the first paper, *On Becoming Me,* students dealt with relationships with parents, the effect of separations and divorces, the effect of having parents who lived across the tracks, early sexual experiences, difficulties and successes in school, and evaluated the process of growing-up. The most originality, as I judged it, was displayed by the lone sophomore in the class: he prepared his paper in the form of an obituary notice, in which he quoted remarks made by his friends and acquaintances about his untimely demise. As a result of this exercise he decided to schedule some activities he had postponed; he wanted to start living a little more.

The second written assignment consisted of poems which, on the whole, contained fascinating insights into students' views of themselves and of college. After reading them all, I asked Dean Robert Rowe if he could furnish money to publish them. He made funds available, and then I asked members of the class if they would permit publication. Four said they did not wish to have their work published; eight agreed to have their poems published as long as they could remain anonymous. The issue of publication fitted well, I thought, with

the idea of creativity. Students had to decide whether they would permit their names to be associated with their work. This was discussed,
to some extent, in the groups, but was not explored completely from
the standpoint of what creative effort may require in terms of risk.
The publication of the poems had several interesting results. Faculty
members were pleased that a book of poems was being published in
the Engineering School. The Dean sent copies to all members of the
Board of Trustees. After the end of the semester, the editor of the
campus literary magazine came to see me to find out how I managed
to get poems of such high quality. He said that the majority were
much better than those submitted to the magazine he edited. By the
end of the year, ME-288 became known as the course where students
wrote poetry. That this was only one assignment was not noted; publication established a reputation.

WHERE I AM

I know where I've been, or do I?
Is where I've been where I think I've been . . .
Or is it only my fantasy?
Did I miss the real where?
The very existence of the question answers it.
Where am I? What? Who?
Can I be at all when I have missed the real?
Can I ever be if I ever miss the real?
My being strives for realness . . .
And in contemplation believes to have found the way . . .
But if I have changed, they have not.
They see the same things in me, expect the same.
And though I try, I am as they see me . . . no change.
Why?
Am I not enough myself to be what I believe I really am?
A creature of habit is a strong one, but yet,
One other, the so desired other, could rule . . .
Could cause the repetitions to cease,
Could give the courage to stand, new, fresh, apart,
Alone, but sufficient, not needing, not requiring . . .
Real.
Could . . . could . . . but does not.
I seek to know why . . . must know why . . .

For knowing fosters doing.
It dominates me.

J. P. M.

WHAT AM I?

Everything must be relevant to another thing.
The tree is relevant
to the soil, or to the countryside.
A wall relates to
a room, a prison;
a book, a chair, a person
take on meaning only when they are
relevant.
What am I?

What I am is relevant
to Time.
Today is confusion, anxiety, despair.
Tomorrow is hope, laughter, understanding,
What I am is only what Time makes me.
What is Time?

Time is a place,
and that place is me.
Time is forever.
I am but a point in that span of lifetimes.
And I must do something—
Something to etch the point of my life
On Time.

Time gives opportunities.
It may give a chance to win,
to succeed,
to make myself a someone
instead of a "who?"
The chance may come only once,
or it may come many times.

One cannot outguess Time.
Time may require
a split-second decision to make the difference

between success or failure.
A split-second in all of Time
may be two minutes,
or four years.

Perhaps these four years
will be my *split-second chance.*
Perhaps that split-second is
Now.

DAVID K. HEDREEN

VISION OF FEAR

Fear chasing me
rolling eyes
drooling mouth
drivel of lust
Haunting my sleep
destroying my days
I am running
running—running
with glue feet
from the glue pot tongue
searching to dissolve my consciousness
Fear bred on ignorance
not yet weaned from myself
Today's ignorance sucked away
today gone without being known
Tomorrow's self
an unsolved mystery

Fear hounding me
wants to eat me
will gnaw my lowest love
Running with blinders
as all have run before me
I fall and am cut
knives of expectation
leaving twelve pieces
running in twelve squared directions
all me but none me

Crying for the poor and sick
for the dead in Nam
for Joe McCarthy
and red underwear
I cry with anybody
for everybody and nobody
but with no concern
tears of distilled water
never tears of blood
The blood of commitment
commitment is life
the breathing soul of self
Fear is death
reeking gangrene
molding flesh
fear devours the grease packing
of my mind
damaged in shipping

Self is truth
truth the coffin for fear
the fear of tomorrow
of tomorrow's tomorrow
Fear of commitment
to lust or love?
hate or forgive?
discriminate or accept?
Repel fear with broken hands
better than broken mind
Bury it in the swamp of expectations
along with relentless pressure
pressure of conforming to every divergency.
Fashion a coffin of experience
experience related to self
But what can relate to sand
Every whisp of wind
forever altering its character
Every grain a parent or friend
an enemy or teacher

Each grain with its own calling
its own direction
Millions of grains
that I have followed
Millions of selfs
But none to be known as
            ME

JAMES KIRCHER

Of the papers required, the one on the principles of observation was, in my estimation, the most difficult for the students. Not only was the concept hard to grasp, but also it was even harder for students to visualize a systematic way to treat observation. As a result, the quality of these papers was lower than of others. The difficulties, however, did provoke questions about the process of observation, questions which had not been asked before.

LEARNING THROUGH EXPERIENCE

The writing assignments were not the only causes of newly learned openness, trust, and risk-taking. Students were learning from class experiences. In the first meeting, after introducing the course and describing the writing assignments, I spoke briefly about learning from one's own experience, and about the ways in which students would become involved during class periods. Before they began to write about themselves, they would need experiences that would give them new ways of thinking about themselves and about their relationship with others. The exercises planned for the first night would demonstrate the ways in which the students would become involved with each other during class periods and would give them some experience in discovering their feelings about themselves and others. The instructions for the demonstration activities were:

Move all chairs back to the walls and form a large circle with everyone standing. Starting on my left, introduce yourself to the group by singing your name and making some motion with your hands and arms.

Without saying anything, mill around inside the circle and try to pick up how people are feeling.

Now, nonverbally, greet people in any way that seems appropriate to you.

Continuing nonverbally, walk up to different people and find the distance from them that is most comfortable to you. Do this slowly, and try it with at least three or four people, including some you do not know.

Around the wall you will find sheets of newsprint and some *magic markers*. Get with three or four others, talk about what you have picked up in the way of feelings in this group, and draw in any way that seems appropriate to you how you think this group is at this time.

After you have finished your drawing, using several sheets if you want to, walk around and look at the work of other groups.

Move out of the group you are in now, circulate around and form another group of four or five, preferably people you do not know, and develop criteria for membership in groups that will help you learn. Use newsprint to put your criteria on.

When you have finished your list, walk around and look at the lists others have developed.

Now form into groups of nine or ten, using criteria you have developed. When you have formed your groups, take a few minutes to talk about how you expect to work with one another.

Nonverbally, for about five minutes, *be* five years old.

Continuing nonverbally, *be* fifteen years old.

Now, without saying anything, *be* thirty-five years old.

Discuss how you felt during the three age periods.

These exercises were to increase awareness of self and of the choices available, to convey a sense of everyone's starting from the same position, to provide an opportunity for self-selection into groups, to encourage awareness of self in process, and to highlight the risk involved in doing nothing as well as in doing something different.

In succeeding weeks, a different activity was planned for each meeting. Sometimes the plans were made by the students, sometimes by me. On balance, I did more planning than they did. I had hoped to learn how to involve them in more of the planning, but did not succeed to the extent I wished. Several students in one group were interested in brainstorming, and volunteered to plan and to conduct the session. They developed several topics for brainstorming, and provided for different roles for members of the group conducting the session. After the session was over, we discussed what they had learned as a result of planning and producing the session. Another group wanted to plan a group competition in the form of a house-building exercise which one of the members had read about. Each group was to decide what types of houses it would build (using three-by-five-inch, and five-by-seven-inch cards), set up an assembly line for construction, and maintain quality control. Completed houses were delivered to a market which set a price for different models. The critique at the end of this exercise brought out the contention that the market did not make sufficient allowance for creativity. The house-building exercise, which took place the third week of the course, provoked a fair amount of dissatisfaction within the groups. A number reported some frustration as a result of attempts which were ignored, to influence house design. Others were frustrated by the teammates' lack of desire to seek creative solutions to the design problem.

Because of this dissatisfaction, the following week I did some work on the use of analogies to stimulate creative thinking. Part of this required one group to develop an analogy, and other groups to build on and extend the analogy. Another part required analogies describing the groups to be developed. Two of these are given below:

Our group is like a quartet on a bicycle going down hill. Every now and then somebody pumps the pedals once or twice.

Our group is like a bunch of people in an orchard. Some are standing on the ground trying to get the fruit within reach. A few are trying to climb up to the top of the tree to reach the fruit at the top. Some are lying on the ground waiting for others to bring them fruit. Others are trying to take the fruit away from those who have picked it off the tree, and some are trying to pick up what they can find lying on the ground.

Probably the most dissatisfaction was produced immediately after the President's Commission on Civil Disorder made public the conclusions of its deliberations. In class I reviewed the comments briefly, and then asked each group to spend two hours working on the following assignment: What can engineers and engineering do to contribute to the solution of the difficulties described in the Commission's report? Two things happened during the discussions which followed. One was the discovery of a considerable amount of prejudice toward blacks. This outraged some, who considered such prejudice unfounded, and who had expected, without really checking, that their classmates were more liberal than the majority of Southern whites. The second discovery was that none had any idea how to tackle such a problem;

they simply did not know how to begin to apply engineering to social goals. One result of this session was a request to invite blacks from Fisk University or Tennessee A. and I. to join members of the class in exploring prejudice and the possibilities of using engineering with social systems in mind. I contacted the Dean of the School of Engineering at Tennessee A. and I. and asked if he had students who would be willing to join ours. He called later to say that their students were near exams before spring holidays and that he could not find any willing to participate.

In the meantime, while waiting for word from Tennessee A. and I., I invited the photographer from that school to spend an evening with the class. I had noted some of his work before our class discussion of prejudice, and had asked him to appear one night. He was somewhat interested in what was taking place in the class and, after several discussions, agreed to bring some pictures and see what would happen. When he arrived, we displayed a number of his pictures and asked members of each group to look at them without comment and then, as groups, to talk about what they saw. Then we all formed a large circle and Zinn, the photographer, began to respond to questions and comments. As questions died down, he began to describe how he tried to innovate and create in photography. He described how he was trying to use his knowledge of biology, in which he had majored at college, television illustration, which he had done for a number of years, and photography, to show cell development from the inside out. This involved, among other things, putting together cell slices and then animating them. The notion was that something new might be revealed in the process. Zinn followed this with a discussion of how he tried to trap ideas. The students stayed with him during the evening, and he stayed tuned in to them. At the end of the course, many rated this as one of the highlights of the program. Several felt less bashful about working at odd hours, and at odd ideas, after Zinn's discussion.

Several times during the evening, Zinn mentioned photography or art displays in Nashville, and also mentioned several plays, each time asking: "How many of you have seen what I am talking about?" Not once did he get a positive response, so finally he asked: "What do you do with your spare time?" Picking up on this note, the next week I constructed an exercise in which students developed limericks,

verses, songs, or posters around the idea of engineers taking part in
outside activities. The production during the exercise revealed a considerable amount about how students thought of themselves as engineers, and especially how often they referred to themselves as tools.
The examples illustrate recurring themes.

> On math, engineering is founded
> With equations we all are surrounded
> Come on, see the light!
> I'll get you aright
> *Activities* make you well-rounded.

> Those who always deal
> with bolts are often
> destined to be dolts.

> Those who always think of tools
> very often wind up fools.

> *Tools* are our *least* important product.

> Set aside the kinetics
> and explore esthetics.

> How do I love thee? Let me count the ways.
> 0000
> 0001
> 0010
> 0011
> 0100
> 0101
> 0110
> 0111
> 1000
> 1001
> 1010
> 1011
> 1100
> 1101
> 1110
> 1111

About half way through the semester, I prepared a course-feedback form and asked the students to respond to it at the close of the evening session. The questions with number of responses, follow.

1. To what extent have you tried to involve yourself in this course?

	10	3	4	6	3		7
Very Little	Some						Very Much

2. To what extent are you satisfied with your own efforts to learn in this course?

	3		4	1	5		15		2	2	1
Very Dissatis- fied	Somewhat Dissatis- fied		A Little Dissatis- fied			Somewhat Satisfied		Very Satisfied

3. To what extent are you satisfied with my efforts to help you learn?

	1		4	4	13	6	2	3
Very Dissatis- fied	Somewhat Dissatis- fied	A Little Dissatis- fied			Somewhat Satisfied			Very Satisfied

4. To what extent are you satisfied with the efforts to help you learn made by others in the class?

1	5	10	7	9	1
Very Dissatis- fied	Somewhat Dissatis- fied	A Little Dissatis- fied		Somewhat Satisfied	Very Satisfied

5. In terms of learning for you, how helpful have the written assignments been?

1	3	10	1	9	1	5	1	1
No Insight At All		A Little Insight		Some Insight		Quite a Bit of Insight		A Lot of Insight

6. Based on what we have had so far during class time,

what have you found easiest to do and what hardest
to do?

Fourteen said the hardest thing to do was to participate in nonverbal
activities. As one said: "Walking around without saying anything (I
feel like an idiot)." The thing mentioned most frequently as being
easiest was group discussion.

7. Based on your analysis of your learning needs and learning desires, please describe what you would consider to be
   an ideal class session.

The answers to this indicated primarily a desire to have a clear-cut
problem, some time to work on it in small groups, and an analysis at
the conclusion of the evening. Typical comments were:

> A class divided into small groups as ours has been seems to
> be the most helpful to me. For example, the night we had the
> brainstorming session and the night we built the houses were
> probably the best classes I have ever attended at Vanderbilt
> in my four years here. It would probably be helpful to note
> that these two nights we completely separated the small groups
> from the class by moving into separate rooms. I feel that I
> can participate more and be more interested in a small iso-
> lated group. I feel somewhat apprehensive about actively par-
> ticipating in a very large group.

> An ideal class would contain some type of action-oriented
> physical exercise and another group-involvement exercise.

> I enjoyed the competition—house building project. Something
> along those lines to promote the necessity for group organiza-
> tion and unified functioning toward a common goal. Some-
> thing constructive which shows the justification of working
> for three hours. A material, physical goal.

Three students suggested that I start the evening with a lecture. The
remainder made no mention of this, although a number indicated a
desire for the teacher to end sessions with a summary and some statement of what proper course each session should have taken. The feed-

back indicated considerable dissatisfaction with the behavior of class-mates. I had been aware of this as I had received complaints from several students. As far as I could tell, however, there was no una-nimity about the identity of offending members. Some thought that only their friends were working, and, as friendship patterns varied, so did the attribution of work. I also knew, or at least thought I knew, that many of the students wished to disguise how much or how little work they were doing. This was evident when papers were handed in or returned. Most of the individuals were careful not to show the con-tents of their papers to others. And, when papers were due, many waited until the last minute to turn them in so that other students would not have a chance to pick up the papers and look at them.

ATTENDANCE

About a month before school was out I attempted to deal with the problem of commitment by lifting all rules on attendance. I re-tained the due dates on papers, but made no requirement about com-ing to class. How many attended after this I do not know, as counting was difficult, for each group met in a separate room, and some met in one member's house. Activities of the different groups varied. For example, one group thought of several ways of involving another group in improvisations. This worked well, and, for the remainder of the evening, the two groups took turns in supplying improvisation cues for members of the other group.

The group that had the highest attendance record, as far as I could judge, consisted of students who initially had not chosen any group and found themselves together by default. After several meet-ings, marked by long silences, they established that one of their un-spoken goals was to become a freely functioning group. When left to their own devices, members of this group decided that the next week each one was to come prepared to do something before the others. The day after that meeting, three students from this group stopped by my office to tell me how astonished they were to find out how much talent they had. One member, for example, presented a magic act with professional skill. This encouraged everyone in the group to work harder at finding other talents and using them.

At the close of one session, five of us remained behind to con-tinue our discussion. At about ten-thirty, a professor from the department of applied math came into the room, leaned against the door and, after listening for several minutes, joined in. At this point the discussion was centering around one member who had an unlisted telephone number, and who had difficulty in making close friends. After another hour or so, I left. The next day I learned that the discussion had continued until one-thirty in the morning, with feedback being provided to different members about their behavior. One of those who stopped by to tell me about the discussion was the math professor, who said he had got some help on problems he would face when he left to become chairman of another department in another university.

For the class's last scheduled meeting, thirty-one of the thirty-seven members showed up. We talked about what had happened, I answered questions for about an hour, and we dispersed. The next day three more students stopped by my office to say that they had intended to come but had been unavoidably detained.

I hope it is clear that I did not try to follow any particular theme during class sessions. I did try to provide a consistent process, that is, I tried to allow a considerable amount of self-determination about what was to be done and how it was to be done. This process was intensified in the latter part of the course when students were left completely on their own. The lack of classic structure ("this is what you are supposed to learn, and this is what you have learned") continued to bother some students. For many it was difficult to see that some of their problems stemmed from a lack of confidence rather than from a lack of knowledge. I pointed out a number of times that creativity demanded a willingness to act in the face of uncertainty, and the ability, or disposition, to bring coherence out of what seemed to be chaos. This was neither persuasive nor comforting to those who felt that their handicap was lack of knowledge.

Another method I used to try to give structure to the course was to provide the class with unidentified excerpts from their papers. I organized the excerpts into different categories, and hoped my organization, together with my comments, would convey some ideas about how learning could be conceptualized. But I was not able to stimulate much discussion of the papers in class both because students considered their papers to be personal communications from them to me and because anything that revealed intensive preparation on the part of a student violated a student norm.

The grade for the course was based entirely on the papers submitted. Each paper was given a fixed number of points; students could gain additional points by using outside resources and could lose points by turning papers in late, misspelling words, or being generally sloppy. I wanted the grading system to be consonant with the element of choice existing throughout the course. When I announced the grading system, I told the students that much of it would be subjective, that I wanted to fool neither them nor myself. This being so, I encouraged them to come and talk with me about their ideas, and to discuss the results of the grades. Toward the end of the semester, we had numerous discussions about the fact that behavior in the class was entirely ungraded. Some felt that, had they known they were to be graded on what they said and what they did in class, much of their sense of freedom would have been destroyed. Others contended that not being graded removed some of the motivation for them. My argument was that I wanted them to be as free as possible and to be clear that what they did represented their own choice, not a choice reflecting what they thought I was encouraging.

From the standpoint of my objectives and my planning, the course was successful beyond my expectations. Students became aware of themselves in new ways; they gained a new perspective on their identity. A few examples from students' papers will indicate the kinds of data used to arrive at this conclusion.

> I want to learn how to see farther than the nose on my face, to look into and beyond the concepts, habits, and assumptions that will surround me all my life. I want to be able to look and really see, to listen and really hear, to sense and really feel. I would like to get my sense and my being to functioning together as an integrative unit.

> It was very encouraging to acquire some knowledge that I feel is a very real part of me, and not just stuck on the surface to be forgotten in the near future.

As students gained a different view of their own identity, they also gained a different view of others. And in the process, they found it difficult to categorize themselves or others in simple terms. One, for example, wrote of apparent contradictions he found in himself, a condition which Maslow (1962) describes in creative people.

> There is probably no way to say exactly how much influence ME-288 has had, since the time spent in class is almost insignificant when compared with the time spent outside of class. It is even more difficult to describe how my attitudes have changed. I have become more tolerant of other people's ideas, and at the same time I have become more ready to disagree with someone's views. I have started to listen more carefully, and to absorb information rather than accept statements at their face value. I have begun to try to combine seeing, hearing, and feeling with a scientific outlook. The idea is something like believing in a miracle . . .

Students learned to see themselves and others as part of their environment. In this process they also became aware of choices they had had but were not exercising.

> It was interesting to note the reactions of the group members during the games of the first few sessions. In particular, the exercise in which the subject closed his eyes and was thrown around the group, relying on his group members to keep him from falling was interesting. My own reaction was one of semi-trust. Instead of remaining as stiff as a board as some did, I tended to try to straighten myself up just in case one of my group members missed me. I remember that Clarence seemed to have even less trust of the group than I did. I am amazed at how this simple exercise so accurately predicted what would later happen in our group. Clarence was the last one to talk freely in the group and I was next to last.

> From the beginning of this course I have been waiting to be guided into learning. After attending school for fifteen and one-half years, my concept of learning has been of a conventional nature. I have always expected to have the teacher dictate the course requirements and in general run the whole show. Finally, I realized, with no small loss of face, that this

wasn't going to happen in this course. Why be spoon-fed all your life? Why not get off your can and do something on your own? Why didn't I realize this sooner? It is an accomplishment that I learned it at all.

I have been able to learn that creativity and group behavior are not things that simply exist but that there are definite techniques which can be applied which will enable a person to learn to improve his abilities in these areas. It is also somewhat of a comfort to know that there are people who spend a great deal of time studying this problem because it lets me know that it is a problem.

As a result of becoming more aware of the environment and of the climate within that environment, students became better able to articulate their growth goals. In the first paper on learning goals, many of their comments were quite global, and couched in generalities, such as "I want to learn how to communicate better." By the end of the course, papers were more apt to contain succinct statements or itemized lists of goals. Two examples will indicate the types of statements made:

Some of the more specific learning goals I have in the region of problem awareness include:
1. The realization that problem-solving does not always rely entirely on practicality and economics, but instead many times upon your own judgment.
2. The need to become aware of the environment of a problem, instead of concentrating only on narrowing the problem.
3. Overcome the fear of making a mistake or making a fool of myself.
4. Overcome my difficulty in rejecting a workable solution and instead search for a better idea. In other words, don't always grab the first workable solution that comes along and assume it's right.
5. Learn to relax and let the incubation take place.
. . . it is extremely difficult for a person to lead a group of his peers. I would like to know why this is so and correct it

. . . Another thing I would like to know is how to feel with people. When I watch television and see Negroes burning cities I just can't understand. With my values and past history I could no more burn down a building than I could fly. But they can, so they must think entirely differently from the way I do. For this reason I would like to be able to learn to put myself in the position of, for example, a Negro in Detroit and know what he thinks and what he feels and mostly what his goals and motives are.

The examples I have cited, and the papers I have been unable to include here, show that students approach learning differently. Those most interested in creativity seemed to be more aware of their learning in this area; those most interested in management spoke about management and group behavior. This is not to say that learning was that clear cut, but the difference is notable. I had hoped that this individualizing of possibilities would take place.

From the standpoint of involving all the students, ME-288 left a lot to be desired. The level of involvement was higher than in previous courses, but I still had much to learn about how and when to transfer the responsibility for involvement from myself to the students.

On the last night of the semester, I asked the students to respond to a final critique. Most of the questions deal with the value assigned to different parts of the course structure.

1. Please rank order the following in terms of your own learning (1 for most valuable):
    Your own analysis of your reactions—1.7
    Feedback from members of your own group—2.5
    The instructor—2.8
    Feedback from members of the class at large—3.5
    Outside reading—4.2

2. Below are listed the titles of the assigned papers. Please rank order these in terms of their value to you (1 for most valuable):
    My Learning Goals (First)—3.2
    On Becoming Me—3.5
    Where I Am—3.8
    My Learning Goals (Second)—3.9

Working with a Partner—4.4
The Climate in Class—4.5
Principles of Observation—4.6

3. Below are listed some of the class activities. Please place
   a 3 beside those that were most helpful to you, a 2 by
   those that were next, and a 1 beside those that were
   least helpful:
   Brainstorming—2.4
   Developing your own learning activities after attend-
     ance was not required—2.1
   Visit of Photographer—2.0
   Developing posters, poems, slogans, and limericks—2.0
   Discussing what engineers and engineering can do to
     contribute to the solution of the riot problem—2.0
   Total class in large circle—1.7
   House Building—1.7
   Drawing impressions of class—1.6
   Nonverbal exercises—1.4
   Telling about a peak experience—1.4
   Telling about something you were proud of—1.4

4. To what extent did the course meet your needs?

	2	5	8	11	2
Not At All	Some	Moderately	Quite A Lot		Completely

5. To what extent did you involve yourself in the course?

	2	9 1 3 2 1	11	2
Not At All	Some	Moderately	Quite A Lot	Completely

6. To what extent are you satisfied with my efforts to help
   you learn?

	2	5 1 1 2 2	10 2 1	6
Not At All	Some	Moderately	Quite A Lot	Completely

7. To what extent were you satisfied with the grading system?

1 1 2 1	3	6	1	6 1	10
Not At All	Some	Moderately	Quite A Lot		Completely

8. To what extent were you satisfied with the fairness of
   the grading?

	2		1 1	10	3	1	1	12
Not At All	Some	Moderately		Quite A Lot				Completely

If I had it to do over, I would mix papers and class activities
as I did in this course, but would do more to assist with structure in
the papers and would work more on the problem of transferring design and control of classroom activity to students. By their senior
year, the set toward learning is pretty deep in engineering students.
Although there may be an overt desire to participate more, there is
little experience to back up the desire. When engagement takes place,
the effect is startling. The content of the poems, verses, limericks, and
papers, as well as activity in class, indicated a vast amount of latent
talent and social consciousness among engineering students. One student expressed this consciousness in this way: "I still want to be an
engineer but I now realize that this is not nearly enough. I think that
one of the greatest problems that our society has today is that we
have too many excellent lawyers, doctors, and engineers, and not
nearly enough compassionate thinkers."

Samuel A. Culbert

Training Change Agents
for Business and
Public Administration

Teaching the behavioral sciences offers unique opportunities to have students confront personally the content assigned for study. Courses can be designed to connect the assumptions and issues in the substantive class material with the student's real life experiences. To accomplish this, an instructor must create a classroom process that focuses each student's energies on finding these personal connections. This process makes for what McLuhan would call *hot* learning experiences as new insights impact simultaneously on a student's emotions and thoughts and he finds multiple applications for a single bit of learning. The fusing of personal and substantive issues can intoxicate students—"turn them on," as they describe the experience themselves. To maximize this sort of connection, I designed (and taught at the George Washington University) a graduate course entitled Behavioral Factors in the Process of Change which dealt conceptually with interpersonal issues encountered in organizations undergoing change.

XI

George Washington University

In arousing students, I believe the teacher has a major responsibility to make learning real, that is, practical and not just inspirational. It is not enough, however well-intentioned, to make students feel excited, interested, inspired, or aroused. An instructor should enable students to carry away concepts and understanding that will be useful in their lives beyond the classroom. This is more likely to happen if the students can acquire the concepts in application, not to abstract descriptions of events, but to their own real, interpersonal experiences.

In seeking to motivate the learning of subject matter that students will feel affects their personal lives, I have experimented with a variety of teaching formats. A recent paper (Culbert and Culbert, 1968) describes briefly how teaching assumptions made in some of the T-group classes taught at the Univeresity of California at Los Angeles were used to formulate a teaching model that relied heavily on a specially designed procedure for assigning course grades. This UCLA model used a particular complex of grades, assigned jointly by the instructor and students in the class, to move a student into a set of personal and interpersonal dilemmas. These dilemmas, in turn, confronted each student with the substantive content of a graduate-level survey course in behavioral science. A more complex variation of this grading procedure was applied to the course Behavioral Factors in the Process of Change subsequently taught at George Washington University. This variation combined high initial structure and shared evaluative responsibilities, as provided by the grading procedure, with a consultant role assumed by the instructor.

Most of the twenty students in the class were enrolled either with the School of Business and Public Administration or with the School of Education. Most of them had already had some professional experience. I could build on their understanding of individuals and of groups to help them learn more about processes for changing organizations in planned and deliberate ways. Consequently, I designed the experiences in the course around the role of the organizational change-agent. Behavioral scientists are involved in change processes when they are members of a task group attempting to make change, consultants helping a task group function more effectively, and trainers working to increase the basic skills of a client group. The course was designed to mirror these functions of the behavioral scientists within the context of tasks that integrate experiential and substantive learning. Accordingly, each student participated in a task group working on a change project and in a consultant group advising a task group. The class instructor took roles of consultant and trainer. Each group was assigned a project; the projects entailed the integration of behavioral-science theories and research about change. Classroom time was available for accomplishing the assignments, but all the groups eventually held additional sessions. In addition to working on its own project, each group served as a consulting team to the other group working on its project. Each *student* consultant had an individual client. In addition, each student shared in a group-level consultation. Thus each student consultant had two assignments: the first to assist his individual client to maximize his personal and organizational learning from occurrences in class (that is, class process); the second to participate as a member of a consulting team helping another task group accomplish its task. To vary exposures among clients and consultants, no two students served as individual clients and consultants to each other. Client and consultant groups alternated evening and Saturday morning sessions, the group acting as consultants one week becoming the client group the next. The two groups planned and timed each session in collaboration. The instructor-trainer reserved the last half-hour of all sessions for training exercises and for lecturettes when they were appropriate.

Individual reports entitled *What I have personally learned about the processes of change from my classroom experiences* made up the final course assignment. These reports were to contain specific documentation about in-class behavior to substantiate each conceptual claim. Wherever possible, concepts mentioned were to be compared with the behavioral-science literature. The documentation was intended to provide training in a key function of behavioral-science consultants, that of documenting conclusions with data from which the conclusions were drawn. Such reporting allows a client to make his own validity check and to assign his own level of confidence to his conclusions.

The most formidable challenge to the instructor in designing experience-based learning is to understand both the content of the course and his own learning goals well enough to construct a design that produces the phenomena he wishes his students to study. In addition to knowing his subject matter well, an instructor must diagnose the needs of the particular students enrolled and make some firm decisions about what context would best suit the learning goals he has decided to emphasize. The diagnosis and design of context are nowhere more delicate than in the design of grading, both because grades and the manner of assigning them carry multiple messages to students and because students invest grades with strong emotion.

I might have given the students total control of their own evaluation. This would have freed me completely to take the role of the consulting behavioral scientist I was attempting to demonstrate through my own behavior in class. However, I think students probably would have spent too much time exploring their impulses to collude in grading, rather than to collaborate in learning, before encountering the content of the course. Initially, I did list myself as having responsibility for evaluating the quality of the team project and the effectiveness of the consulting efforts. However, I turned these evaluations over to the student teams toward the end of the semester when the students became so personally involved in the course process that I felt they would not only learn from this task but also from any impulses they might have to collude.

It is important to make clear what I am *not* asserting. I am not claiming that the grading scheme provided a direct motivation for the students to learn what I wanted them to learn. Rather, my hypothesis was that the grading scheme would involve students in learning activities paralleling the role of the organizational consultant. Perceiving the grade to depend on performing the task in the role of client and, in the role of consultant, on aiding the client group to function effectively, the students would be likely to enter those roles with a readiness to take them seriously as tasks to be accomplished. From their experiences in performing in these roles, in turn, would come connections to the substantive learning of the course.

While some students claim that my classroom structure, emphasizing grades, diabolically hooks them on their own craziness about university grading, I find that using grades within my particular model maximizes learning potential. This use of grades does produce an initial connection to each student's involvement, but it has primary utility as a *means* for posing specific personal and interpersonal dilemmas, dilemmas that parallel the substantive learning of the course. The reward-coercion power of grades is quickly relegated to a secondary, if seldom disregarded, role. The presence of this residual concern is sufficient to motivate the student initially to confront the learning dilemmas of the course but insufficient to command his deep involvement. As the students perform the roles of client and consultant, learning to function effectively in these roles and learning to understand their functioning conceptually become far more salient than the rewards and coercions of their grades. It is these experiences in roles that ultimately deepen the students' involvement.

One-sixth of the course grade was assigned to each student on the basis of his *group's project;* each group member received the same grade as the instructor's total evaluation of his group's project. This grade was used to encourage interdependence among the members of each client group. I intended it as one motivation, among others, for individual members to diagnose their team's needs and contribute to their group what they thought might be needed for group effectiveness, perhaps at a cost to their own personal goals. Thus a student might find himself putting aside his need for personal recognition in order not to interfere with the group's progress in its task.

One-sixth of the course grade was assigned for *individual contributions to the group's project;* each group member was differentially evaluated by his own team, self included, within the constraints of a 3.33 grade-point budget. This grade was intended to force the two groups to evaluate their members differentially. It provided a built-in reason for each group to examine its own power structure, the kinds of behavior that were rewarded or censured, and the motives behind these evaluations. Each member had a formal means of exerting influence, although the total group had to make decisions about what process it would invent to manage this influence, since influence that goes unmanaged in task groups and organizations has a way of interrupting planned change. This grade was also to demonstrate the importance of giving and receiving feedback periodically about one's performance in the group. This provides task group members with an opportunity to learn from experience. The task group's objectives provide an action context for evaluating, and possibly making use of, interpersonal and intrapersonal feedback. A third use of this grade was to focus the students' attention upon the importance of finding out the norms against which their behavior is understood within a new social system, that of their particular work group.

One-sixth of the grade was assigned for *individual consulting contributions* to a client; each consultant was individually evaluated by his client group from a grade-point budget determined by the clients' evaluation of the consultation they received from the consulting team. The contingency between the consultants' contribution, as a group, and the grade-point budget, from which the efforts of individual consultants could be rewarded, was intended to provide a strong motive for collaboration by consulting team members. I hoped that each student, in his role of consultant, would experience a pressure to concern himself with the impact that his consultation was having on his client. This grade provided a structured reason for each consultant to compare continually the effect of his consultation with his own diagnosis of what action he thought his client needed to take and with his client's perception of what he (the client) thought he needed to do. This grade also directed the student's attention to the quality of the relationship the student, as consultant, was able to form with his client, since the client was charged, eventually, with presenting his contributions to his work group when it undertook to grade the consultants individually, using a limited grade-point budget. The client was challenged, to conceptualize his learning, by a consultant who experienced structured pressure to contribute to his client's learning. I planned that the interaction between consultants and clients would keep the attention of clients focused on two things: the needs of their task group, and the relevance of the client's own actions to the changes going on in the group. During the evaluation period, the clients were challenged to conceptualize the contributions made by their consultants and, thus, to become very involved in another system (their consultant) which had undergone change.

One-sixth of the course grade was assigned for *individual contributions to one's own consulting team;* each consultant was differentially evaluated by his own team, self included, with the grades contingent upon the clients' evaluation of the team level consultation. This grading process involved the students in their second evaluation of self and teammate. It asked team members to differentiate their own and others' effectiveness. Playing a large part in determining this portion of the grade was the judgment made by other members of the consulting team of each student's performance in collaborative participation. (These dual criteria correspond to the ways in which many professional consultant teams are evaluated.) Once again, the client's group-level evaluation determined the grade points available for the evaluations and the students were asked once again to make self-assessments with real and hard consequences.

Two-sixths of the course grade were assigned to each student, by the instructor, on the basis of *individual papers* relating personal experiences in the class to the substantive learning of the course. This assignment was to focus the attention of the students on the process of classroom events and on their personal reactions to this process. Understanding process is the key behavioral-science strategy for managing and interpreting planned organizational change.

The effectiveness of this grading procedure ultimately rests on students' providing one another with the raw behavioral data (perceptions, thoughts, personal theories, assumptions, experiences, and feelings) on which evaluations are made. This exchange of data establishes the reality context in which each student deepens and expands his personal connections with the course content. The richness of this teaching method, then, is directly related to the richness of the behavioral data produced and the opportunities the students have for exchanging these data. The motivational theory on which this grading procedure rests demands that communication among students be frequent and serious. But ample communication among students was not only necessary for the postulated motivations to occur; it was also necessary if the students were to feel capable of carrying out their grading duties at all. The alternate, intimate functioning as client and consultant, and the long sessions spent in group-building at the beginning of the course, were designed to produce this necessary depth of communication.

PROCESS OBJECTIVES

In designing the classroom format, I made a number of assumptions that contributed to the depth of student communication and involvement. These assumptions, implicit in the design, were critically important in creating the climate for learning that my class enjoyed. Since I thought of these assumptions as goals for classroom process, I call them process objectives. I set out to:

1. Make the content of the classroom process the same as the substantive content of the course. The connection between substantive content and experience is a very personal one. Although explicit from the outset, it takes a while for students to make this connection personal (emotional), and, frequently, the connecting events are different for individual students.

2. Make each student's experience, whatever it might be, a valid opportunity for learning. The challenge to the instructor is to create a classroom climate receptive to individual students working on whatever aspect of their experience seems most relevant to the explicit goals established for the learning experience. This means that, while the learning goals of the course content are specified, the paths to these goals must be individually designed.

3. Connect students with the values of applied behavioral science (Tannenbaum and Davis, 1967) and provide them valid opportunities to evaluate for themselves the applicability of these values. Applied behavioral science is a discipline heavily laden with values—those of humanistic psychology. To provide students with these values, without giving them real opportunities to test their applicability results, in my experience, in the values being held only loosely by students, who need very concrete and personal experiences to elevate themselves from descriptions of what should happen to accounts of what has happened and what can happen.

4. Produce situations where students learn and build on the experiences of others as well as of themselves. Observation of others is potentially a powerful medium for increasing students' understanding of the content under study. This potential is most powerfully activated when observation takes place with understanding of the personal experience accompanying another's involvement. The classroom offers this possibility best when students have some continuity of observation of one another and when there are opportunities to quiz others about the nature of their experience.

5. Get students actively involved in one another's learning. Students learn more deeply when involved with the blocks to learning erected by others. One is often too personally involved to conceptualize immediate experiences for oneself, but there is an additional capacity to do this when helping another to conceptualize his experiences. The content learned is more visible, as are the personal obstacles that blur the learning.

6. Help each student to become the architect of his own development. The challenge to the instructor is not only to provide freedom to students in the directions they will go, but also assistance in helping students handle the responsibility of this freedom. Students require additional support and confrontation to diagnose accurately their personal situations before designing the action steps that can best respond to their developmental needs.

7. Help students identify with the feedback part of the evaluation. The often-overlooked key to aroused learning is that students learn best when they are experiencing considerable personal self-esteem and acceptance. High self-esteem implies a valuing of all one's experiences with a focus on the search for the meaning in an event rather than on an evaluation of whether or not there was meaning.

8. Create a climate in which students are open to learning from personal and conceptual differences. Too often students form associations based on similarities, and view differences as threats to group cohesion. Students' learning is significantly heightened when differences are posed so that the assumptions underlying a different point of view become understood, and tensions created by different ways of viewing the same phenomena are not prematurely dissipated.

9. Find ways of helping students see the natural everyday applications for their classroom learning. In many respects, this objective is identical with that of making the classroom process the same as the

substantive content of the course. However, some differences are present in even the most straightforward extrapolations of classroom learning. Conceptualization is always a necessary bridge from the present to other situations, whether family, social, or work. Hence, it is essential for students to increase both their ability and propensity to conceptualize classroom experiences in terms which apply to outside applications.

I had those process objectives in mind when I formulated the design for this course. My overall intent was to provide students an initial structure, broad in spectrum, of course goals, content, and rules. I believed this structure would give students the greatest freedom to become deeply involved with the content of the course as well as with one another. (This is in contrast to the typical, open-ended, T group format where the lack of concrete goals and content necessarily entails a search for structure or focus which, in some ways, constricts freedom.) In the design of this class, interpersonal relationships had primary importance in being vehicles for the individual's learning of course content. This type of structure can ignite a number of activities.

CLASS ACTIVITIES

I came to the initial class meeting with three main goals. First, I wanted more specific information about the students. I needed this to double-check the appropriateness of the course design and the professional context that I had planned for the course. Second, I needed to get the students' approval of my plan to lengthen the times of class meetings from two to three hours and to add week end meeting time. In exchange for the additional class time, I mentioned that required extra reading would be substantially reduced in the classroom model I was proposing. Third, I wanted to place the experience-based nature of the course in a context where the students could relate it to the substantive material the course was designed to cover, and I wanted them to be able to feel confident in deviating from the more typical format for university teaching.

Term papers, collected at the end of the course, disclosed that the most important part of the first classroom session was the confidence and excitement I conveyed when telling the students about the course format. Many students wrote about the insecurity they felt in departing from more conventional classroom format, although many also mentioned that they had been in classes where similar, but more time-bounded, unstructured experiences had taken place. I distributed copies of a syllabus describing the course design, grading, projects, and time schedule and then spent about an hour answering specific questions. Emotion in the class was intense and even somber as I began the second hour of this meeting, outlining the values implied in the technology by which applied behavioral scientists approach organizational change. I drew heavily in my discussion on a paper by Tannenbaum and Davis (1967) and on a discussion in the assigned course text by Bennis (1966). The students were active in this discussion and I could see the beginnings of enthusiasm as they began to talk about their personal connections to the course content and anticipate the classroom sessions to follow.

I assumed the design responsibility for the team-building on a Friday night and Saturday morning. I began by presenting a brief orientation, outlining for the students their deceptively simple task. They had merely to divide themselves into two groups. I told them that, in my role as consultant, I would be glad to make additional comments as we went along and that I thought the course syllabus gave them sufficient information to begin. A salient, but undisclosed, secondary goal of mine was to familiarize students with behavioral process, which is the core of the behavioral-science technology of change.

The initial group discussion stressed commonalities. Students made comments that seemed to imply that any two groupings of ten would be as effective as any other. With time, some of the students searched for criteria, with one student finally saying, "Here we are, adults, and we can't even choose teams as well as when I was a kid playing baseball." Another student responded, "Yeah, but then you probably knew who were the best players and weren't so afraid of hurting someone's feelings." In response to this interchange, another student, who had earlier professed to be highly skilled in the technology of change said, "I'm starting a group," and, pointing to some other students who had been urging a quick decision, went on, ". . . and I want you, you, and you to be in it. And anyone else up to ten who wants to join us." A group quickly formed and began to have a meeting in the middle of the classroom. They quickly elected the convener to be a parliamentarian-type leader, while the others first watched and then formed a second group. But, instead of getting on with the task, the groups continued discussing such membership criteria as personal preferences and personality factors. Some students saw their memberships as temporary from the beginning and walked back and forth between the two groups trying to make up their minds.

When the students gathered the next morning, the two groups simultaneously disbanded and the students again formed one large group. After some rather diffuse discussion, which left a number of students with expressions of bewilderment, I decided to intervene to provide them with more understanding of the process going on. I began by noting that, while we were back in the large group from which we had started, I did not think that the group was back where it had started. I mentioned that the preceding events had raised questions about the importance that students were placing on personal information as well as on formal behavioral-science skills, and that the spontaneous presence of the large group made it appear to me that many of the students wanted more information about others before making committed decisions about team composition. The students spent the morning interacting in the large group, with almost no assistance from me, apparently gathering information about one another. After lunch, cliques of twos, threes, and fours, developed during lunch, banded together to form two groups. Pairs of clients and consultants were made by individuals, within their own groups of ten, negotiating for specific pairings with the persons in the other group with whom they most desired to work. Each of the two groups appointed representatives to clear up any cross-group conflicts over two students mutually choosing the other as a consultant. Then the groups asked for their task assignments.

I presented the groups two tasks and asked each group to choose one. I had intentionally designed each task to be so broad that it could quickly be accomplished by the groups' scanning the literature and agreeing upon a single point of view. The literature of behavioral science contains many explicit commentaries which fulfilled these assignments. The task chosen by Group B was to "develop a model for implementing planned organizational change"; the task chosen by Group A was to "develop a set of criteria for evaluating planned organizational change." These assignments, allowing a great deal of interdependence between the two task groups, provided an added impetus for the groups, when consulting, to become involved also in the content on which their client was working. At the end of the afternoon session, I discussed briefly some of the current behavioral-science literature that was related to the classroom dynamics we had experienced. I continued this practice at later sessions and built up in this manner, as the weeks went by, an optional reading list.

Both groups spent most of their early sessions as clients attending to the intragroup organizational issues of distributing responsibilities for their task and consulting projects and clearing up difficulties encountered in using their new behavioral-science vocabulary. The two task groups developed very different leadership climates. Group *A* established a highly democratic group climate, and spent considerable time attempting to get consensual agreement on all decisions without regard to the magnitude of a decision's consequences. Group *B* was initially organized along moderately autocratic lines, electing for its leader the student who formed the first group on Friday night of the team-building weekend. Tempered by that earlier experience, he reluctantly accepted the role of leader. (His group developed rapidly until the consultant team initiated a leadership crisis which I will report shortly.) Both groups did, however, make outside assignments to their members, thus starting the research process for their tasks almost immediately. Semantic problems with the new vocabulary yielded some very impressive learning confrontations. Using the somewhat technical terms contained in behavioral-science literature, the students soon discovered that they were having enormous difficulties communicating with one another. Each group spent considerable time agreeing on personal definitions for the same primary terms they had used in three to six previous courses in behavioral science, recognizing explicitly that they were no longer fully confident of their previous learning.

During an early brief lecture, I discussed the options students had in taking the role of consultant. I did not want to give too much direction. I did want each student to have a chance to take whatever role naturally evolved as he attempted to perform the consultant functions. I did, however, suggest some preliminary target-setting interviews with clients, which consultants might use as a partial guide in their initial observations. The consultant groups themselves developed a stop action procedure that enabled them to meet periodically. After a caucus, they would either intervene in the entire task group or ask for time to meet with their individual clients. Over the course, a coffee break routinely took place at 9:30, during which client-consultant pairs usually took the opportunity to compare notes. The differences in task group leadership styles had an early effect on the interventions by consultants, who frequently intervened to point up, for example, how the Group *A* democracy was wasting precious time and how the Group *B* autocracy was suppressing minority points of view. The eventual effects of the conflicts which arose over these group-level stylistic differences were to challenge each consultant group to figure out how to make the other team's decision-making process work more effectively, and to confront each group with their first inclinations to change others to be more like themselves.

By the time Group *B* had had its second task-group meeting, the pump for a crisis had been primed. During an intense meeting, the Gorup *A* consultants decided to inform each of their individual clients, during the coffee break, about the particular way the Group *B* leader had been suppressing their contributions and running the group to get most recognition for those viewpoints and theories that most corresponded to his own way of seeing things. Unbeknownst to the consultants, one of the Group *B* members had, by himself, designed a twenty-five-page, fully documented, intervention model, which he planned to distribute during the next group session. He intended to try to influence his group to accept his model as their final team project. The dynamics in this session were as dramatic as any I have ever seen. Most of the members entered this meeting determined to make their own ideas more prominent and with the secondary notion of wresting the control of activities from their present leader. While these themes were being played out, the member who had designed the completed model naively distributed it and asked for a group decision. Many of the group members behaved as if they had not received the paper. The leader thumbed through it cursorily and assigned it as take-home reading to be discussed at some future class meeting; some members wanted to discuss whether they should consider the content of the paper before everybody had had a chance to make his contribution.

By the end of this meeting several key events had taken place. The leader had resigned with a passionate speech stating that he believed the group would turn out a better product if he were not a leader. The member who had distributed the model had made a very emotional statement when he saw the resistance with which his effort met. An excerpt from the tape of the meeting gives the reader the flavor of what took place:

I've worked with groups for twenty years and never had this feeling before. I've learned more about myself in the last two weeks than I have in years. The values Sam mentioned a couple of weeks ago were the ones I've regarded for my whole life. Then the feedback I received showed me I was controlling and distrustful. I realized that all the other times in groups I've had a role with built-in power. This is the first time in my life that I've realized that while I have all these values, I never really lived up to them before. You know I've never in my life been this mad at anyone before.

Perhaps most exciting of all was the way the entire class was "turned on" by their recognition that they had experienced one of the most basic of all phenomena found in the literature of the behavioral sciences; namely, rate-busting. (Rate-busting occurs when one worker increases his output beyond the rate of that production management expects and above the rate at which other workers perform. Typically this overproduction meets with censure from other workers who fear that management will expect them to increase their production similarly.)

The task groups made fairly rapid headway on their assignments despite the fact that considerable amounts of class time were spent in hammering away at group process. Individual students divided up their research of the literature and copied handouts for other students. Frequently, students made brief presentations to go with their summaries. This system served a dual purpose for many of the students who were taking comprehensive exams at the end of the semester. Most important, the students consistently used their own experiences in class as examples through which to evaluate theories they were reading about. As the class progressed, the emotional involvement of the students deepened. I began to overhear conversations indicating that, out of class, substantial time was being spent by groups of two's and three's discussing class issues. Students were borrowing the tapes I was making of the class meetings, and spending time listening to them. However, it was not until I read the term papers that I became fully aware of how much outside time was spent. Students mentioned daily lunches together, long late-evening calls, and a two-hour Saturday seminar that extended through the entire week end. In her term paper, one student mentioned a somewhat obvious liability that attended all this excitement:

> The long hours came as a big surprise to my husband and me. Had we known about it ahead of time, he probably would have talked me out of taking the course and that would have been a great loss to me! My husband felt so neglected and bitter toward the end that it was quite a relief for me when the course ended. He also resented my involvement on such a personal level with people in a situation in which he was not included. For this reason we have decided that should I ever get involved in something similar it would be best if I were to do it away from home.

The client-consultant pairs took root and seemed to add meaningful dimensions to the students' learning. One of the situations in which initial resistance and boredom were overcome is recounted in this narrative:

> Working with Charlie as a client was a frustrating and fabulous experience. He was so task oriented that I thought we would never talk about anything else. I called him, chased him, haunted him, but all he wanted to talk about was his part of his team's model. I tried different approaches: I collected verbal feedback about him from people in the class and gave it to him. I gave him all my notes pertaining to his group with all my thoughts, questions, and ideas, and when I asked him what he thought of them (on April 4), his reply was that my notes were well done. I could have kicked him. I kept telling him that now it was his turn to give me some feedback, but he acted as if he didn't know what I was talking about. Then I told him some of my problems. He sincerely tried to help me but he still kept silent about himself. As objectives for our meeting on April 4 I wrote the following in my notebook (which I gave to Charlie): "Charlie is a dilemma. Has closed the door on me. No signs of feedback or collaboration. Either I (a) stop trying in which case I would let him down, or (b) keep chasing and annoying him." That was the night

he presented his paper. I was kind of annoyed because I had asked him earlier in the week if he had any plans for this evening and he told me he didn't. If he didn't at that time I felt he could have let me know when he did. Anyway in my notes which went to Charlie I wrote: "I feel that our relationship is even worse than before we started. Have no inkling of what Charlie will do next. Why doesn't he trust me? Resolution: one more try, and if that doesn't work, I'm going to ask Sam for advice."

Well, I did ask you for advice. At the time I was kind of reluctant because in a way I felt that I was betraying Charlie by tattling on him. On the other hand, I felt that it was in Charlie's best interest, and besides I had let him know that I might do this. I can't tell you how glad I am that I did confide in you. Had you not known the problems I was having you might not have given me feedback on April 29th, and I might not have ever found out that Charlie had indeed learned an awful lot from the course. (You told me that Charlie was magnificent this morning, when we had separate sessions, and that he has used this course.) Edie, who is in Charlie's task group, reconstructed the incident for me, and I called Charlie to hear what he had to say about it. The change in Charlie overwhelmed me. We talked for over an hour and he told me how he was afraid to open up, to expose his feelings, to entangle with personalities. At the time he had written a good part of his paper. He read what he had and we discussed it. He even asked me if I felt that his working with a woman made it difficult for him! For the first time we had really talked to each other. On April 25 I gave him my entire notebook. (I told him that I had promised myself that if he really changed I would do this.)

After vigorous struggles around the meaning and accuracy of established theories, both task groups decided to go beyond the literature to create their own solutions to the assignments. Both groups relied heavily on their own experiences as microcosms of organizations. They went through phases of experiencing or data generation, processing their data by seeking the reasons for events happening as they did, seeing what generalizations they could formulate from their experiences, and then testing established theories against their experience-based model or criteria. The students' reactions to this theory-building were often electric. This is illustrated in the following transcription of a conversation that took place just after Group *A* had completed its project and one of the members, Bob, had mentioned that he had been functioning for days with only four hours' sleep each night.

Bob: I don't really feel whipped; I'm turned on, caught up, uh, intrigued with the class, the group, the process. It's here, it's in the group, caused by the group, uh, well, it just occurred to me, a term that Ken used earlier, this is almost a religion. There is a possibility to this essence, the creative essence of a group that I think can turn me on. It can turn me off too when it's missing—just horribly turn me off.

Tim: Then would you want to use creativity as another criterion in our model, or maybe spiritual?

Len: You're right, it's really visceral. It gets me in here, from within, a real, gut feeling.

Bob: At the beginning of the class, the sort of thing we talked about excited me and scared me because Sam seemed to be listing up an impossible amount of things we could accomplish. I said, "Shit! That's great!" And then we got into what was happening and I thought, "By God, we're not going any place." That turned me off. And as has been pointed out to me, I was hostile, but then these things began to work through and I see us; by God, we're making some good progress on this stuff! And then I started getting these spiritual reactions, gut reactions, whatever it is, but you know, an excitement over what we can do. That we can interact, we can put together.

Ken: You know there's not a much better word than "exciting" to describe what we're feeling. Because it's different, because it's challenging. Hell, if we're being excited, why make it "visceral?" Put down "exciting" as a criterion.

Group *B* had its project in good shape but was having difficulty finishing the loose ends until one of its members pointed out,

"The reason we're having difficulty gaining closure is that we don't want the group to end."

Students made numerous reports of what appeared to be their deep and creative connections to the behavioral-science literature on change. Below is an excerpt from a term paper in which a student links his classroom experiences to the theories under study in what seems to me to be a very sophisticated way.

> It seems to me that I can now directly relate Bennis' idea that "change is more lasting, if not more traumatic, in decentralized organizational settings." I think this is because of the total personal involvement present in the decentralized organization as opposed to the partial involvement I find in the autocratic centralized organization. More simply stated, my other university classes were structured to have group organization arbitrarily selected by the instructor. And surely, as if to verify the entire concept, I never met with the members of my group except during the first night. Our objectives were individual and the oral presentation we made was less than graduate level. The embracing of the "usual" way helped effect my learning in the "usual" way—I'll do well to remember any of what I learned in time for final exam. In contrast, my learning experience in the decentralized organization of this course is very real, live, and completely fresh in my mind. It was challenging and meaningful to the extent that I vividly remember most of the minute details of every process I had to experience to effect change.

My own role as training consultant dwindled with time. Over the semester I used my thirty minutes, at the end of meetings, in a variety of ways. When I thought something was blocking a group's progress, I would invite that group to spend ten minutes discussing a question or issue that I would pose for them. Typically, these questions were aimed at uncovering the thoughts, feelings, or concepts that I thought would produce the data necessary for the group to overcome their block. Initially, the students needed substantial help in taking the consultant role. The absence one night of a member of the consultant group allowed me the opportunity to take the consulting role for an evening and then discuss my performance with the class. However, for the most part I stayed in the background, watching the drama of the classroom, and spending time in free-wheeling discussions with students on what they were doing both in class and out. The structure of the class itself seemed to be doing the hard jobs of teaching and confronting; this took the pressure off me and allowed me to be open and receptive to the students.

The team projects ultimately reflected the students' capacities to collaborate and invent. Toward the end of the semester, the students decided to experiment with pooling their resources. They rejected a number of suggestions about ways of joining together on a single project that would cover both assignments. They did, however, invent a procedure demanding considerable energy during the last work sessions. Representatives of the two groups formulated a design whereby the groups spend these sessions working simultaneously on their own projects while two members of each group were on loan to the other group. These members were replaced every thirty minutes and each group analyzed the other group's progress after five rotations, when all their members had watched and had an opportunity to contribute to the other group. After sharing these thoughts with the other group, the students agreed that the rotation process had infused a new technique into the course.

Upon completion of the substance of the projects, the students spent time in individual groups discussing the medium in which they might make their presentations. Both groups strayed from the ordinary. Group B decided on a video tape of their criteria in action, with a diagram and guide of what the viewer should be observing. Group A demonstrated their model by using a panel to present its elements and periodically asking members of the observing group to apply these elements briefly to concrete examples.

The grading, at the end of the course, worked out almost exactly as I had hoped it would. The students were very serious about this task and struggled for hours with their decisions and in presenting their reasons. Each group agreed to make decisions about the other group independently, and to provide opportunities in class for exchanging viewpoints with the students being evaluated. This produced an equitable evaluation process yielding a number of fruitful confrontations. Before reaching their final evaluations, the students spent some time considering some personal needs for A grades. In all but one instance, they decided that the accuracy of the grade earned overruled other needs. The needs put forward for *A* grades, by the way, contained some interesting commentaries on the overall system of university grading. One student claimed he needed all *A*s this semester in order to be allowed to take his doctoral comprehensive examinations. Two others stated that they had barely maintained the graduate school requirement for a *B* average and were facing possible dismissal as the graduate school's standards had been revised upward during that semester. A fourth student claimed that she would not be able to pursue her studies beyond the Master's level without an *A* grade in the course; on this basis, she was awarded one of her own team's three *A*s for the group project.

By and large, I evaluated the individual reports highly. Of particular value to me was the way in which students used their reports as opportunities to explore analytically issues having personal relevance. I had specified only broadly the focus of these reports and had not explicitly spelled out the possibilities for the themes many of the students developed. These themes included (1) one student's struggles and conflicts in being viewed first as a woman and second as a professional; (2) another student's analysis of how his anger and aggression influenced the structure of his group's report; (3) a philosophical paper contrasting the way in which Kierkegaard might have performed had he taken this class, with the student's assessment of his own behavior in class; (4) a student's discussion of the way in which the class process provided him freedom from his previously high need for structure and from personal discomfort in enduring ambiguous situations.

One report came as an unpleasant surprise to me. This was from the student previously described as autocratic leader who had been exposed by the consultant group. He had missed the Saturday evaluation sessions at the end of the course because he needed to study for his final comprehensive exams to be given the following week. He had, however, made exacting arrangements with the other students and was consulted by phone on several occasions during evaluations. He had arranged with me to turn his own report in after his heavy exam schedule. The central theme of his report concerned authority relationships and contained a number of severe data distortions of such relationships as he viewed them in the classroom. Apparently, for this student, the confrontation was too strong to be met without self-protection.

The students in this course were given the freedom to choose their own moments and their own ways to connect the concepts of behavioral science with their tasks in the course and with their own inner thinking. This is in contrast to the usual pedagogy in which learning is to be exhibited precisely at testing time and not necessarily either before or afterward. However, it is important that the freedom that I provided for the students was not produced merely by removing restrictions from a traditional course. Therefore, I designed a different structure, one which would provide some way of supporting the tentative and uncertain steps the students would have to take in this strange new setting. I believe that the primary supports for the new freedom were both structural and technological. Structurally, the design for the course produced phenomena that partook of the content being studied, and, therefore, I was free to insert technological aids into the proceedings as they were needed.

Both the syllabus and the task-group assignments were phrased in terms that told students what needed to be done, but not how it was to be done. (The syllabus presented the rules for grading and advised students of the boundaries for procedures. The task group assignments communicated the specific requirements for conceptual output.) This gave students the freedom to discover and use whatever individual paths seemed to make the most sense as they progressed toward their objectives. Similarly, learning objectives were worked out individually within the boundaries of the task-group assignments. The common assignments to all members of the class insured that individual objectives would be similar enough to present a continuing, high potential for students to see the relevance of one student's learning to another's. The design of boundaries and conceptual requirements allowed me, as instructor, to make some key technological inputs. Given these inputs, I was able to use my own classroom participation to demonstrate my commitment to help students learn from the individual paths they chose to travel. I think this placed me in an optimal position to accelerate the rate and depth of learning. Moreover, I strongly believe that the study of applied behavioral science can best proceed by starting at points of furthest understanding and pushing forward to see what else can be discovered by experiencing, through real actions, what is already known. When my students and I felt ourselves at the very edges of the conceptualizations our own actions were exemplifying, and understood that new discoveries were just beyond our grasps, we began to stretch ourselves beyond our previous limits. This is what made our heightened ("turned on," if you will) experiences real.

John A. Seiler

Training Managers
in the Laboratory

Schools that train students for the skillful performance of a role—be it teacher, artisan, doctor, or diplomat—function most fully when they distill, in their classrooms, the essential qualities of life related to the role their students seek to play. The responsibility of teachers, once they have achieved such a distillation, is to train students to learn from the experience of role performance and to learn more effectively and more rapidly than would be possible during a similar period on the job. Until a role has become professionalized, that is, until preparation for it has become part of a ritual and it thus comes to enjoy a privileged monopoly, as with medicine and law, role trainers cannot help but be aware that they compete constantly with apprenticeship for the favor of their potential students. Formal schooling offers the inherent advantages of professional, full-time instruction and the opportunity to stop and study action at will. Apprenticeship is blessed by real action, by practitioners of experience, and by renunciation

XII

Harvard
University

while learning. To compete successfully, particularly against the short-run attractions of apprentice training, the formal instructor must gain first-hand familiarity with the practice of the role for which he offers preparation, and extrapolate changes in the practice of that role over the foreseeable future; conceptualize the basic characteristics of the environment in which the role is practiced and translate or synthesize those characteristics in a school setting; become expert in devising strategy and tactics for helping students become aware of what it is in themselves and in their synthetic environment that enables them to achieve the goals associated with the role they are learning.

With this somewhat rudimentary concept of what is involved in education for practice, the author and a number of his associates on the faculty of the Harvard Business School have been developing a course called the Laboratory in Organizational Behavior.

After World War II, the Harvard Business School incorpo-

rated in its revised curriculum a course, called Administrative Practices, to instruct students in how to get things done through people.
This course was the seed of what is now called Organizational Behavior, one of the two basic areas of instruction and research in management from which the other, older, and more specifically business
courses derive their basic tools. (The other basic area deals with mathematics, decision theory, managerial economics, and other forms of
symbolic logic.) The history of the Organizational Behavior area is
characterized by a contest between knowledge and skill. At one extreme has been the application of concepts, theories, and research results; at the other, the confrontation of issues arising in classroom relationships between students and instructors. Mediating between the
forces in this contest has been the practice of discussing cases which
pose real-life problems. Sometimes knowledge has been ascendant,
sometimes skill. In neither case have instructors been satisfied that
budding managers have been educated as well as they should have
been. In the early 1960's, knowledge was in control.[1] Course instructors were deriving confidence from seeing how much more adept their
students were at technical analysis than they had previously been. At
the same time, these instructors were quietly concerned that this increase in technical skill was not matched by the sensitivity and practical effectiveness that some former students had displayed. Some instructors, trying to rejuvenate old, multilevel, here-and-now discussions in their classrooms, were rediscovering how monumental are the
difficulties of being didactician, case discussion leader, participant,
and observer, all at the same time.

Spurred by a school-wide curriculum revision in 1962, an attempt was made to escape the pendulum swings between knowledge
and skill by designing a sequence of three courses each with its own
substantive and pedagogical focus. The first was a case-practice course
devoted to analysis and employing an integrated conceptual scheme
(Seiler, 1967a). The second was a course in organization design that
tried to find a middle ground between knowledge and practice. The
third was the subject of this paper, a third-term course that sought to
put students into a life-experience to which they could profitably bring
all they had learned about organized human behavior—to give them
a place to test out hypotheses, humanize concepts, begin to learn new

[1] See Lawrence and Seiler (1965) for course content typical of this
period.

responses, and otherwise internalize learning. Although the temptation is great to dwell on the agonies and exultations of the first few rounds of this third course and to recount in detail our attempts to adapt 100-to-1 student-teacher ratios to a personally confronting set of class activities, wisdom demands that we review only briefly our first, necessarily halting steps and quickly pass on to the latest editions of the laboratory course where seeds of transferable pedagogy most likely lie. The first three years of the course's development were largely devoted to looking for a meaningful task. We began with the basic idea, derived primarily from our experience with sensitivity training, that what our students most needed, now that they were chock full of knowledge and adept at prescription, was to become immersed in an interpersonal experience of their very own. They needed to reconceive their experience and relate it to the kind of organizations they would be members of in the not-too-distant future. That remains our basic idea, but the settings and tasks in which that process has since taken place have changed dramatically.

In the first year, we tackled the problem by assuming that our students, who virtually live, eat, and sleep together in conglomerates one hundred strong, had developed a sufficiently complex society after six months together that we could use their own formal and informal organizations as the focus for analysis, testing, reorganization, and drawing parallels. We divided the classes into three groups of thirty-three men each and asked them, on the basis of their past experience, to make sense of their own classroom behavior and to do something about it. It seems obvious now that so sharply withdrawing the usual props to social intercourse was too traumatic for such large groups who had had so little tutoring in self-analysis. Over the next two years, we experimented on two dimensions. First, we supplied some structure for the behavior that was to be analyzed. This structure first took the form of our organizing groups to do research on self-chosen aspects of their current social and work organizations—that is, research on the *section,* as the one hundred-man group is called. As they proceeded in this research, we periodically halted formal activity to pursue questions about the personal and organizational problems students were encountering. In other words, we tried to focus our sensitivity training on the full social development of the section and, simultaneously but more microscopically, on the specific behaviors of students engaged in pursuing this section's goals. The next year, responding to students' feelings of frustration in trying to create any meaningful change in the behavior of their sections, we shifted the focus of research to smaller organizations created by students within the course and assigned research topics such as intergroup stereotypy, problems of interpersonal communication, competition between peers, and distortion of communication up-and-down hierarchies. As our students' aspirations became more realistic, however, the confusion about the difference between task and process came more clearly into focus. This confusion should have come as no surprise, since we set our students the task of studying the processes of their own research organizations, then halted them in midstep to do here-and-now analysis of what was going on in the process of doing research. It seemed clear, by this time, that we had far underestimated the importance of setting our students organizational tasks that had nothing whatever to do with the study of social processes. It took us three years to overcome our enthusiastic bias toward doubling up the force of the course by having students study themselves as a long-term organization and simultaneously having them study themselves studying. (It is hard enough to describe what we wanted them to do, to say nothing of doing it.) Quite obviously, the instructors should have studied themselves more than they did when they were designing their self-study course.

The second dimension we worked on during the second and third versions of the course was the formal orientation and training of students in self-analysis. We had assumed initially, as we each had done in our own T group experiences, that our students would develop skill at self-analysis simply by being exposed to the material to be analyzed and by being required to make sense of it. But the mass-production aspects of our ninety hours of student time over a period of three months demonstrated that we needed to provide some ideas of observation and relatively simple practice in it, interpersonal feedback, and analysis before we cast our students into a full fledged organizational experience. During this same period of course-development, sensitivity training, as an educational movement, has been tending toward beginning with more structure than it did some years ago.

LABORATORY IN OGRANIZATIONAL BEHAVIOR

The essential goal of our laboratory course is to provide conditions sufficiently similar to those the student will find as a working manager so that he can put to work the ideas he has learned in his previous courses dealing with human behavior in organizations. Since the student is expected to derive from his contact with these ideas his own, unique style of making sense of organized human behavior, the laboratory functions most effectively by providing the full range of organizational behavior against which the student may test and re-define what he believes to be the most workable set of ideas for him.

The simplest and, perhaps, most candid way of describing the laboratory's goals is to state what measures we took of each student's performance when we assigned him a final grade: We ascertained how well he performed in his role in the simulated organization (meas-ured by his peers); how well his organization performed in the simula-tion (measured by economic indicators); how well he could sense the underlying themes in a work-group meeting and take effective action to increase group productivity (measured by an essay based on tran-script material provided by his instructor or by himself); how effec-tively he could, under the usual constraints of a formal examination, develop organizational designs and design implementation, given a case description of an organization in difficulty. To do well by these measures, a student should have been helped by the laboratory to en-rich his ideas about how he functions in a work situation, how other members of his organization function, how the organization functions, and how he can act most effectively in such a work situation.

Probably the only way one can know what a course like this entails—a course which is based almost wholly on experience—is to travel vicariously through its sequence of activities and sample some typical aspects of the course. The first exposure of a student to the course came in the form of an introductory paper distributed before the first class was held. Excerpts from that paper follow:

> The LOB course has goals and procedures which dis-tinguish it rather clearly from other first-year courses. It is important that you know in advance what some of these dis-tinguishing features are. With this course, we take one step beyond the case. In case discussions you analyze, make de-cisions about and take action on someone else's problems. In the laboratory, the problems are your own, singly and col-lectively. The course requires relatively less outside prepara-tion time than other courses, and proportionately more in-class

time than other courses. Instead of preparing cases to discuss when you get to class, you will usually be creating cases by your own work experience during class time and then using those cases as a source of learning during more class time on the same or another day.

During the first week of the course, you will be engaged in a number of activities designed to prepare you to learn as much as possible about organizational behavior from later course experience. Some of this initial training will require outside preparation of cases and readings, so the first week's class schedule will probably vary from day-to-day. Beginning with the second week, however, you will likely find that you will be working at LOB most of every afternoon on the days the course meets.

After the preparatory first week, there will be a second week devoted to exploring, making sense of, and drawing implications from the organizational aspects of a group research assignment in another course. A third week will be devoted to organizing into corporations. In the four subsequent weeks, you will be acting as a member of a business game corporation. In whatever organizational role you assume, you will be engaged in making three sets of decisions a week. Between the second and third decisions of each week, you will have an LOB class in which to make emergency adjustments to the way you are working. During two afternoons early the following week, you will have more leisure to analyze your organizational and interpersonal behavior and to try out new ways of working together, before it is time again to get back into the decision pressure of the game. The final two weeks of the course will be devoted to review of the business game experience by successive confrontations between various organizational units within each corporation and, finally, between the three corporations of each section. You should keep a journal throughout the LOB course. You will need a record of events and of your feelings about those events when it comes time to report on and discuss your experience in the last weeks of the course.

On the first day of class, students were conducted through an

outline of the course with the aid of the table. As the reader can see
from the vertical axis of the table, there was a primary distinction
made between work at an objective task and work at trying to understand how things were going and how they could be made to go better, that is, process work. The horizontal axis delineates the three
major phases of the course. The first phase, occupying about six meetings, was devoted to training to do the process work. The second
phase, the equivalent of about fifteen classes, was organized around
playing a business game (McFarlan, McKenney, and Seiler, in press).
The game required the organizing of corporations of about thirty
men into an executive, his staff, and three divisions, each with two
plants, and the taking of responsibility for decisions about marketing,
production, and finance. Each corporation was to go through three
years of simulated life, divided into twelve quarters of specific decisions about production volume, manning, cost, pricing, market promotion, finance, and so on; each quarter's decisions would be fed to a
computer after three hours of decision time. The laboratory's classes
were to be devoted to understanding how one's organization or sub-
division was faring and how it could be made to function better in
human and organizational terms (as opposed to terms of market strategy, inventory policy, and so on). The third and final phase of the
course, about six meetings in length, was to be a time for reflection on
what had occurred while the game was being played, at a time when
the game was complete and results were known.

   Another document used at the beginning of the course, (and
which, to the parents of such a course, seems to be essential for our
understanding of students' ideas of what this laboratory was supposed
to be about), discussed the basic reasons for such a course, in terms
of some typical dilemmas in which students in the course, as well as
others in real life, sometimes find themselves because of lack of adequate information. Called *Information Exchange in Group Work*, it
is included, in abbreviated form, in an appendix following this chapter.

   In the first phase of the course, students began their exposure
to process analysis by discussing several cases of groups at work—essentially using this material to make the distinction between task and
process and proposing interventions which might have been made by
a group member at what they considered to be critical points in the
dialogue. Then they set about, with a group task of their own, to try
this sort of analysis on dialogue they, themselves, generated. Often, the

Types of Work in the Laboratory in Organizational Behavior

Major Phase of the Course	WEEK I	WEEK II	WEEK III	WEEK IV
	Orientation and Training in Process Work		Organizing and Working in Business Game Corporations	
TASK WORK	Analyzing cases of group behavior; learning an observation scheme; performing a sample task.	Writing then discussing group process paper with your other course team; drawing implications for future group work.	Corporate staff to be trained in game technology, staff training of corporation members; organizing corporations.	Practice decision set and conduct first three quarters of game business.
PROCESS WORK	Observing, analyzing, discussing immediate behavior of your own work group.	Observation of process of past and present group behavior; using feedback to improve group performance, present and future.	Observation and analysis of organizing process; feedback and change where necessary.	Observation and analysis of practice decision set; feedback and change where required; observation and recording of process in first three quarters.
PRIMARY WORK SETTINGS	Section and small work groups.	Other course teams.	Corporations.	Corporate units.
REPORTS		Other course's group-process paper due April 5, 5, P.M.	Descriptions and supporting reasoning for organization design, procedures, job assignments, etc., due April 14, 5 P.M.	Brief report of any organizational changes and why. Due before first actual decision set.

Major Phase of the Course	WEEK V	WEEK VI	WEEK VII	WEEK VIII	WEEK IX
	Organizing and Working in Business Game Corporations			Confrontations on Business Game Process Issues	
TASK WORK	Conduct quarters 4, 5, 6.	Conduct quarters 7, 8, 9	Conduct quarters 10, 11, 12	Individual and group report-writing; group and intergroup discussion.	Continuation of Week VIII and review.
PROCESS WORK	Process analysis, feedback, experimentation and change based on first three quarters; observation and analysis of next three quarters; short run feedback and change between quarters 5 and 6.	Process analysis, feedback, experimentation and change based on second three quarters; observation and analysis of next three quarters; short run feedback and change between quarters 8 and 9.	Process analysis, feedback, experimentation and change based on third three quarters; observation and analysis of final three quarters; short run feedback and change between quarters 11 and 12.	Retrospective process analysis plus observation of current feedback behavior; interventions and change as required.	Same as Week VIII.
PRIMARY WORK SETTINGS	Corporate units	Corporate units.	Corporate units.	Corporate units.	Corporate units and the section.
REPORTS	Same as Week IV; due by 5 P.M., April 25.	Same as Week IV; due by 5 P.M., May 2.	Same as Week IV; due by 5 P.M., May 9.	Individual, plant, division, and corporate staff reports of primary intra- and inter-group game process analysis. Due dates to be announced.	Corporate reports analyzing primary game processes. Due date to be announced.

tasks these preliminary groups worked on were decision assignments made by other courses that the students were taking simultaneously, one of which was a marketing research report on which we required a written paper from each group for our own purposes, indicated in the table. Once this initial training had been completed, our students were ready to organize their business-game corporations. A prospective student, curious about the Laboratory in Organizational Behavior, could get a picture of what he himself might later experience by listening to a participating student's description (Seiler, 1967b) of the course and the method.

"It's March, two weeks before vacation. The Marketing course has assigned you and seven other students a research report to do on the characteristics of the listening public of a local UHF-TV station. You've no sooner got that assignment in mind when in comes the instructor you'll have next term in LOB. He hands you an additional assignment. You're to keep track of how your Marketing Research (MR) group operates because you'll have to write an LOB report on your group's functioning after your MR group has turned in its report. And that's not all. You'll have to distribute copies of your report to your fellow group members and then sit down with them and talk about your various perceptions. These assignments are both big jobs. They span the Spring vacation, and you thought you'd get a chance then to relax! How do they always manage to keep you just a little off balance? Luckily, a couple of others in the group are staying around Cambridge over vacation; they volunteer to do the MR telephone interviews. But no sooner do you get back (from Bermuda, perhaps?) than this crazy LOB starts.

"Orientation papers tell you that, instead of two hours' preparation and an hour and twenty minutes in class, you'll be mostly in class for three hours and twenty minutes. There's a lot of talk about learning to exchange information among the people you'll be working with. There are suggestions as to how to go about it so that the information will be relevant, so that people can accept it, and so that you can use some of the same data to operate better. There are cases about students working, complete with transcripts of their meetings. You're supposed to figure out what's going on and what you'd do if you were one of them. And there is a special way in which you're supposed to observe people working together to record what they're doing according to some categories of work-oriented and emotion-oriented behavior.

"Then you get another surprise. It's your MERC IV assignment. (MERC stands for Managerial Economics, Reporting and Control.) Your MERC assignment turns out to be a group job in LOB, too. The report you've got to write goes to your MERC professor and, once that report's been turned in, your LOB professor wants you to get together with your group and talk about how you did your jobs. You find this reasonably interesting, actually, because your group could have done a lot better job if they hadn't got to bickering about who was going to take the lead. There was really a pretty simple answer to it, but you missed it.

"The next week you get a day out of class to write up the report for your Marketing Research group. You sweated on it last Friday and Saturday, and then the MERC assignment intervened. You feel that your group was out for minimum-effort on the MR report, just a passing grade. As you see it, things went smoothly until one of the guys started to goof off. The others let him know how they felt, so the goof-off offered to write the report. Too bad he wasn't much of a writer! But everyone felt he had to be given a chance to make up for doing nothing. Then you spend an afternoon talking over the reports with your group. You find out that the others had thought you were trying to take over the group at one point. You had wondered why no one was listening to you for a while, there. But after the afternoon's discussion, you feel pretty good about the group. You look forward to working with them on the business game.

"Then comes an evening of reading about the game and how LOB is supposed to fit into it. With that behind you, you spend a couple of hours with your corporation (composed of four MR groups) nominating and electing an executive board. This turns out to be the honor event of the year because you pick men for these jobs on the basis of professional respect. You get appointed as a plant manager. In the subsequent section discussion, it's interesting to see how the three corporations differ. A has a strong leader. He unilaterally chose two of his executives and had a completely open election discussion before the whole group. B (your corporation) has a participative leader and its election discussions were somewhat more polite. C is going to be run by a committee under its president, who will be

the master strategist. They held strictly secret balloting. You wonder
whether these differences will turn out to be significant in terms of
subsequent performance. But you don't wonder for long. There isn't
time.

"Soon you have a thick business-game rule book to study.
You're attending corporate meetings to set policy and procedures.
You're working with your company's organizational development
man, who helps you plan some initial meetings of your plant. He gives
you some material to read and tells you about a lot of evaluation devices and exercises he has available for your use.[2] You work with your
plant group to assign tasks and work out relationships. Then you start
the practice move—pro forma income statements, raw material inventory, market research, depreciation, cost per unit, product development, promotion—on and on. All those boxes to fill in; no time to
figure out what's going on; up all night after the practice, figuring
out what went wrong. A corporate meeting is scheduled in the early
morning. Everyone is sprawled around one of the dormitory lounges.
The president spurs you on. Then the first real move comes up. The
computer printouts come back. Two more moves over the next thirty-
six hours. Incredible! But you did make some money!

"So it goes for four weeks. Regular classes Monday through
Thursday. On Thursday afternoon a printout comes back; a decision
is needed by 7 P.M. The next printout is back at 8 A.M., Friday; decision is called for by 11. Then follows an LOB evaluation and attempts to get the guys working better together. Another printout shows
up at 3 P.M.; decision required by 6. Then, if things aren't going so
well, a corporate meeting after supper and divisional and plant meetings all weekend.

"Monday and Tuesday afternoons are all LOB time. You try
to figure out what's wrong and fix it. Is this what business is like? You
decide medical school would have been a vacation! Midway through
the game, things start coming apart. Your plant has a fight with the
other plant over a decision on product pricing. Your product prices
are too close together. Then, when you try to make a deal on a transfer of inventory to the other plant, you can't settle on a price. The
division manager tries to mediate but it doesn't work.

"The president calls in the LOB instructor (he's a consultant

---

[2] A set of immediate feedback exercises were made available to give
corporate autonomy and to give relief to the thinly spread instructors.

during the game) to meet with the division while all of you try to figure out what's wrong. After a while he points out that the division manager, younger than either of your plant managers, has taken sides with you, and the other plant is apparently defending itself. Well, true enough, you and the division manager *have* been pretty close. Once all this gets raised, a lot more attitudes get expressed and you seem to begin to work things out. The instructor withdraws, but drops around once in a while to sit in and see how things are going. You hear from others in the section that he's been consulting with a lot of them, too. He's even had some sessions with the three presidents about their relationship with the chairman of the board (an instructor from another course area who works with the section strictly on business game aspects of the experience). Your organizational development man is busy, too. He runs some corporate-wide attitude surveys and turns up some communications problems. The divisions, it seems, really aren't helping one another. One is very successful, the other two aren't. The president is concerned, but nothing seems to happen.

"You remember that you are responsible for grading your men at the end of the game. In turn, you will be graded by the division manager. It's pretty serious—30% of the course grade. Another 30% is based on corporate economic performance; 15% comes from reports like the MR; and 25% is contributed by the final exam. So your OD man organizes meetings on evaluative criteria, and then you have a practice grading program. You have to sit down with each of your men and discuss your evaluation of him. The grade distribution *is* pretty high on the scale; but still, when you give an average grade to one of your men and high grades to the rest, you find you've got to level with that man. You begin to think over how you'll handle this at the end of the game. Final results come out. Damn it all, what happened? Your corporation started out as number one of the twenty-one corporations, and it ends up as number ten. One of your corporation's other divisions was tops, but yours never quite made it. You spend two weeks, the last two of the course, trying to figure this out. But first, there's that final rating. You can't give all your people top grades, so you learn a lot about evaluating subordinates. "Fair but firm" seems like a good policy, but it's tough having to face a fellow with a poor grade. Then you have to sit down and write the same kind of report on your plant as you did on your MR group. The meeting with your plant really opens up some things. You hadn't realized how unapproachable you'd been. It turns out that your group thought you wouldn't allow a change in job assignments. That assumption seems to have been behind a big problem—coordination among functional units. It probably would have been better, you now decide, to have set up product managers. You wish you could spend more time in this plant discussion, but a division rehash session is called. Since there has already been a crisis resolution in the division, there isn't much new on that score, except that you find out more about the division manager's problems with the corporate staff and how they kept him from being of more help to you. Next, you have a corporate meeting. There is some good discussion. The president takes a lot of flak and handles it pretty well. His notion of decentralization, it turns out, was too simple. You really needed some leadership, but he thought you'd resent it. You wonder if he hadn't been right about that. But how could you have known at the beginning what you know now?

"The section meets to compare notes. Each corporation distributes a statement of its major successes and failures before the meeting. You find out that the differences in the way the corporations organized themselves initially really meant something. The corporation with the open discussion and strong leader turns out to have been number one in the first-year corporate standings. Your outfit, with its decentralization and bottoms-up management was in the middle. The third corporation, with its secret ballots and committee management was near the bottom. The discussion, you find, really shakes up some of the myths about participative management. It turns out to be a lot more complicated than that.

"That's it, except for the final exam. It's given in two parts. The first is a transcript of a meeting between the executives from last year's course and the LOB instructor. Those boys really were competing with one another. They vented a lot of their problems on the instructor, just as you do with the old man. But the instructor was sure making it tough on his students, not taking a clear position, just raising questions. You develop your analysis of what was happening and suggest how you might have behaved if you'd been there. The second part is tougher. You are given the case of a company that can't seem to attract, keep, or develop enough good managers. A consultant is called in. He does some research and comes up with some attitude patterns that spell a difficult situation. You're told by the executive vice president to recommend a plan of attack on these problems.

You've really got to devise an organizational development program, figure out how to implement it and, at the same time, act appropriately for your position in the organization. You really sweat over that part of the exam.

"After the course has ended, you're asked to give your evaluation of the course by filling out a long multiple-choice questionnaire covering all aspects of the work. You score some parts higher than others; but overall, like most of your fellows, you score the course at 5.5 on a 7-point scale. In the space provided for suggestions, you recommend that the game be split into halves, with a week between them to reorganize and get onto a more productive track. You feel sure your corporation could have come out on top if you'd only had a chance to back off a little and see what became so clear later during the postgame discussions. You go off to your summer job looking for a chance to use some of your new understanding of organizational behavior. You turn your assignment to study the inventory control system of your division into a fully fledged organizational analysis, but you're smart enough to play it cool with your boss. He actually thanks you at the end of the summer and asks you to be available from time to time during the following year to help work out the implications of your summer's work. You think maybe you'll go back to that company after graduation. A brief reevaluation questionnaire is distributed by LOB in the fall. It's designed to see whether you've changed your mind about the course. This time you and the class rate it 6 on the 7-point scale." So much for being a student.

What the instructor does and feels in such a course is unique. He begins in the usual classroom manner during the orientation phase of the course. From that point onward, however, he has a choice to make. He can largely withdraw from events and only attend to the proper scheduling of activities. The course carries itself, in a sense, if the assigned tasks have been well designed. This choice is particularly attractive if there is an unfinished article or book crying for attention.

However, teachers, being the kind of people they are, rarely choose the passive role. The idea that students can be learning something significant in the absence of an instructor is abhorrent for most of us, so we stay on the scene as much as possible, if only to keep the idea from spreading. To stay on the scene means to invade the students' bailiwick, since students do their course work in odd nooks and crannies, there seldom being enough small rooms to accommodate the

rather large number of groups involved. So the active instructor becomes a foreigner in his own course. The role he usually adopts is that
of the consultant. But consultants scarcely ever are in a position to act
without the invitation of consultees. Does the instructor sit in his office
and wait for a call? The most successful answer to this awkward problem is to inform students that the instructor will visit work meetings,
on a rotating basis, to keep himself informed of developments so that
if and when his help is requested, he may act in an informed manner.
That gives him at least semilegitimacy for being present in his classes.
Then it is his task to demonstrate that he can be useful. To do so, he
must be alert for the first crisis, particularly one at the top of his students' simulated organization. If he steps boldly but with finesse into
that crisis, bringing relevant parties together but avoiding forced reso-
lutions, he can begin to make himself valuable. Usually the competition for the number one performance positions will make sure that the
instructor's talents are used thenceforth. In fact, the instructor will be
likely to find that what could have been a respite turns into a very
time-consuming task, indeed. There are many complexities in the laboratory instructor's role—not the least of which pertains to the evaluative component of his job. But these difficulties can be overcome. For
those who like to engage in a teaching-learning process which takes
place on the run and in unexpected forms, this kind of course can be
exciting and can provoke all kinds of new ideas.

APPENDIX: INFORMATION EXCHANGE IN GROUP WORK

About Norms Governing Discussion Topics: One work group,
led by a student who expressed a great deal of enthusiasm for the
course, agreed at its outset to discuss group members' basic motives
and to analyze their origins, much as a therapy group might do. No
one questioned the wisdom of devoting time and effort to work of this
kind, even though it obviously involved information that was beyond
that necessary for the solution of the group's working problems. Several group members felt anxious about what this agreement might
demand of them. As a result, the group developed a norm of appearing to discuss important motives but never actually doing so. They
were able to do this by talking over anecdotes of personal history
which were relatively favorable to the speaker. As a result, and as the
group agreed in its process analysis at the end of the course, not only
was the group's avowed intention thwarted, but the norm of unau-

thentic information exchange invaded the discussions of information which *was* relevant to solutions of their day-to-day working problems. There was speculation on the part of the group's leader about his own motives in suggesting a "full disclosure" policy, i.e., did he do so, he wondered, because he knew this was the surest way to *avoid* full disclosure? Why hadn't he encouraged a norm of gradually increasing open communication of feelings relevant to task achievement, instead of a norm which was so likely to fail in achieving its espoused purpose?

About Leadership: Reluctance to share feelings about the leader of the group (on the part of the leader and on the part of his group) has been widespread. Choosing a leader was an uncomfortable process in which many aspirants held back or disguised their aspiration for formal leadership for reasons of modesty, fear of losing, or of being harshly judged by their overly critical peers. Simultaneously, and for the same reasons, the group found it difficult to talk openly about the necessary qualifications of a leader. As a result, choice of a formal leader was usually made arbitrarily—the oldest man, first nominee, the most aggressive group member, and so on. Usually no limitation on the leader's authority was discussed nor were any other ground rules decided upon or even raised for discussion. Members usually did not voice objections to these procedures for establishing a leader in the group for fear of seeming to criticize the chosen leader or of having a "sour-grapes" attitude. It was fear of appearing critical, too, that prompted the group to leave all the functions of leadership in the one man's hands, as impossible as such an assignment was. Thereafter, members typically withheld feedback to their leader as he tried to exercise an undefined role under difficult circumstances and without benefit of information about how he was doing. Members who were dissatisfied with the leader either began to withdraw or, in a few groups, to conspire outside the group to replace the old leader without hurting him by open discussion of his performance. This conspiracy required further concealment of information within the group. As the new leader began to take over, the old leader drew incorrect conclusions about why his power was waning, others outside the conspiratorial group further withdrew and the conspirators were left to carry the workload, alone. The group ended up with a bewildered old leader, with resentful and withdrawn individuals, and a subgroup which reproached others for the withdrawal which left only a few holding the bag. With new secrets designed to protect old ones, these groups had created the conditions in which exchanging relevant socio-emotional information became increasingly difficult.

About Participation: With surprising frequency, inadequate information exchange fostered the development of nonparticipants. During an early meeting a member perceived his contribution as having been ignored or discouraged in some way. Fearing that the answer to why he got such a reaction would be painful, he next tried to be heard by actively criticizing the contributions of other members. The group perceived his criticism as rejection and, without questioning why he was reacting as he did (for fear of expressing the irritation they felt or of invading his privacy), they sidestepped his criticisms. The critic then became increasingly preoccupied by why he was not being heard, and, as a result, he, himself, listened less well leading to his being further off-target in his comments, and further ignored. In some cases, the nonparticipant, to assuage his feeling of guilt at not participating more, volunteered to write the group's final process analysis report, although he was least capable of doing so, having been a nonparticipant. When the group report turned out poorly, the sense of mutual rejection was reinforced.

About Intergroup Relationships: The failure of a group to confront its internal working problems may complicate its relationships with other groups. A number of examples of this problem arose when the course required that pairs of interdependent work groups observe each other at work and try to help each other see and deal with their respective working problems. Often, the helping group acted on unnecessarily inadequate information: (i) it observed weak points in the other's meeting but failed to recognize its own ignorance of the complex relationships underlying those weaknesses; (ii) in failing to recognize its ignorance, it unwittingly touched on internal conflicts which the other group was unable to discuss by itself, let alone in the presence of outsiders; (iii) it was aware of its own good intentions but unaware of how closely the other group was scrutinizing the "helping" group's behavior for some sign of sympathy (perhaps signified by such seemingly trivial evidence as whether there was a willingness to clarify a communication); (iv) it used terminology it was familiar with, assuming incorrectly that the other group derived the same meaning from these terms. In order to overcome these obstacles, the helping group would have had to be willing to expose its own experiences from which its helping ideas had been derived, i.e., expose its own internal conflicts, but this it felt it could not afford to do. Instead, it swamped the other group with undigested observations, used private language, defended its views, protected its own sensitivities but ignored those of the other group, convincing the others that it did not want to understand but only to display cleverness and superiority. When the other group counterattacked, the helpers, convinced of their good intentions, felt wronged, and the intention retrogressed further.

About Authority Relationships: In past laboratory courses, most of the socio-emotional issues associated with authority relationships have arisen around the instructor, although it seems likely that the design of the present course will create more numerous and varied superior-subordinate relationships. The problem most often experienced in this area revolved about the superior's roles as an evaluator. As he worked with his subordinates, for example, he sometimes unwittingly assigned work in an inconvenient schedule. For fear of being evaluated as unwilling to put effort into the job, the subordinates refrained from informing the superior of his error. Actually, they felt that the "error" was intentional, having been motivated by some pedagogic scheme which the instructor was unwilling to reveal. When the schedule was not met, the superior began to feel that his subordinates were behaving irresponsibly. They, in turn, felt that he had been toying with them arbitrarily by setting an impossible task, then becoming irritated when it was not accomplished on schedule. The subordinates felt they could not express their opinions of the injustice in the superior's acts for fear of being further negatively evaluated. The superior felt he was being open about his feelings but was meeting a blank wall. His behavior became more and more expressive of negative evaluation, and so on.

Malcolm S. Knowles

Teaching-Learning Teams
in Adult Education

The graduate program in adult education was established at Boston University in 1960 with the dual purpose of extending knowledge about adult learning through research and of equipping adult education practitioners with the competencies particularly required for the effective management of learning experiences for adults.

My central mission in this program has been to develop and test a theory of learning that would be more consonant with what we know about the maturation process than are the traditional theories of pedagogy. Specifically, I speculated that as a human being moves through the process of maturing, he experiences changes in at least four critical characteristics that affect his learning: His self-concept shifts gradually from that of a dependent personality toward that of an increasingly self-directing person; as this shift occurs, he learns better if he is given increasing responsibility for his own learning. He accumulates a growing body of personal experience, which has

XIII

Boston
University

increasing value for his own learning and the learning of others. As he himself attaches increasing value to his own and others' experience, he learns better in situations in which the experience of the learner is used as a resource for learning. His readiness to learn becomes determined decreasingly by biological and academic factors and increasingly by the developmental tasks of his emerging social role. He learns better when learnings are timed to coincide with the needs and interests stimulated by these role requirements. His time perspective shifts from one of postponed application ("Accumulate subject matter now for possible later use") to one of immediate application ("Learn things now that will help in coping with today's life problems"), so he learns better those knowledges, skills, attitudes, and values that are relevant to the problems he faces in life at this moment.

Taking these speculative propositions as working hypotheses to be tested empirically, I have attempted to develop a graduate curriculum and teaching technology that would be as congruent with the propositions as I could make them. The principles and techniques that have emerged from my experiments are applicable, with adjustments for differences in levels of maturity, to the teaching of undergraduates—and, indeed, of all children and youth.

The graduate program in adult education at Boston University is currently populated by about three hundred students, most in their thirties, who have begun graduate study after several years working in educational institutions, industry, social agencies, health agencies, government, and religious institutions. When they enter the program, they are given a self-diagnostic worksheet on which are listed twenty-nine competencies the program is designed to develop. Each student makes a preliminary self-assessment, on a scale from weak to strong, of his present level of achievement in each competency. On the basis of this self-rating, a first-year program of learning experiences is laid out. Thus, each student enters his first course with some exposure to the concept of self-directed learning and some practice in self-diagnosis of learning needs. Every course, field experience, and independent study project in which he engages from then on is designed to deepen his understanding of the process of self-directed inquiry and to sharpen his skills in engaging in the process himself and helping others engage in it.

The total program consists of a dozen courses (only a few of which any one person would take), a variety of field experiences, independent study in adult and higher education, and opportunities for additional course work in the humanities, behavioral sciences, foundations of education, communications, and business administration in other schools and departments of the university. The dozen adult and higher education courses range from highly cognitive courses, such as The Nature of Adult Education to highly skill-oriented courses, such as Methods of Adult Education.

All of these courses, however, follow a process design that includes, during the fifteen three-hour sessions of a one-semester course, a number of basic phases.

Phase 1: Climate setting and resource identification. This phase, which usually takes up the entire three-hour first meeting, includes: orientation to the broad purpose and scope of the particular course; introduction of the students and faculty, with brief descriptions of their special concerns or interests as well as of the special resources they have to contribute to the substance of the course; a brief survey of the process design of the course, with the rationale for it; a review of the resource materials—including bibliographies, textbooks, and collections of documents—and resource people relevant to the course; suggestions as to how the students might prepare most effectively to participate in the second phase of the design. The social climate that is established in this phase is informal and relaxed. In my role as teacher, I serve as a procedural guide and information resource, concerned primarily with establishing a warm, empathic, and collaborative relationship with the students. My attitude is one of genuine respect for their concerns and resources though I value the resources I can contribute to the process of mutual inquiry.

When the enrollment in a given course is more than about twenty-five students, it is too time-consuming to have individual introductions, so I use group introductions, for which I have experimented with various techniques including: *The inquiring reporter,* in which each group is asked to choose one person to compose a feature story about the personalities and resources of the members of his group and to report it in three minutes to the total group; *the living newspaper,* in which each group is invited to select one feature of a newspaper—a news story, editorial, book review, column, or sports article—and present a description of their group in that format; *the television variety* program, in which each group is told it will have a three-minute segment of a television variety show to present its group, through interview, panel show skit, song, comedy, or news program. I have found that this procedure works best when subgroups are limited to six persons and when they can have at least twenty minutes to plan their presentation. This type of activity produces immediate ego-involvement, sets the norm of participative learning and mutual sharing of resources, and induces a spirit of creative inquiry.

Phase 2: Diagnosis of needs for learning. This phase, which typically occurs in the second and third meetings, consists of three elements. The first element is the development of a *model of specific competencies* (knowledge, understanding, attitudes, skills, interests, and values) required for excellent performance of the role of adult educator in the content area of the particular course. I have experimented with several techniques for developing such a model including a straightforward presentation of my own ideas of the desired competencies, with criticisms from the students; a group interview of a

panel of experienced professional adult educators; and the pooling of
lists of competencies compiled by groups of students based on their
search of the literature. This last technique, supplemented by ideas I
contribute to the pooled list, produces the model to which the students
have the greatest commitment. For example, in a recent course on
The Nature of Adult Education, I presented to the class a number of
competencies I had extracted from a long list developed by Martin
Chamberlain (1960–61) and validated by a jury of national leaders
in the field. "The adult educator: understands the role adult education has played in American society in the past and is playing in
the present, and has aspirations regarding its role in the future;
has broad knowledge of the present scope and trends of adult education as a field of social practice in terms of its aims, agencies, content,
personnel, programs, methods and materials, and operational problems; understands and is interested in the concerns and issues affecting
the adult education field; has a deep insight into the relationship between the education of youth and the education of adults; understands
the basic processes of adult education." I invited the students to test
this list against their ideas and experience. By general agreement they
added three more competencies. "[The adult educator:] has a broad
overview knowledge of the research that has been done in the field;
understands the existing theories about the psychology of adult learning; has a basic understanding of the nature of the adult education
movements in other countries."

The second element of Phase Two is an assessment, by the
students, of their *present level of achievement* of the competencies
specified in the model. The assumption behind this procedure is that
the extent to which the students themselves experience a gap between
where they are now and where they want to be will directly correlate
with their degree of motivation to invest energy in reducing the gap.
My own feeling is that students are more likely to experience such
gaps by analyzing actual performance than by giving intellectualized
answers to questionnaires or pencil-and-paper tests. Accordingly, my
efforts have focused on devising critical incident cases, skill practice
exercises, simulation games, role playing, and videotape self-observa-
tions, in which students get feedback on their actual performance of
the desired competencies. In the Nature of Adult Education course,
I suggested that those students who wished to experiment with a mutual self-diagnosis process might spend the week, between the second

and the third sessions, scanning the literature with a view to constructing a diagnostic exercise. In the third session, the thirty students who had prepared exercises were paired, with each member of a pair giving his exercise to the other. The remaining fifteen formed into three groups of five to share the results of their individual self-diagnoses. Many of the exercises devised by the students were much more imaginative and demanding than I would have dared present. Most of them were of the critical incident variety, such as "If the editor of the *New York Times Magazine* asked you to write an article on the part adult education has played in the historical development of this country, what would be your five main points?"

The third element is pooling of the individual learning needs that are revealed in the self-diagnosis process. For this, the most efficient technique is to put the students back into groups of five or six, have each group pool the needs of its members into a common list, and then to build a master list of needs from the composite reports of all the groups. After such a master list of needs has been laid out on a blackboard, I get some feeling for the frequency distribution among the needs by going down the list and asking the students to raise their hands for the three needs that are of highest priority order for each one. In the Nature of Adult Education course, there were clusters of identified needs around each of the competencies included in the model, except for the one, about the scope of adult education as a field, which the students felt they could get from their own reading. In addition, there were about a dozen students who expressed highly individual specialized needs that did not fit into the more generalized competency model.

Phase 3: Formulation of course objectives. This phase takes place immediately following the compilation of the master list of needs. It consists simply of translating the clusters of needs into behavioral objectives. In the Nature of Adult Education course, the objectives became: to develop an understanding of the historical development of the adult education movement in America and its role in the evolution of our culture; to develop an understanding of the philosophical issues about which adult educators are currently concerned; to develop knowledge of the main theories of learning and their implications for the education of adults; to develop an understanding of the methods and materials uniquely appropriate to adult learning; to develop insight into the implications of what is known about adults as learners for the education of youth; to develop knowledge of the nature of adult education movements in Western Europe; to develop knowledge of the present status of research in the field of adult education.

Phase 4: The planning of learning experiences.   This phase typically occupies the period from the fourth through the sixth or seventh week and consists of three stages. The first stage is the organization of learning-teaching teams. Usually a team is organized for each objective, but sometimes one team will take responsibility for two or more objectives. These teams are organized by asking each student to make a first, second, and third choice on the basis of the priority of his needs. If more than eight students select one topic as their first choice, negotiations are entered into to try to get students with strong second choices to move over to a smaller team, because teams of more than eight persons have difficulty organizing for work. In the Nature of Adult Education course, for example, there were seven teams, one for each objective, ranging in size from four to eight persons. A dozen members chose individual projects, and organized themselves into three mutual help groups, in which the members simply shared their experiences in their independent studies.

The second stage is the preparation of the teams for doing their work. Before the teams split for their first meetings, I review the tasks they have undertaken, which vary from course to course. In the Nature of Adult Education course, the task of each team is to learn all it can from the literature and from resource people on campus and in the community about the respective content units and then to plan how the teams can best help the rest of the class to get the essence of what they have learned. Their ultimate goal is to conduct a miniature learning experience for the rest of the class. The tasks of all teams were reviewed in open meeting, so that all the teams understood the tasks of other teams and so that problems of territorial conflict could be resolved.

The first time I used learning-teaching teams, I found that it took a couple of weeks to work out their group dynamics, so that they did not get to working on their tasks until almost their final meeting. Thereafter, I would give the students some process coaching before they formed teams. This coaching usually took the form of inviting students who have had previous experience in learning-teaching teams to suggest ways in which they can organize themselves for work more efficiently.

The third stage is that of team learning and planning. During the first meetings of the learning-teaching teams, which typically take place in the fourth session, members usually probe one another's interests and resources more deeply than was possible in the large meetings, review their resource materials, and then divide responsibility among themselves for carrying out their research. During their second meetings, team members typically report to one another the results of their investigations and pool their thoughts on the most critical questions and issues requiring further study. During the third meeting, agreements are reached about which elements of their content units must be developed for their classmates and how this is to be done. During this sequence of meetings, the instructor, often assisted by a group of advanced doctoral students, is available for consultation by the teams on both their content tasks and their group process.

In every course, when the learning-teaching teams are being organized, members of the class are invited to volunteer for a team working on evaluation. This evaluation team is given responsibility both for planning procedures and tools for evaluating the course and for proposing a plan for grading. Only once in the last ten years has a class opted out of responsibility for doing its own evaluation and grading.

Phase 5: Presentation of learning experiences. This phase typically runs from the seventh through the fourteenth weeks, thus permitting seven or eight teams each to have a full three-hour session in which to present their learning activities. It has become standard practice, however, to reserve the last half-hour of each session for the instructor to comment and for the total class to analyze each team's design. In the early years of our experiment with learning-teaching teams, about half the team presentations tended to be fairly stereotyped transmissions of information by lecture discussions, film discussions, panel discussions, symposiums, and the like. The norm became established that every member of every team must have equal time "on the air." As the students gained more experience with learning-teaching teams, this norm has given way to the norm that presentations should be creative and effective, regardless of how few students have the chance to show off. Most team presentations have become highly creative experiments in participative learning, with such designs as microworkshops, simulated field experiences, participative cases, televised lectures, group interviews of professional leaders, and original dramatic presentations. Almost all teams prepare handout materials, ranging from annotated bibliographies to elaborate collections of manuals, reprints, guidelines, and instruments—many of them reproduced outside the university.

   Phase 6: Course evaluation and grading. The fifteenth session is always reserved for course evaluation under the leadership of the evaluation team. Although the evaluation teams have experimented with a variety of patterns, the final session usually is fairly predictable and includes: (1) The results of the inquiry into the theory and practice of educational evaluation. In the course on the nature of adult education, for example, the presentation typically reviews the current status of the research literature on educational evaluation; in a course on administration, the presentation is on program evaluation; in the course on methods of adult education, the focus is on tools and procedures for measuring behavioral changes. (2) The findings on the students' evaluation of their course. Many evaluation teams have experimented with rating scales, postmeeting reaction forms, interviews, and other evaluation procedures, the results of which are fed back to the class. (3) The collection of final suggestions from the class about improvements that might be made in future offerings of the course. Both written questionnaires and buzz groups have been used for this purpose. (4) The determination of grades for individual students. In all but a few instances the system that has been adopted for arriving at grades has been some form of self-grading. Evaluation teams have experimented with a wide variety of procedures for providing students with objective data about their performance to assist them in grading themselves responsibly. In some instances, they have repeated the diagnostic exercises used to develop the model of specific competencies, thus giving the students some kind of before-and-after measures. Another favorite technique is to provide feedback and consultation by fellow members of learning-teaching teams, by interteam triads, or by pairing of teams. A procedure used quite often is to assume a *B* to be the standard grade and to require the student to submit evidence to the evaluation team of superior performance that would warrant a higher grade.

   After ten years of experience, our learnings from this experi-

ment in group self-directed learning are based largely on impression-
istic data—a base typical in the first phases of action research. Our
impressions are supported by a growing volume of student reports collected through course-evaluation procedures. First, it is overwhelm-
ingly clear that undergraduates in our American colleges do not, on
the whole, learn the skills of self-directed inquiry. They enter graduate
school still dependent on their teachers to diagnose their needs for
learning, to formulate their learning objectives for them, to tell them
what they need to know, and then to evaluate what they have learned.
They do not know how to ask questions that can be answered by data;
they know how to ask only those that can be answered by authority
or faith, yet they reject the answers of authorities and faith because
these conflict with their need to be self-directing. They have not
learned the value of their own experience as a resource for learning,
and they have not learned the techniques for learning from their ex
perience. But it seems equally clear from our ten years of experience
that students *can* learn to be self-directed learners if they are plunged
into educational activities that require it, if they are well coached in
the required skills, and if they are supported by a respectful environment. Most of our students have become fully fledged, self-directed
learners by the end of one semester's immersion in the process; a few
take a year; I have known perhaps half a dozen who never were able
to accept it.

Second, it is clear that the basic orientation toward learning
that most students have developed in their earlier schooling is one of
competitiveness. This orientation is manifested initially in our program by a defensive reaction to the self-diagnostic phase, in which
embarrassment about engaging in a process that reveals weaknesses is
frequently expressed. After all, one gets *A*s by showing how good one
is. The competitive attitude shows up most sharply and is least functional in the early operation of learning-teaching teams, when struggles for control, self-assertion, and one-upmanship hinder the teams'
task of learning together. It frequently reveals itself, also, in the presentation designs constructed by the learning-teaching teams; often the
best ideas for designs are discarded because they do not provide an
opportunity for all members of the team to show off equally. It becomes a real problem at grading time, when the emotionally-charged
need to be best or at the top gets in the way of using evaluation procedures for meaningful self-assessment. This attitude of competitive-

ness can be changed to one of self-acceptance and collaboration by à sequence of experiences in an environment that rewards and reinforces the latter attitudes. This behavioral change takes longer than the development of basic skills in self-directed inquiry; in fact, it is my impression that a noncompetitive orientation to learning does not become fully established until the final stages of a master's program.

Third, most students find that learning to become self-directed learners is euphoric and ego-expanding. This observation is supported by numerous evaluative statements obtained from students at the completion of their degree programs. They report that, when they came into the program, they viewed education as a chore, a self-degrading necessity, or, at best, a mostly-irrelevant means for gaining a degree which conferred status. But when they really mastered the art of self-directed and collaborative learning, education became a thing of beauty, an aesthetic experience, a life-enhancing activity. As one student wrote in his evaluation, "It's like a narcotic—I've become addicted." That is what our program is all about—continuing education.

Solomon Cytrynbaum

Richard D. Mann

Community as Campus
—Project Outreach

Student activism and rebellion of the past few years, the continuing effects of white racism, and the demands from black students for a relevant education have generated an atmosphere of crisis in American higher education. In response, administrators and faculty have expressed varying degrees of support for innovations aimed at increasing the social and personal relevance of the college experience. Radical challenges to the traditional view of the college classroom as a bastion of rationality have only rarely had any significant impact on teachers and administrators preoccupied with a narrow domain of cognitive and abstract concerns. Very few of the twenty-three hundred American institutions of higher education have welcomed social action programs, opportunities for experiential or interpersonal learning, or major reorganizations of curricula. Those innovative programs that have been adopted have frequently been viewed as ancillary stepchildren

XIV

University
of Michigan

who must be endured (Manion, 1967; Sanford, 1967b; Harrison and Hopkins, 1967; Sunderland, 1967).

Project Outreach is an example of such a stepchild; its parent is the course in introductory psychology at the University of Michigan. In the process of maturing from a vulnerable and wide-eyed infant into a robust, precocious and somewhat awkward adolescent, Outreach has generated a number of challenging questions about the goals and values of higher education, the boundaries of the teacher-student task relationship, and the nature of effective teaching. Psychology 101, An Introduction to Psychology as a Social Science, is currently a four-credit-hour course offered to about fourteen hundred University of Michigan students each fall and winter term and to about two hundred students during the summer. It is taught by graduate students who are appointed as teaching fellows in the Department of Psychology. Each term about thirty-five teaching fellows are responsible for approximately fifty discussion sections averaging twenty-seven students each. Sections meet three hours weekly for lectures, discussions or other learning opportunities, and teaching fellows are free to use the fourth hour as they wish. The evolution of the course has been such that the discussion section belongs to the teaching fellow; there are no common texts, lectures, or exams. Each teaching fellow functions autonomously, though responsible to his peers and a faculty coordinator. On the whole, this group of teaching fellows enjoys, and values, teaching, and in the past it has spent a great deal of time and energy discussing and thinking both about individual classes and more general teaching-learning issues. The teaching fellow peer culture serves not only as a system of informal control but also as a potent source of stimulation, support, and rewards for creative teaching-learning innovations.

In the spring of 1965, this group of energetic graduate students and their faculty coordinator, the junior author of this chapter, worked on several persistent and common sources of dissatisfaction among teaching fellows. The most pressing were concerns about the passive, receptive, learning styles manifested by some students; the inability of the teaching fellows to connect with some students despite a manageable class size and considerable opportunity for students to participate in discussions; the frustration of the teaching fellows with the more traditional, segmented survey of such discrete, substantive topics as statistics, motivation, learning, and other areas often judged to be of little relevance to their students; and their desire to revitalize the fourth weekly common lecture hour. So the fourth hour was turned over to the teaching fellows to be redesigned. A subgroup met over the summer and gradually evolved a series of substitute activities, called Outreach, to make it possible for students to break out of the classroom into the laboratory of real life. About eight teaching fellows made the initial arrangements and, in the fall of 1965, about three hundred students were offered, among other possibilities, the opportunity to spend from three to five hours per week working with adult patients on the back wards of a state hospital, working with children and adolescents in a residential treatment center, tutoring an OEO trainee, or participating in self-analytic sensitivity training. Usually, students who chose to participate in service-oriented projects met afterward with a supervisor on campus to share experiences, feelings, concerns, questions, and what they had learned. Outreach is therefore a rubric for a variety of diverse services, social-action activities, and opportunities for experientially oriented education as well as for a number of discussion groups focusing on problems not usually considered to be part of an introductory psychology course. Only the groups in sensitivity training have a faculty consultant. As in the introductory course, project supervisors in Outreach are totally autonomous and are responsible for their projects and students.

From its tentative and rather risky beginnings over three years ago, Outreach has exploded into a huge and sometimes unwieldy enterprise. This growth has been accompanied by a proliferation of new and unusual projects, an increasing number of participating students, numerous requests from students to continue participating beyond one term, and a continuing capacity to attract a large group of graduate-student supervisors with diverse departmental affiliations. Currently there are about forty-four projects being offered in six major areas. These projects serve about fourteen hundred students each term; they are supervised by about one hundred and twenty graduate students, eighty or so experienced undergraduates, and some permanent staff from the participating institutions and agencies. A sixty-page booklet is required to describe all the current projects for students so that they can make fairly knowledgeable choices. In the area of social institutions and social structure, a project on psychology and the law includes discussion, observation, and participation; topics include civil disobedience, drugs, legal insanity, divorce, and homosexuality; students can also serve as jurors in mock trials at the Law School and visits courts. Other projects in this area include: Psychology and Religion, Teen age Community Structure, Israeli Kibbutz, Psychology and the Elections, Psychology and the Military, Psychology and World Politics.

In the area of conflict and strategies for change, an action-oriented project on university reform gives students practice in planning and testing strategies for radicalizing and changing educational environments. Other projects in this area include: Psychology of Conflict, Psychology of Aggression and Violence, Radicalism and Technology, Psychology of Non-violent Action.

In the area of understanding the self, peers, and interpersonal relations, a semistructured group working on nonverbal interaction enables students and supervisors to design and participate in nonverbal experiences and exercises to learn about nonverbal styles generally and the self in particular. Another project, on cross-cultural relations, uses unstructured groups in which students from different countries and cultures attempt to understand one another and learn about others' backgrounds. Other projects in this area include: Male and Female Relationships in a Changing Society, The College Experience, Roles and Games People Play, Sensitivity Training, Value Conflicts and Stereotypes, Drugs and Social Behavior, Toward Black Consciousness, White Racism, Children's Play.

Disturbed children, adolescents, and adults are studied through arrangements with numerous mental hospitals, residential schools, clinics, and other organizations in the Ann Arbor area. Students usually take on actual work with patients in limited and educational ways. In the area of education and child development, students in Outreach assist teachers and do limited teaching tasks in public and private schools and in the OEO tutorial program. Projects in the area of the arts and the mass media include: Psychology of Art, Psychology and Modern Drama, The Garbage and the Flowers, Television and the Mass Media, Values in American Cinema, Psychology and Literature.

The current edition of Outreach is regarded by some with considerable ambivalence, but the small group of teaching fellows who have been party to the growth and development of Outreach is proud of the fact that, despite the size of the program, a tendency toward bureaucracy, and an increase in the number of content-oriented projects (a somewhat disturbing development to those who primarily regard Outreach as a source of experiential and personal learning for their students), Outreach remains fairly open and supportive to the large number of bright, creative graduate students and experienced undergraduate students who take roles as supervisors in Outreach projects. The model of peer supervision has been developed most systematically in the projects in sensitivity training. Groups of cotrainers meet weekly to discuss their groups and to take part in sessions on theory or technique; they can also participate in any of the different kinds of weekend training sessions available. Inexperienced supervisors who want eventually to lead groups can observe and participate in a variety of groups. The supervisory and training program for sensitivity-group trainers has developed to the point where a graduate course is being proposed to legitimize these experiences as part of the graduate student's professional training and development.

One of the most surprising and reassuring observations about Outreach is that the initial fear of casualties, expressed by some supervisors, faculty, and others, has never really materialized. In nearly four years, with more than seven thousand students, there has not been a single case where it could be determined that a student had suffered serious or long-term physical or emotional injury as a direct result of an Outreach experience. (One should not exclude the possibility of unreported cases or ignore the fact that some students have reported that they have been temporarily shaken up by their Outreach experiences.) This negligible casualty rate is quite striking, since presumably naive freshmen are placed in close contact with seriously disturbed patients in maximum security units, since about half the students in Outreach (including one group which went to Washington for a nonviolent peace protest) are transported by bus or car on a weekly basis to and from projects, occasionally under poor weather conditions, and since many students have participated in intense and emotionally demanding experiences in sensitivity groups. These risks, as well as the anxiety arousing nature of many of the projects, have not discouraged students from continuing in Psychology. The contrary conclusion is suggested by the unusually large increase in the number of concentrates and majors. All of this suggests that many undergraduate students are much stronger, more independent, and more competent than they are usually assumed to be. Some data from the students' own reports suggest that those who participated in Outreach were more involved, modified their career plans more often, and became more concerned about life and social problems than students who chose alternative fourth-hour activities. However, the Outreach students also reported that they had learned less psychology and new information than their peers (Jorgenson, 1966). The increasing demand for supervisory positions from graduate students (many of whom are not in the Psychology Department), and experienced Outreach alumni, and the continuous and mutually satisfactory relationships between Outreach and about twenty hospitals, clinics, agencies, and schools should also be noted.

Outreach also has less happy aspects. Its size, complex stepchild status, and structural unwieldiness can become an administrator's nightmare. About four weeks are required, during each term, to type, mimeograph, and collate seventeen hundred copies of the sixty-page descriptive booklet for students. The University's transportation and room-service staff, who regard Outreach as an extracurricular activity, have complained that the program is straining their resources, and funding from the University has been somewhat unreliable. For the past two years, Outreach has financed a good part of its own operating expenses through private donations, grants from the Wolverine Fund, the President of the University, the State Department of Mental Health, participating hospitals, agencies, and school systems. As a last resort, this year (1969) students have been charged a laboratory fee and contributions have been solicited from teaching fellows and supervisors. The mixture of pride and inconvenience experienced by some administrators and faculty affiliated with Outreach is delightfully revealed in the following quotation, taken with permission from a recent memorandum sent by the acting chairman of the Department of Psychology to the Office of the Assistant Dean of the College of Letters, Science, and Arts (LSA):

> As I am sure both you and Dean Haber are aware, Project Outreach presents some of the same problems (and satisfactions!) as a highly precocious and physically robust progeny does to middleaged parents. While the conception of this offspring was not wholly accidental, I believe that not even the most avid of its progenitors was quite prepared for the vigorous development that took place during the first two years of its existence. Clearly, the organism found an environment well suited to its genetic characteristics and it now begins to appear that just keeping it clothed and fed is starting to put some strain on the resources not only of its parents but of the more extended family as well.
>
> I recognize, of course, that no departmental program, much less any segment of any such program, can be permitted to monopolize the available resources of the College. However important we or you feel that this particular educational experiment is, it cannot be allowed to infringe unduly upon the other aspects of the total instructional responsibilities that we have. Thus far, however, this program has operated on what can only be described as a "shoestring" basis. While there have undoubtedly been demands on classroom space and some limited cost to the University in connection with supervisory appointments, when viewed in the context of the number of

students involved and the contributions this program is making toward the educational enrichment and the community relations aspect of the University's program, it is a source of some embarrassment to me (and I think it should be to the College) how little support this program has actually received.

We speak frequently of the need for educational innovation and the support of experimental programs beyond what is required for the routine operation of our standard curriculum; and with good justification in my view. To be blessed with such a highly adaptive approach to higher education as Project Outreach represents and to have it cost as little as this program has is truly, I think, a credit and an honor to those persons who have been responsible for its inception and administration during the past two years. Obviously I look on this program as a source of considerable pride from the Department's point of view and clearly I feel the College should view it likewise.

The most challenging educational question raised by Outreach is that of how one integrates the experiences of students with the course content. A teaching fellow faces a number of dilemmas when he makes a range of Outreach projects available to his students. If he is sincerely committed to helping his students integrate their Outreach experiences and the course content, when and how will this occur? If he decides to devote half a class period a week to discussing Outreach, or if students are encouraged to bring up relevant Outreach data at any time, the teaching fellow must be prepared to accept the fact that the class will not have the necessary time to survey, in a prescribed sequence, the topics he had in mind. Even more perplexing for a teacher who hopes to prepare his students for advanced work is a student's preference to commit his time and energy in the course to a concentrated study of a particular problem area in which he became interested during his Outreach experience. How does a teaching fellow respond to a student, in the Northville State Hospital project, who wishes to concentrate almost exclusively on psychotic processes, the impact of a mental hospital as an institution, and therapy with psychotics? How does he deal with a black student who prefers to read about the personal and meaningful issues being raised for him in the black consciousness project, rather than study a series of readings that seem irrelevant to him at that point? What about the bright, sensitive, but antiintellectual student, who is convinced that he learns best through his own direct experience, not through abstract words and symbols, and proposes to participate in at least three projects? What about the student who worked hard to understand why he was feeling so competitive toward his sensitivity-group trainer, who read up on authority relations in groups, and who now expects to deal with these same issues in class?

Another problem is the inevitable, exceedingly difficult dilemma about grading that strikes at the heart of the traditional view of higher education. Since Outreach represents a quarter of the student's commitment in the course, it should theoretically count for at least 25 per cent of the final grade. Therefore, how does a teaching fellow assess a student's performance in a hospital ward, in a sensitivity group, or his participation in the Washington Peace March as a part of the nonviolent project? How much and what did he learn? Is requiring the student to list the symptoms of schizophrenia or the dimensions of authority conflict a fair sampling of what he has learned? If not, should he then be graded on his empathic skills, his openness to experience, his tolerance for complexity and ambiguity; or should he be graded on his ability to draw reasonable inferences from his observations? Should satisfactory attendance be sufficient?

In this, Outreach, and the introductory course as a whole, have generated ripples of concern throughout the College. It is reported that, for Psychology 101 students as a whole, the average grade is slightly closer to an A than to a B, and that there seems to be little relationship between these grades and those in other courses. Thus, a student may have a D average in his other courses but an A in Psychology 101 (Milholland and Stock, 1968). Since an alternative to the current grading system such as pass-fail has not been available, more and more teaching fellows have been resorting to self-grading, or giving all the students in their classes As or Bs. The result is that administrators, deans, and counselors no longer place any credibility in grades in Psychology 101. It is clear that Outreach is not solely responsible for this development, since a number of teaching fellows and faculty have been pressing for something like a pass-fail option for some time and such a proposal has recently been submitted and approved. The problem indicates considerable disenchantment with grades and the related issues of evaluation, impersonality, and power. Efforts to innovate evaluation do not always involve an eager student pressing an ambivalent teaching fellow, as the pressure goes both ways: there are some students who have an investment in the current grading system and resist faculty initiative toward self-grading, pass-fail, or other innovations in evaluation.

These concerns mask a more basic and fundamental challenge to current conceptions and practices within American higher education. As an educational innovation, Outreach derives a good deal of its vitality from offering learning opportunities that are socially and personally meaningful. It legitimizes feelings, intuition, and affective and interpersonal learning along with traditional cognitive content. In this sense, Outreach challenges a number of values and assumptions about students and learning that are sacred to the traditional university culture, especially those values of truth, quality control, and accreditation. American universities and colleges tend to set the pace in maintaining, legitimizing, and promoting values that reward students for academic excellence. Efforts at change to the contrary and with few exceptions, there exists in American higher education a deep and resistant commitment to the proposition that students should be selected, and their performance evaluated, primarily on the basis of relatively detached, impersonal, objective, uniform, frequently verbal and cognitive criteria, even though lip service is often paid to nonintellectual factors (Jencks and Riesman, 1968; Sanford, 1967b; Harrison and Hopkins, 1967; Manion, 1967; Stern, 1962; Fishman and Pasenella, 1960). Thus, "formal systems of higher education in the United States provide training in the manipulation of symbols rather than things; reliance on thinking rather than on feeling and intuition; and commitment to understanding rather than to action" (Harrison and Hopkins, 1967, p. 432). Faculty are central to the maintenance of this dominant culture. They are usually selected, recommended for tenure, and promoted on the basis of their intellectual output, scholarly prominence in their field, status as researchers, skills of grantsmanship, and record of successful mobility from institution to institution (Jencks and Riesman, 1968; Knapp, 1962). They are rarely rewarded for their teaching skills, ability to design innovative arrangements for learning, ability to communicate intimately with students, or effectiveness as a model of concerned social activism. Accordingly, they shift more and more into research, and into information-giving and -processing roles, frequently at the expense of concern for the personal and social development of their students (Knapp, 1962).

This dominant culture reflects on students and on the teaching-learning process in the classroom. Generally, for those students who do not drop out, rationality, intellectual abstraction, critical thinking, emotional detachment, objectivity, and verbal manipulation become highly developed and valued and are rewarded (Bloom and Webster, 1960; Harrison and Hopkins, 1967). Faculty are less and less able to recognize and reward idiosyncratic brilliance, creativity, or learning (Jencks and Riesman, 1968). The most critical implication of the dominant culture is the fact that educational innovations, such as Outreach, that are characterized by concerns about students' emotional life, personal relationships, and social action needs, and which view the teaching-learning transaction as a vehicle for creating and sustaining concrete personal, interpersonal, and social fulfillment are generally excluded from our universities, or are exceedingly difficult to incorporate into the classroom process. Public statements to the contrary, one finds in American college classrooms little sustained commitment to educational objectives that integrate cognitive activities and emotional responses with a number of learning dimensions (Mann et al., 1969; Bower, 1967; Biber, 1967; Thelen, 1967; Sanford, 1967b; Kubie, 1965), or that view the educational process in terms of a more generalized conception of personality development, growth and change (Green, 1967; Sanford, 1967a; Bradford, 1965; Rogers, 1961), or that are addressed to the domain of experiential learning and to opportunities for interpersonal growth, for the realization of personal authenticity, and for putting the student in touch with his values, joys, hopes, fears, and essentially with himself (Leonard, 1968; Jencks and Riesman, 1968; Sunderland, 1967; Harrison and Hopkins, 1967; Bugental, 1967; Rogers, 1966b, Bennis et al., 1964).

The dilemmas created by Outreach and similar projects make clear the conflict between the two cultures within the university. How shall we resolve the conflict? How can we make the resources of the traditional culture, and of the real-world culture of the student's experience, available for the intellectual and emotional tasks of teachers and students? If we want to encourage the development of a teaching-learning process that attempts to integrate the two cultures, the goals of higher education must be reconceptualized, by our reappraising the relationship between teacher and student in terms of goals and strategies. This reappraisal, *teacher-as* typology, is a way of talking about the interrelationship of teacher, student, and task. The teaching-learning transaction can be characterized in terms of six related goals, each with a fairly distinct teacher-task strategy, each involving characteristic behaviors and skills, each resting on distinct assumptions about learning and about students, each depending for success on distinct types of student motivation, each capable of certain positive, negative, or distorted results. Taken as a whole, the six roles—the teacher as the expert, the teacher as formal authority, the teacher as socializing agent, the teacher as facilitator, the teacher as ego ideal, and the teacher as person—constitute the teacher-as typology. Since the teacher performs these roles simultaneously, with the salient role often changing quickly from one type to another, conflict and strain arise. For example, the expectations of the students may strain the personality dispositions of the teacher. We have constructed a scoring system to capture, moment-by-moment, the dynamic and complex nature of the interaction between student and teacher. The scoring system is presented in detail in Mann, et al. (1970, chapter 1).

The way in which each teacher-as type could help teacher and students to accomplish the work (the simultaneous pursuit of task and emotional goals) they have to accomplish, may be illustrated by a description of a hypothetical classroom in which a teacher (or as in the case of Outreach, a teaching fellow) is confronted by students full of newly-discovered ideas and questions about their Outreach experiences, and full of unresolved emotions about them. The teaching fellow, Mr. *S*, is prepared to lecture on socialization practices, provided none of his students raises a question for discussion. His class visited the back wards of a state mental hospital for the first time the previous night, so, before he starts his lecture, he asks for questions. After an initial silence, one girl asks if the patients at the hospital are the way they are because of their heredity. Mr. *S* hesitates for a moment, curious about her reasons for that particular question. Then he launches into a lecturette suggesting that constitutional factors may predispose certain individuals to psychotic disorders. (Later in the term he discovers that the girl's mother is a chronic psychotic and that the daughter is concerned about the risk for herself and her future children.) As he lectures, *S* notices that some students appear depressed and uncomfortable and others seem to be inattentive and distracted. Recognizing that he has lost the attention of most of the class even though the information he is communicating is not very threatening, he asks the students why they seem depressed and uncomfortable, and gets no answer. *S* breaks the impasse by relating how disturbed and shocked he himself was after his first trip to the hospital. He says that it took him almost five visits to get used to the setting and to get over his discomfort with the patients. In response to this opening, a number of students comment on how horrified they were by the smells, the slovenly appearance of the patients, and the inhuman manner in which the ward attendants treated the patients; how they were taken aback by the patients' childlike behavior and by their passivity; how they were annoyed that patients had nothing to do but sit around with nobody appearing to care about them. One girl reported a wonderful conversation with a patient who appeared so perfectly normal that she could not understand why he was hospitalized.

Mr. *S* now asks students how all this made them feel. A few students say they feel hopeless and cannot see that there is anything they can do for the patients. One girl says she felt so sorry for the patient she talked to that she wanted to take him home with her. Two male students are so angry at the conditions they saw that they talk of picketing the State Department of Mental Health. *S* agrees that the conditions are bad—there is only one psychiatrist for an entire building housing four hundred and fifty patients. He points out that many of these patients have spent most of their lives in mental hospitals and that many of them will be in institutions permanently. He asks if anyone has ideas about why the discharge rates are so low. One student suggests that just being a patient in that place could make anyone disturbed. When *S* asks the student to elaborate, he replies that a patient's individuality could be undermined by things like having to wear institutional clothes; other students chime in and note other ways in which patients are treated as children who cannot be expected to behave like adults. *S* now refers to some literature on the patient's role and on the extent to which behavior management and custodial care are the prime concerns of the hospital staff. Several students vehemently attack the staff for focusing almost exclusively on control and obedience, rather than on helping the patients prepare for discharge. *S* then points out that some patients, when they are not drugged, can be very difficult to handle; that in fact they can hurt or kill themselves, attack others, or destroy property. A short silence follows; several students look doubtful.

Now S tells about a recent lengthy car trip he had in a snowstorm, during which a friend had a psychotic episode in the car. He describes some of the events which occurred, says how frightened he was at first, how difficult it was to control his friend's erratic behavior, how he felt then and later about the whole episode and about his friend. Some of the events from the view of hindsight seem amusing in a tragic way; he relates a few. Then he suggests that, given this experience, it is not difficult for him to understand at least why the hospital staff is so constantly preoccupied with behavior management. One of the students rejects this as insufficient justification for what they saw going on at the hospital. S agrees and emphasizes again the need to understand both what is going on inside the patient and the impact on the patient of the hospital as an institution. S then asks the class if they can see any similarities between the role of the patient and the role of the student. There is no response. Time is running out; S suggests that they may want to think about this question and discuss it later if they like. As the class breaks up, the students burst into conversation among themselves.

The teacher-as typology has been presented elsewhere in detail (Mann et al., 1969, chapter 5), so a brief description of the six task strategies that can serve to bridge the gap between the dominant cognitive and secondary emotional culture aims in the classroom will suffice.

The teacher as expert has the major goals of transmitting the relevant findings, fundamental concepts, and analytic perspectives of his field and feels obliged to ensure that his students have mastered them. He uses the characteristic behaviors and skills of lecturing, scholarly organization and preparation of material; he asks questions, hands out dittos, discusses questions and terms, and draws the attention of students to other experts and resources. He assumes that students learn established truths by being exposed to them by the teacher; that fundamental concepts, vocabulary, and principles must be acquired before more sophisticated, independent study can occur; that passive learning is not incompatible with creative output. This strategy rests on an assumed need of students for active mastery, achievement, and intellectual competence and on the belief that curiosity and intrinsic interest in the material will motivate students to learn. The teacher is expecting students to acquire and retain knowledge and wisdom and to remain curious about the field. Factors that militate against this outcome are the student's fears of being or appearing to be stupid or incompetent, of failing in his own eyes, or of being overwhelmed or publicly shamed by the teacher. In extreme cases, the negative results of this sort of teaching are resistance to information, devaluation of the credibility of the teacher and the field, and total or partial ignorance. Lying between success and failure is the possibility that the student will come to consider that the source of all knowledge is external and will adopt rote learning to master knowledge.

The teacher as formal authority is typically required, by the institution in which the classroom is embedded, to be not only an agent of instruction but also a powerful source of control and evaluation. He is responsible to a group of comparatively unknown administrators and external agents who expect him to insure uniformity of standards; he is encouraged to cooperate with the university officials in seeking students' compliance with the university's rules, regulations, and standards of decorum so that the administration or the university is disrupted or politically embarrassed as little as possible. Functioning as a formal authority, the teacher must define course objectives, clarify guidelines, and specify requirements. The assumptions about learning and about students implicit in the teacher's functioning as a formal authority are that students need externally-imposed structures and guidelines as well as feedback because they cannot be trusted to control, discipline, or evaluate themselves; learning is indicated by one's position on a teacher's presumably uniform set of standards. Some teachers view the power inherent in their functioning as a formal authority as a necessary deterrent to student self-deception about his ability or performance. Challenges by students to a teacher's control or power often encounter arbitrary, punitive action such as dismissal from class or more subtle indirect reassertions of control through the manipulation of grades or requirements. It becomes important to the students to know what the teacher expects, to be clear about the demands and limits of the course, to find out what the teacher will reward, to function in a learning environment that has some routine, and to be assured that rewards for excellence will at least be reasonably uniform and objective. Behaviorally, students may indicate their acceptance of formal control by requesting permission to speak, by complaining about the irrelevance of other students' digressions, or by efforts during office hours to have the teacher control a particularly annoying fellow class member. By accepting and supporting the teacher as a formal authority, the students are often forced to adopt a dependent stance in the face of external sources of evaluation, and are often denied both the responsibility for decisions and choices as well as the opportunity to engage actively in a process of creating their own learning environment. Some students may, nevertheless, support the teacher as a formal authority because of their needs for dependency and conformity and their difficulties in handling responsibility in an unstructured, ambiguous environment. Some students may also feel the need to test their potency against a strong authority figure. Other students may actively rebel against formal authority, engage in acts of sabotage, become insolent or idle, or develop other forms of passive aggression.

The teacher as a socializing agent has, as his primary goal, the selective recruitment and acculturation of neophytes into his own culture, discipline, intellectual style, or value system. He tends to identify bright, exciting prospects who possess the right temperament, values, or other qualities, to provide encouragement and adequate preparation for future work beyond the immediate course by introducing these students to the concerns and activities of those already working in it and by clarifying the courses and occupational possibilities that lie ahead. He encourages a student's decision to take further courses in the area, his vocational explorations, summer jobs, research possibilities, his desire to discuss issues of interest with other members of the field, his defense of a teacher's position in class discussions, and his interest in pursuing particular topics in more depth. Students who have internalized some part of the teacher's orientation begin to derive a sense of self-esteem from the performance of mutually valued activities. Students reject the teacher as a socializing agent for a variety of reasons. Some students will resist what they perceive to be excessive or illegitimate pressure on the part of the teacher; some may actively mistrust the teacher's intentions; some may consider that the teacher is collecting disciples to enhance his own stature.

The task strategies, of transmitting expert knowledge, of controlling and evaluating student performance, of recruiting and socializing students into the teacher's own culture, are consistent with the goals of the dominant university culture. If we look back at our hypothetical classroom, we shall see that the learning in which those students were participating is not covered by any of these three strate-gies. Students in actual Outreach projects may not be willing to re-main passive learners who are presented with information, truths, and evaluations from powerful, influential, and authoritative, external sources. Their experiences may lead them to question certain conclu-sions accepted by the dominant culture; for example, the notion that there are established and unalterable truths segmented across disci-plines. Students in Outreach projects may also question the necessity of enduring superficial survey courses before being permitted to pur-sue an interesting problem in depth; they may reject the claim that knowledge is ordered in a hierarchal or pyramidal fashion. Under-standably, students may begin to question the assumption that edu-cation will naturally flow from the process of being accredited by passing exams. Accreditation in itself may seem irrelevant to students who are attempting to deal with issues of race, war, mental illness, ghetto life, identity, alienation, and the like. They may begin to feel the need to use their own feelings, values, attitudes, and intuition, as well as those of their peers, in coping with problems of social or per-sonal relevance. All of these consequences and others call for task strategies appropriate to personal concerns. The teacher as ego ideal, as facilitator and as person, seems to us the legitimate task strategies for these and similar issues outside the content.

The teacher as facilitator regards the more troublesome per-sonal and situational impediments to students' learning in different ways. The teacher as a facilitator acknowledges the relevance of un-intellectual influences in the learning process and accepts some degree of responsibility for dealing with them. Thus, the teacher's goal as facilitator is to foster the intellectual and creative growth of the stu-dent by helping him move beyond whatever is blocking his attain-ment of his own goals. The teacher as a facilitator seems to be guided by a series of assumptions about students that differ substantially from those characterizing the teacher as an expert, as a formal author-ity, or even as a socializing agent. He has a great deal of faith and trust in students and in their potential for learning, given good learn-ing climate. He has a deep respect for students and for their capacity to be responsible and competent and to choose and attain their own goals for learning. He attempts to serve primarily as a resource person, clarifier, reflector, and path-clearer for his students. As a task strategy, the teacher as facilitator incorporates what Rogers has been advocating over the years. In a series of papers on teaching and learning, Rogers (1961a, 1961b, 1966a, 1966b) has consistently argued that the most meaningful, lasting, and productive learning occurs in a facilitative learning climate. These assumptions often lead the teacher as facilitator to concentrate on two general sources of impediments to learning. On the one hand the notion that students can make progress in personal growth as well as in intellectual output to the extent that the learning climate minimizes fear of failure, self-abasement before authority, or discouragement resulting from excessively high standards, leads the facilitator to confront emotional and interpersonal blocks to learning energetically, in a variety of ways, direct or subtle. On the other hand, the facilitator's operating more like an administrator than a counselor by addressing himself to a variety of situationally determined impediments, may involve his experimenting with innovative classroom structures such as student centered or self-directed student groups (Beach, 1962; McKeachie, 1963); with 'T' group methods (Weir, 1968; Argyris, 1965); with a cooperative class structure (Haines and McKeachie, 1967); with a variety of tips for teachers (McKeachie, 1968), or with independent study programs (Baskin, 1962). He may also try to help students gain some influence over their lives as students (Sunderland, 1967); to obtain relevant field experiences; or to bring ungraded or self-graded courses into being (Anderson, 1966). If we could capture the pedagogical fervor that often characterizes the teacher who strongly emphasizes the facilitating strategy, we would note the teacher's rejection of any effort to impose his answers and even his questions upon the students, who need more than anything else to develop questions and answers relevant to their own lives. This leaves the learner responsible for defining the problems and issues to which he wishes to address himself; for searching out in his own style the kind of cognitive, affective, or interpersonal data he feels are most useful; and for arriving at his own answers, solutions, and truths, by using the teacher and his classmates as resources. The facilitator therefore listens hard to what his students are saying, attempts to clarify what students are saying, and is attentive to the processes that may impede the functioning of the class. When students are tense, anxious, depressed, or hostile to the point where work and productivity are affected, he is likely to call for a discussion of the issue. The teacher as facilitator is likely to be high on what Dixon and Morse (1961) call empathic potential. The facilitative strategy works well for students who are ready to do creative and independent work. Some develop a real and meaningful commitment to the responsibility for defining and achieving their own learning goals, even though, at first, the prospect may frighten them. However, faced with uncertainties and myriad pitfalls, some students become rigid with anxiety and deny personal responsibility for the failure or success of their learning. Different students enjoy varying degrees of success in using the innovative structures the teacher makes available. Anxious, dependent students who are most comfortable with the highly structured, traditional lecture, where expectations are clearly defined, are often unresponsive to the teacher as facilitator.

The teacher as ego ideal presents a model of enjoyment and excitement in teaching and working as a professional in his field. Ego ideal functioning rarely occurs in isolation from other task strategies. For some students this model is a compelling one for identification and emulation (Adelson, 1962). The ego acts as if he feels brilliant, more fully alive, more liberated, more potent, and more sensitive than his admirer. The teacher as ego ideal interprets a student's involvement, sense of excitement, and bursts of energy and vitality as positive results. At times students give the appearance of having had their batteries recharged by the teacher; they may unwittingly be imitating him. But a teacher who can so completely involve himself in a particular set of ideas or kind of teaching may provoke disruptive feelings for students. Some may become concerned about being too attracted by the teacher and feel that their identities are threatened by the extent to which they are fusing with the teacher. Some students may feel overwhelmed by such a display of energy and lapse into passivity. Fantasies of being scorned by a narcissistic teacher who expects students to match his activity and responsivity are equally disruptive.

The teacher as person comes closest to meeting, in class, the demands for authentic interpersonal relationships (Sunderland, 1967; Bugental, 1967; Bennis et al., 1964). The aim here is to engage students in authentic and mutually validating relationships within which both the student and teacher feel sufficient trust and freedom to share their ideas and personal reactions, not only to course material, but also to matters that may fall outside the usual definition of what is relevant in a classroom. The full range of human needs is very much a part of the teaching-learning transaction. This is what McKeachie and his coworkers (1966) seem to have found in the relationship they observed among students' affiliative needs, teachers' affiliative cues, and performance. Typically, functioning as a person may involve the teacher in sharing anecdotes about his days as a student, about his family, or his political activities. He may share his concerns about his effectiveness as a teacher, about his ability to relate to some students, or his feelings about particular students. He may express momentary irritation or pleasure. In this sense he makes the expression of subjective motions legitimate. He may describe the haphazard routes by which he or other "great men" arrived at their chosen professions, and, by puncturing some of the myths students construct about teachers, he may enable students to view teachers as ordinary mortals in pursuit of manageable goals. In a variety of ways, the teacher as a person communicates that what happens in the classroom is not separate from the way he conducts the rest of his life; consequently, the same is true for students. This gradual and sometimes agonizing growth of mutual trust, respect, and affection can be a liberating and rewarding aspect of the teaching-learning experience for both student and teacher. The sense of being more than a product or another name on a class list can help build self-esteem, especially for students who have strong affiliative needs or who are committed to testing, exploring, and confirming different parts of themselves (Bennis et al., 1964).

Some students have a great deal of difficulty handling the more intimate aspects of the teacher as a person and exert considerable pressure in the direction of mutual impersonality. Because of a real or fantasized history of painful experiences with previous important authority figures, because of strong fears of being rejected if they expose more of themselves, or because they hide what they consider to be totally unacceptable parts of themselves behind masks or cautious behavior, many students recoil from more personal contact or confrontation with teachers. Della Piana and Gage (1955) found that, while some students are more oriented to feelings and personal relationships, others are mainly task oriented. The latter may worry that affiliative and self-indulgent goals will supersede what they consider to be the legitimate work; namely, learning information and facts. In these circumstances, teachers may be accused of having abdicated their responsibilities by becoming one of the boys. Other students may worry about what the limits are and who will stop things if they begin to go too far and get too intense and threatening.

Reports of several efforts to construct typologies of teacher-

task strategies and to search out dimensions of teacher behavior are
available in the literature (for example, Adelson, 1962; Anderson,
1966; Trow, 1960; Jackson, 1963; Rogers, 1966a; Isaacson et al.,
1964; McKeachie, 1965, 1966, 1967; Wispé, 1951; Grimes and Allinsmith, 1961). Much of this literature overlaps with or can be translated easily into the terms we have used to describe the six task strategies of the teacher-as typology.

Illustrations of the way these six task strategies are used may
be found in the performance of Mr. S in our hypothetical class. Despite
the digressions and the alternations between emotional and substantive
focus, the discussion in our illustrative classroom shows a certain coherence. Teacher and students focus attention on the issues at hand
and there is little that is not relevant. The amount of emotional distress is not sufficient to be disruptive for any period of time. Mr. S is
able to encourage at least some of the students to use their feelings as
part of their effort to understand the hospital and their own experience. He has been operating within the framework of the teacher-task
strategies we have been developing. He seems to use them all fairly
flexibly to realize his own objectives and in response to his judgment
of what individual students—and the class as a whole—are thinking
and feeling. At certain points during this session, we see him functioning as an expert as he delivers brief lecturettes or information
about the hospital as an institution and about the etiology of psychosis.
In showing his feelings about his first visit to the hospital, and, in the
anecdote about his friend, he shows himself to be an authentic, feeling
person as well as one who can function as an energetic ego ideal when
faced with a group of depressed students. While he attempts to respond to the students' changing view of reality, he does not lose sight
of his task objectives. His emphasis on the need to develop a greater
understanding of the reasons patients are treated as they are communicates something about the way he operates as a professional psy-
chologist; that is, he is manifesting his intellectual style as a socializing
agent. Although issues of formal authority, power, and control do not
appear to be crucial in this session, the manner of structuring the discussion suggests some elements of this strategy as well.

This idealized, balanced movement across strategies presumes
the availability of particular capacities, resources, and skills. The effective teacher must have considerable intellectual competence in order
to act as an expert, he must be sufficiently familiar with the literature

of his subject, to be able to deliver on a moment's notice a coherent lecturette on the current topic, or to be able to direct students to the appropriate resources. In such semistructured discussion, he needs skill to be able to pull together a series of seemingly unrelated themes, and to focus attention on a particular issue, problem or question. This skill is especially critical when a number of students are sharing their experiences of different projects. Mr. *S* shifts from his initial stance as an expert to that of facilitator as he becomes aware of the students' depression. By asking the questions he did, he not only made the expression of feeling legitimate, but also gained useful information about what was troubling different students. His display of energy and of his capacity to communicate enable the teacher to be seen as a charismatic ego ideal—a strategy that may be effective with some depressed students. Finally, we see Mr. *S* taking the risk of presenting himself as a real, vulnerable, and authentic human being throughout the session. He is able to risk emotional encounters or threatening revelations in situations where his self-esteem may be at stake. Had the occasion warranted, he might have found it necessary to acknowledge his ignorance, admit that he was wrong, angry, or frightened. The teacher as a person is willing to increase tension or to confront a student in the class if he thinks it will help the student or the class as a whole. He is willing to trust his intuition and therefore to take emotional risks without necessarily knowing how the episode will end. In this sense, he is prepared for expected distress or antagonism from students, but he is also on the lookout for the unexpected.

The ability to shift from one strategy to another is illustrated by the manner in which Mr. *S* approached the question of the relationship between heredity and psychosis. Despite his curiosity about the reasons behind the question, he sensed the student's anxiety and abstained from probing further. He responded to the substantive rather than to the emotional component of the question, possibly with the thought of exploring the issue again at a later date. This form of forbearance is frequently based on a realistic time perspective of a group's development. It differs from the premature abdication of expert and formal authority strategies that is often seen in classes based on student-centered democracy. Authority issues, problems of freedom and intimacy require time to be worked out in groups (Slater, 1966; Tuckman, 1965; Mann et al., 1967; Bennis and Shepard, 1961). For example, Gibb's (1964) data and ours suggest that the trust and realistic respect necessary for successful facilitation and for developing authentic relationships is likely to come about only after a stable, multilateral authority structure has been established. Moreover, socializing efforts require an accurate picture of the student's goals and aspirations and the extent to which he is committed to them, and time is required for both the teacher and the student to develop a clearer sense of where the student is headed. Premature intervention on the part of a socializing agent may be disruptive for the student whose plans are not firm.

There does not seem to be any single teaching strategy, technique, or structure generally effective for all types of students, at all times, under all circumstances, with all teachers. Neither does there seem to be any remedy for dealing with disruptive feelings. Faked solutions such as premature abdication, insincere and undeserved expressions of trust, affection, respect, admiration, or reassurance are sensed for what they are by most students and discounted. There is no substitute for honest recognition of difficulties and for joint efforts by teacher and students to solve problems realistically. These efforts may include privately reducing distressing emotions, exploring alternative paths and courses of action, or attempting to use and bind feelings rather than to eliminate them. For students, such as the more challenging, rebellious males, it may be necessary to generate even more tension before productive work can occur. We have observed that confrontation about the teacher's function as a formal authority can help establish a stable authority structure for some teachers.

Our discussion of the teaching we think can bridge the gap between the traditional culture of the university and the immediacy of students' experiences may be summarized briefly. Outreach is an educational innovation affiliated with the introductory psychology course at the University of Michigan. Its range and diversity of projects reflect, to a large extent, an effort to respond to the more experiential, interpersonal, and social-action needs of students. Outreach presents dilemmas and challenges to the dominant university culture, which essentially views the classroom as a bastion of rationality preoccupied with impersonal, abstract, and cognitive concerns. Innovations such as Outreach demand a reconceptualization of the teaching-learning transaction to legitimize the pursuit of experiential, emotional, and interpersonal goals as well as the more traditional cognitive or content goals. The teacher-as typology, specifying six distinct, yet related, teacher-task strategies for achieving these goals, is such a reconceptualization. Illustrations of this may be found in the ways in which effective teaching moves flexibly among the six roles specified by the typology.

PART **THREE**

No one teacher's manner of conducting a class can become a simple recipe for others, particularly when learning does actually catch up both teacher and student in a single adventure. When a prescription is simple, the techniques too easily become separated from the

DESIGNING CHANGE

conditions that determine their success or failure. The final two chapters turn to educational theory and offer guides to the educator with which he can select techniques applicable to his own situation.

Leonard M. Lansky

Changing the
Classroom

The authors of earlier chapters in this book have described their ideas, insights, trials, and tribulations in trying to change the college classroom. The first step for each was a tough one—the teacher's look at his own role. Each came to the same liberating conclusion: to teach does not mean only to lecture. Another degree of freedom occurred when each teacher asked what he wanted to accomplish in the classroom, "What are my goals?" and followed that question with the more difficult one, "How might they be accomplished?" These questions and the answers led to other problems and some common discoveries. Each teacher learned, either again or for the first time, that he too was in the classroom, and that his acting as lecturer and evaluator—as expert and boss—were major determinants of what occurred as well as keys to much dissatisfaction. Thus, his reproaching the students with laziness, lack of involvement, lack of appreciation for knowledge, shortsightedness, resistance to change, interest in sports,

Some Psychological
Assumptions

sex, social life, and so on, would not serve to justify his pedagogy. Each teacher then found himself engaged in a complex diagnosis of a complex place, the classroom. The variables in the diagnosis included the course content, the departmental structure, the scope of the program all of which had some bearing on his planning a strategy for teaching. The different author's strategies have elements in common. Most teachers discovered that the students could be resources for one another, rather than separate competitors for grades. Most teachers found that involvement lay inside the students in their needs, goals, skills, wishes, ideas, hopes, and fears. Each teacher learned that the processes in the classroom were relevant to the subject matter, even in topics other than psychology or sociology. Most teachers discerned, sooner or later, some of their needs being gratified in the roles of lecturer and evaluator; and those needs had to be examined as the teaching role became wider and different. Resistance to change caused

293

conflicts in the teachers. Several learned that their conflicts and previous views about teaching were uncomfortable blinders when they tried new ideas. Some made the error of trying to get the student started by lecturing and discovered that this modeling had itself set a tone they did not want. Each teacher became alert to some students' willingness to follow new paths and others' strong resistance to changes in the usual roles of teacher and student. Trust was critical and often challenged. Key questions were, "What is in it for me? What is your game? What are the new rules?" Each teacher got "hung up" to some degree in the evaluation system: grades are important for students. Each teacher rediscovered that concepts are not the only things being learned in the classroom; students reinforce or develop skills, attitudes, and values as well. Each teacher designed a program in which the students had to take some responsibility for their own learning. Each teacher found that, when students and teachers shared responsibility and talked about working together, a problem-seeking, problem-solving orientation took over from the usual, single right-answer model.

Insofar as errors, difficulties, problems, and the like were not seen by teachers or students as irrevocable failures, both achieved one major educational goal—a willingness to try new things and to take a problem-solving attitude toward education and learning. "I don't know," or "I am confused," or "I am wrong," became incentives to learn, not negative judgments about the person. The right answers do feel good and understanding does feel good. The point is, however, that being confused and in error need not feel bad or wrong. But the success of the innovations was greater than the success of achieving one goal. Most reports indicate that the classroom became relevant for teachers and students; both felt that the new learnings obtained were valuable—sometimes in surprising ways. Relevance did not mean relevance only to our culture today; it meant that the student and teacher grew together in their understanding and in learning ways to get more understanding. This could occur from studying history, mathematics, poetry, or oneself. All of one's experience became relevant when the whole self could be used in the classroom. Perhaps the success reflects merely the newness of the teaching strategies. After thirteen or more years of one dominant classroom model, almost anything new would look good to college students. While there probably is some Hawthorne effect in the teachers' and students' reactions, I do not think that that effect accounts either for all the results or for their special flavor. It seems that the teachers did, to varying degrees, base their strategies on some sound social-psychological assumptions and facts, and then applied the strategies to the teaching-learning situation in their classrooms.

The following list of assumptions and facts bearing upon the issues that concerned these innovators before, during, or after their attempts at changing the classroom is only one selection from a large set of possible assumptions and facts relevant to the college classroom. Some of the items overlap; some might be ordered differently. It is a task for the future to discover a small set of assumptions from which all the others might be derived.

Individual differences affect learning situations. Individual differences among students and groups are more important for teaching strategies than are similarities. When rewards (grades) hinge on the passing of tests, the outcome limits the range of personal investments and strategies by students. Differences in motivation and types of skill are not put to use; any capacities that do not help answer test questions may lie wasted because they can actually hurt grade-getting. Personal—individually unique—investments are minimal when the teacher's curriculum, lectures, and tests make up the course. But if the teacher focuses on the differences in students' needs, skills, interests, attitudes, and values, the teaching strategy changes. The students' individual differences become relevant for their learning.

Learning is ubiquitous. Learnings fall into several categories, for example, those of content (ideas and concepts), skills, attitudes, and values. Thus, the issue for a teaching strategy is not how to get students to learn, but how to enable them to learn certain things—certain concepts, attitudes, and so on. The current revolution in education reflects a growing awareness that the Quiz Kid kind of knowledge is not the primary goal; because of the rapid growth of factual knowledge, it is one of the least important. The passivity of students, the dropout rate, the poor reasoning reflected in political and economic decisions on all levels of our society—urban blight, pollution, racial tensions, increased armaments, and so on—are overwhelming evidence to support the view that our educational model has failed. We have been too oriented toward and too concerned with memorizing the simple correct answer to the simply stated factual question. Factual knowledge is only one resource in the search for meaningful problems, the development of skills and values, and the assessment of

alternative answers. Different students need and use different facts at
different times. Instead of a content-factual orientation, we need a
problem orientation. Instead of trying to teach students a common
content in the hope that they will need most of it some day, we need
to focus our attention on problem-solving skills and clarifying attitudes
and values. At present, these topics go untaught. Our innovators made
them salient.

Feelings are real, always present, and relevant for learning.
A dominant view in our society goes counter to the statement that
feelings are real. Indeed, we are taught that feelings interfere with
our learning and with the smooth operation of our society. But we
know that feelings are always present. We are only beginning to learn
how to use them effectively in the classroom without changing the
classroom into a therapeutic situation. The narratives in this book
make it clear that, unless feelings are considered and are used, the
classroom becomes irrelevant.

Learning includes content, skills, attitudes, and values.   The
things that are learned in the classroom can be categorized in many
ways, but four will do. In every classroom, the student is learning a
number of skills. In the traditional classroom, he is learning again and
again that he must keep silent, pay some minimal attention to the
lecture, and be sure to pick up the changes in tone or other cues that
will indicate what material will be useful in forthcoming tests. These
are complex skills and are learned with different degrees of success by
different students. Similarly, the student is getting continual reinforcement for an attitude and value that says that the formal learning situation is irrelevant to the most important things in his life. He develops
the attitude that the formal learning situation is relevant only insofar as
he can obtain the necessary grades to achieve the status that his academic degree might mean for him. We are saying this rather simply,
but the issue does boil down to this kind of attitude and value. A different orientation to the classroom could lead to the students' learning
different skills, attitudes, and values.

Specific learnings and results are only probable.   At best, a
teaching strategy can increase the probability of specific learnings. The
more specific and concrete the goal, the more sure is its attainment if
limiting procedures are used. On the cognitive side, programmed instruction can effectively teach sets of concepts in a standardized way.
Similarly, elementary physical skills—swimming, sewing, following a

track on radar—can be taught by methods which work more with the similarities than with the differences among persons. However, if the teacher wants students to carry their ideas and skills beyond the classroom; if he wants them to use their judgment in the future and to seek new problems; if he wants them to feel that they and others are growing, competent persons; his teaching strategies must exercise only limited control over the students' behavior. For these goals, which are more difficult to attain than are simple verbal memories or simple physical skills, less is known about the teaching strategies. However, the experiences described by the innovative authors of this book are tests of these assumptions.

Human reactions are voluntary and involuntary.   People do not completely control their reactions to any situation. This assumption is an important one for understanding learning. Most learnings occur unconsciously. I am quite unconsciously reinforcing certain cognitive-perceptual-motor skills as I write. On one dimension, the skills add up to bare legibility, and the increments of learning make the habit of poor handwriting harder to break. However, I can become aware of the problem: the example of handwriting popped into my head. Then, deliberately, I tried to slow down, to keep the slant of letters constant, to use more space for each letter and word. Thus, an opportunity for new learning occurred spontaneously.

Man is motivated both to reduce tension and to seek tension. For many years, the tension-reduction model of motivation has been the dominant one in American psychology. Man eats when he is hungry, sleeps when he is tired, studies to avoid failing in courses, and so on. Recent research and reflection have restored to psychological thinking a view long known to philosophers and to everyday citizens; namely, the notion that man is curious, likes problems, seeks challenges, and does things to become aroused and excited. Students know about this basic motivation; each has his own challenges in everyday life. The innovators devised such challenges in their own subject matter by asking each student to look at the behavior of his own classroom or small group.

Man can examine his own acts, feelings, and needs.   People can look at their own behavior and become aware of their ideas, feelings, skills, attitudes, and values. By such introspection, people make available for change, through conscious learning, what was previously habitual or not in their awareness. By bringing the self and self-awareness into the classroom, a revolution occurs. Relevance begins with, indeed means, relevance to me. Relevance is personal. Insofar as each student's reaction to the materials, the course design, the other students, and the teacher can be talked about, the course is relevant. This assumption seems to be sound psychology. Its truth is not easily accepted; and once accepted intellectually, it is difficult for both teachers and students to act upon it.

Self-examination is learnable, uncomfortable, and resisted. Self-disclosure and self-examination are threatening. In a sense, this assumption is a restatement of others in a different form. If people are always learning and feeling and are not aware of their motives, many actions and habits will tend to persist because of unconscious investment in them. This conception can help the teacher with his own resistances and with those of the students. However, as with other things, no one factor is enough; love is not enough, good will is not enough, knowledge is not enough. The student and teacher must work together to learn how to examine their own activities and to take suitable action. As several authors testified, they knew about resistance to change but were not quite aware of its operation in themselves as they planned their courses. Thus, one author reports that he began the course with a series of lectures—just to get things started. Then he could not understand why groups of students presented their team's ideas as lectures or as question-answer sessions which bored everyone. When insight came, the teacher realized that he had both kept control over content by lecturing and had served as a model for the class.

Learnings are promoted by feedback. In the traditional classroom, with the focus on specific content, the feedback is the teacher's responses to the tests and papers. We have already commented on the limitations of these methods. Programmed methods can provide more immediate feedback on smaller learning units, be they content or skills. Other people, if they will share their perceptions, are an excellent source of complex feedback on skills, attitudes, and values. By using small groups, by asking groups to look at their own functioning, by being open to feedback, the designers of the new courses encouraged person-to-person feedback. However, there are resistances in our culture toward giving feedback that results in self-disclosure, and several authors report resistance by some students to these new methods.

Small groups make more complex and frequent feedback possible. A primary reason for small groups being used in many of the

innovations recounted in this book is that, in a small group, every individual can have a chance to be seen and heard. Each individual can
have his contribution assessed publicly by the others. One can get
feedback on many dimensions of one's ways of operating in a small
group. In a large group, if work is to get done, everyone must focus
chiefly on the task itself. In a small group, however, the group will
have more time to look at its own processes and at the interactions
among individual members. Thus, the small group techniques lend
themselves especially well to students' learning interpersonal skills, examining attitudes and values about learning, and learning about one
another.

Teachers are models for students. Students have a complex
set of expectations about appropriate and inappropriate roles of teachers in relation to students. What the teacher does and says carries
great weight in the classroom. When the teacher goes against normal
expectations, students tend to be distrustful and to look for inconsistencies between words and actions. Thus, the openness and sharing of
the teacher in attempting the new methods becomes very critical. Under normal circumstances, the teacher decides what is required, the
classroom method, lectures, and assignments. The teacher also decides
on the value of a student's learning. This complex set of expectations
is firmly entrenched in students at all levels. Autonomy and responsibility are foreign to current education; similarly, a problem-seeking
attitude is relatively rare. Such expectations about the teacher's role
and a realistic concern for grades are barriers to change in the classroom. For example, how can students show feelings (neither right nor
wrong in themselves), and feel free to make errors from which they
will learn, if they are accustomed to being rewarded for hiding feelings
and communicating only the correct answers? These issues were faced
by each of the innovators in this book.

*One major goal of liberal education is to create self-propelled
learners.* Liberal education should be liberating. It should help students to develop skills to use on their own. In short, one major goal of
education is the growth of a person. This item has been discussed
several times above. The typical classroom procedures do block the
possibility for students to take responsibility for their own growth.
Thus, it is not surprising that they do not take such responsibility or
show it.

Shared responsibility for teaching and learning creates self-

propelled learners in teachers and students. The whole teacher and the whole student go to the college classroom. In the traditional model, only part of each gets involved. Thus, the classroom becomes relevant for only a small fraction of their lives. The fraction that is involved is much too small and is the wrong fraction for the overall goals of liberal education to be attained. When both teacher and student share the responsibility for planning and carrying out the curriculum, both learn much new content, many new skills, and both examine and perhaps change many of their attitudes and values. One striking finding among the innovators was that they had to learn new skills as consultants, listeners, organizers of materials, and helpers with individual and group struggles on attitudes, values, skills, and concepts. The shared responsibility for planning also led to a shared responsibility for evaluation of the students' growth. The students and teachers alike discovered that they were dissatisfied with the usual criteria for judging what had been learned and how well it had been learned. Thus, several new ideas emerged for assessing the activities during the classroom work. One conclusion seems to be that the notion of grades as we now know it is not very useful.

The above assumptions and facts add up to rather simple conclusions. The teacher's self-awareness seems to be one requirement for changing the college classroom; self-awareness is difficult to achieve. Students resist the new methods because the methods go against their expectations and because they demand open expression of feelings, self-disclosure and self-awareness, all of which are threatening. There are great resources within the students' individual differences in skills and feelings. In every instance cited, small groups helped students to use their own resources and to take responsibility for their own learning.

Unless the planner can spell out for himself what he wants to achieve in terms of content, skill, attitude, and value objectives, he is going to have great difficulty in planning and in executing changes. Once he has specified his goals, he will still have problems, but he is more likely to solve them if he knows what he is after. It is important to be as specific as possible in order to be alert for potential incompatibilities among objectives.

The second major task, after specifying and listing the goals, is to list the resources available. Knowles (in Chapter Thirteen) notes that there are resources in students, in the community, in the library, in the university, in the teacher himself, in the group, and in possible assistants. An important strategic decision to be made at this point is about how the resources will be made available to the students. For some objectives, it will be necessary for the teacher to make the resources known and available very early in the course. For other objectives, it will be useful to dole them out as they are needed. For still other objectives, the better strategy may be to have the students locate their own resources.

The third major task in planning for change in the classroom is to prepare oneself. One must be prepared to have difficulties and even failures in one's best laid plans. Discouragement and resistance will occur. It is useful to make contact with other persons who have tried such innovations, and from whom one can get emotional support when things go wrong. One might draw upon graduate students and undergraduates who have taken such courses or who have tried such innovations in other parts of their own working lives; students who have been through such an innovative experience with you can be extremely helpful. The experience of working with you to solve problems, of seeing that you have problems and can come up with solutions affects your students and becomes a resource for them.

The fourth major task is to build into the program from the outset a systematic feedback mechanism. One of the great temptations is to focus more attention on the content of the course, especially if there are problems. The collection of data on how the program is working must be planned in advance and be automatic; otherwise there will gradually be no time for feedback and evaluation.

Finally, as some of our innovators indicate, one should be aware that the second time and the third time and the fourth time should be better than the first time. It takes considerable experience and practice to develop the new teaching habits. Our innovators attest to this; nevertheless, they remain committed to the struggle.

Roger Harrison

Classroom
Innovation

Our purpose is to draw some guidelines from behavioral science that
will enable the university teacher to design innovative courses and
classroom situations that will work.[1] A classroom that works is one
where both the learning processes and outcomes occur as intended,
and where the qualities of social interaction between students and
teacher and among students are as designed. This chapter is not intended as a treatise on behavioral science applicable to learning; it is

[1] I am very grateful to Howard Perlmutter and Donald W. Taylor for
their contributions to this chapter. The counsel and collaboration of the former
was critical in understanding and overcoming the discouraging difficulties in
classroom innovation which plagued my early attempts to design and implement self-directed learning. The latter, in his role as chairman of the Department of Industrial Administration at Yale University, displayed extraordinary
patience and forbearance for my experiments and for their sometimes unfavor-
able outcomes, as well as serving a valuable role as consultant and critic. I
especially appreciate the encouragement and the help in clarifying theory which
was given by Diana Boyce.

XVI

A Design
Primer

an attempt to extract from that body of knowledge some practical implications for the conduct of teaching in the university classroom. Presented are principles and concepts that have relevance for the decisions teachers have to make when they depart from the well-trodden paths of tradition and strike out into the wilds of educational experimentation. I have called this chapter a primer because that is all I know how to write. The applied art has not advanced to the point where we can write advanced works on social engineering and design. The most I aspire to is to transmute some of my own experience into concepts that indicate the choices that have to be made in designing educational systems for higher learning and to explain why I believe some choices are better than others.

Before going ahead, I should like to be clear about the value-position from which I am writing. This is not a chapter about how to design learning situations for any learning goal whatsoever; it deals

rather with the problems of maximizing values I believe are important. The values are basically the same as those put forward in a
previous paper on the design of cross-cultural training by Harrison
and Hopkins (1967). I believe there are close parallels between the
problems of transition from one's own culture to another and the
problems of living and learning in a society in flux such as ours. In
our culture, people are required to become increasingly adaptive and
responsive to change. This fact implies a number of changes in the
appropriate goals of university education, and these changed goals underlie the design principles of this chapter. Instead of educating in
preparation for one career, we need to educate for multiple and se-
quential roles, even while we do not know what the demands of the
roles will be. Going beyond an educational period confined to the
period of youth, we need to build education as a lifelong process taking place both inside and outside formal institutions. We need to con-
vert students from institutionally-directed education to self-directed
education. We need to move students from reliance on authoritative
sources of information toward developing and evaluating their own
sources. We need to move from a focus on the content of learning to
an equal and sometimes greater concern with the process of learning.
That is, we need to be at least as much concerned that the student
in our classroom learns how to continue to learn as we are that he
learns the facts, principles, and theories we present to him there. We
need to change educational systems in which the learner is primarily a
passive recipient of learning, by designing systems in which students
actively create their own learning. We need to move from a criterion
of learning that stops with achievement measured in the classroom, toward a focus on application in the real world.

The rapid pace of change requires the student to "own" his
learning. He should be prepared for active, self-directed exploration
and inquiry throughout life. A major design objective is thus to maximize freedom of the learner.

I further believe that there is a relevance gap between the
focus of much university education and the situations in which that
education is to be applied. The gap is not so pronounced where the
aim of education is instrumental—the acquisition of specific knowledge and tools for producing goods and services. It becomes large
when questions of values, goals, and emotionally charged choices are
involved in the application of learning. We are better at training

people how to do things than we are at helping them learn to make choices; we teach students what they need to know to serve the needs of a profession, or organization, but we give them little help in deciding whether the goals of that profession or organization are worthy of commitment.

I believe that our higher education usually makes it easy for our students to split their values from their behavior—a splitting that is central to the alienation endemic in our culture. The separation of facts and theories from values and emotions that we foster in the name of rationality and objectivity continues into organizational and professional life, where it contributes to performance without commitment and action without responsibility.

Since this chapter is primarily a design primer rather than a critique of university education, I shall not belabor the connection between rationalism in the classroom and alienation in society. I do want it to be clear that I believe classroom design should lead wherever possible to significant encounter for the student with the values, choices, and dilemmas embedded in subject matter, and that the encounter should be as real, involving, and emotionally significant as possible. This does not mean anti-intellectualism. Rather, it is a bias in favor of involving the student in a real way with meaningful and important issues requiring choice, commitment, and consequences.

All classrooms are complex social systems. However, university classrooms have had a ritualized, stereotyped character that makes it possible for both students and teachers to perform their respective roles with very little understanding of the forces and processes involved in the system. Everyone knows it is the role of the professor to lecture, make reading assignments, give examinations, evaluate assigned work, and assign grades reflecting the student's achievement in a course. Everyone knows it is the student's role to attend lectures, identify and take notes on those contents the teacher regards as important, and to do the same with assigned reading. The whole is to be held ready for production on demand: in class, in papers, and in examinations.

We are introduced into this ritual at the age of about six, and we stay with it until we are in our early twenties—longer if we become graduate students and teachers. Graduate students learn the ritual so well that usually it is not necessary to train them to be university teachers; they have played opposite the teacher so long that they know the role—they can be said almost to have understudied it. Although it is a nervous, scary experience to face one's first class as a university teacher, this is usually because we do not know if we will be able to live up to the demands of the role, not because we do not know what those demands are. Most of us quickly learn to perform adequately if not brilliantly, moving with little stress from the audience to the stage. The stereotyped presentations made by the students described by Torbert and Hackman (in Chapter Seven) are a good example of the learned ability to switch classroom roles.

When our rituals fail to produce the expected results, we face a sudden increase in our need for knowledge and concepts that will help us separate what is efficacious in our teaching and learning from what is merely ritual; we need concepts that will furnish better guidelines to what is wrong and what to do to correct it than a system of blind trial and error. Since most of us are trained more in the ritual of the classroom than in its art and science, we resort to trial and error for improving our classrooms. We begin by trying to improve our practice of the ritual: better lectures, assignments, tests, and so on. We experiment with smaller classes, with ungraded assignments, and with group grades for group assignments.

As we tinker, we encounter and learn the dynamics of the classroom social system in a way we could not when we merely played our parts within the ritual. We find the system resists some changes, accepts others. Some changes have intended effects, others go badly awry. Some roles we prescribe for students and for ourselves require skills, abilities, and attitudes that they or we do not have. We encounter apparent contradictions: an innovation works in one classroom and not in another, and we begin to search for the reasons.

My own curiosity about the social psychology of learning systems began when I tried to apply, in the classroom, some of the practices I had learned in the conduct of sensitivity training and consulting in industry. To my surprise, it seemed that giving students freedom to direct their own learning was more likely to produce apathy than involvement. To add to my confusion, I found that my *groupy* techniques were eminently successful when I conducted weekend training in leadership for student leaders at other colleges and universities, but when I tried similar things within the framework of regular courses at home in my own institution, students were confused and suspicious.

I began to discover that if I wanted to change my classroom I had to learn to use or to neutralize the forces already existing in the system: rewards and punishments and students' reactions to them; values and standards about the appropriate behavior for students and faculty; needs and wants present in students but unmet by the university environment. I began to understand how the students' personal development prepared some of them to welcome and use freedom in the learning situation, but caused others to shrink back from freedom, or abuse it, appearing either too irresponsible or too dependent to use it effectively. I began to see how the pressures from other parts of the university organization and culture limited the measures I could take in my classroom; for example, I found that when I reduced the pressure of grades on my students they often used the extra time to work on courses of other teachers who were not so lenient.

As my understanding of the forces became more detailed and systematic, I found that my experiments and innovations worked better. Students were more highly motivated and they produced better work. The outcomes of my educational experiments became more predictable. I gained greater skill in diagnosing what was going wrong and in intervening to save a failing experiment. Out of these experiences grew a rough framework of concepts and principles that serves as a guide in deciding what is important to provide for in designing successful classroom experiences.

The overall aim of this chapter is to help the innovative teacher to understand what changes in values, attitudes, skills, and behaviors are implied by his design, both for his students and for himself. He should be able to identify probable sources of resistance to change and be ready to work with them, counting the resistance as part of the job of innovation. The design of learning systems, like politics, is the art of the possible. The ideal classroom will not exist in any university we shall see within our lifetimes. We hope to be able to push much closer to the ideal as our knowledge becomes more systematic, detailed, and accurate.

The value, that we train students to "own" their learning, implies choices among alternative learning processes in the classroom. In this section, I shall discuss three types of learning: conceptual, instrumental, and rote. Ultimately, I think, we are concerned with learning that not only results in the mastery of the content of a discipline, but also trains the student how to learn. Traditionally, we have been more concerned with learning content than with learning how to learn. If we are to produce active, self-directed, lifelong learners, however, the latter becomes as important as the former—perhaps even more important. Specific content may eventually become obsolete or irrelevant to the learner; what he learns about how to explore the world, to gather and evaluate information, to make hypotheses and test them will never be out of date.

The processes of conceptualization and theory-building are central to the task of learning how to learn. Practically, the learning activities of discovery and application are the realization of these processes. By discovery, I mean that we expose the learner to a variety of experiences, events, facts, and phenomena, expecting that he will find the relationships, categories, and concepts that order and explain his experience. The teacher provides the experiences and the student actively makes sense out of them, finding the meaning in the events. The teacher has provided the conditions for learning, but the learning process remains the property of the learner. In the case of discovery, the learner goes from the concrete experience to the abstract theory or concept; hence the learning process is inductive.

Application or hypothesis testing is the deductive obverse of discovery. The concepts and theories are given, and the learner's work consists in applying them to the solution of particular problems or to understanding experience. The teacher provides the organizing concepts and the learner uses them as tools to manipulate events or to understand them.

Both the inductive and deductive learning processes are active and contribute to learning how to learn. In each case the learner has to do something with what is given him: build theory or test it. Both can encompass the experience of encounter. The experiences of which the learner is asked to make sense inductively can be designed to exhibit values and have emotional impact as well as to be intellectually stimulating. The application of concepts and theory to action may have value implications and dilemmas of choice.

Two examples from my own teaching illustrate the processes. In one course in the psychology of administration, I wanted students to learn and test a theory of motivation deductively. I presented the theory, using lectures and reading assignments. Then I asked my students to conduct interviews among first-year students at the university in which they were to elicit as much information as possible about the motives and needs of the first-year students and test whether the theory was adequate to account for what they found. Where their results deviated from the theory, I encouraged students to modify the latter, thus beginning the inductive process that should always follow the failure of a concept or hypothesis.

In a different course on group behavior, I asked students to keep a diary of significant events, which occurred during the biweekly unstructured meetings of the course. At the end of the semester, they were to derive concepts and theories of group behavior from these records of experience. In this example, the students moved inductively from experience to the discovery of concepts.

In both these examples I was concerned not only that the students learn about psychology, but also that they learn about how to use theory and how to learn from experience. I was concerned about the students' learning how to learn as well as about their learning of content. I believe that rote learning is greatly overused in the university classroom, with the result that students commit to memory a great deal of material that never gets related to anything more significant than the next examination. The problem is not that the material which is learned by rote is unimportant, but that we often assume that, once it is learned by that method, the teaching-learning job is done.

Since rote learning will probably be with us for the foreseeable future, we need to find some way of counteracting its tendency to make students passive and uninvolved in learning. For example, the effective modern language methods reduce the rote learning of vocabulary to a minimum and never allow it to interfere with active use of the language in conversation. When we move toward an emphasis on active use of each bit of information to accomplish some result, we are going away from rote learning and toward instrumental learning. The terms of the learning equation shift from *X goes with Y* to *to accomplish result X, do operation Y*. This is obviously a more active process of learning and is more consistent with our values.

Some of the innovative courses described in this book have large components of instrumental learning of techniques, those of Runkel and Seiler, for example, and the one by Horn, especially, is built around instrumental learning principles. We should, however, be aware that our choosing to provide students with tools always involves consequences for learning how to learn. The student who works out his own methods of approach most owns his learning. The student who has a wide and free choice of methods and techniques that can be applied to his own goals also has a good deal of ownership, especially if he is required to make the choice on his own. Horn's chapter illustrates this very nicely. Obviously, one cannot always make the ideal choice, especially when there is a good deal of content and method to be learned. But the consequences of overcontrolling the instrumental learning of students may be severe. This is illustrated by an example from industrial experience. A large American chemical company extensively recruited research chemists in Europe for a time during the 1950's to compensate for a shortage of chemists trained in the United States. After several years' experience, however, the company decided that the Continent was not a good source of research personnel. The company discovered that young chemists trained there found it hard to take individual responsibility and to carry projects forward. As one manager put it, "They are so used to having the professor tell them what to do that, if you give them a project, they wait around for someone to tell them how to do it. They have no confidence in their own ability to conduct research." These chemists had learned a general method for doing research (ask the professor) which did not work when they were left on their own. They had also acquired an image of themselves as low in the ability to generate their own approaches to problems. Though they were well-trained in their basic discipline, their instrumental learning about how to solve problems required a relationship to authority that was not available in this organization.

To summarize my point of view regarding the selection of learning processes in the design of classroom experiences: I favor giving a high weight to learning how to learn. Conceptual learning processes give the learner most freedom and ownership of the learning process and can best prepare him to be self-directed and independent in his future learning. Both inductive and deductive processes are advantageous: the former being the generalization of concepts and theory from experience, the latter being the testing of theory and its application to the solution of problems.

The lower learning processes have less desirable consequences. Rote learning tends to develop a passive and dependent orientation to learning, and instrumental learning is often tightly controlled by the teacher's selection of goals and means to the goals. However, instrumental learning can in part be given back to the learner when the teacher encourages exploration and experimentation in the choice and practice of means to goals.

MOTIVES, NEEDS, AND GOALS

An understanding of the motivational aspects of classroom design is badly needed in American universities. A theory of motivation can help the classroom designer make intelligent choices about the needs and incentives upon which he will base his designs. First of all, man is a wanting animal. When one need is satisfied, others arise and become motive forces. While it is possible to satisfy a particular need, it is not possible to satisfy all the needs of a person. Although we tend to think of human needs as fixed and static, they are actually changing and dynamic, first one and then another emerging, becoming potent, achieving satisfaction, and then fading into the background. Give a man bread and he wants respect; give him respect and he wants love.

Universities, like other social systems, control the behavior of their members through the application of incentives (rewards and punishments). For the incentives to be effective, they must actually meet important and currently active needs of the members. Otherwise the incentives will not control behavior and the system will begin to break down. When our assumptions about the people's needs turn out to be inaccurate, things can go wrong very fast. The behavior of others in the system becomes unpredictable and uncontrollable. This is happening on university campuses all over the world where many students are becoming inexplicably unresponsive to the incentives applied to control their behavior. It is a reasonable hypothesis that the students' needs have changed, while the incentive systems have not.

Our model of motivation postulates three basic human needs actually or potentially active in everyone. The model is a modification of an original conceptualization by Maslow (1954). *Physio-economic needs* are those for very broadly defined creature comforts: anything from the most basic essentials of existence like food, water, shelter, and clothing, to such unessential but comfort-producing incentives as automobiles, dishwashers, and shorter working hours. Social systems for the production and distribution of goods and services originally take much of their motive force from physio-economic needs. *Social needs* are those for love, acceptance, belongingness, and closeness to others. This need includes all wants and desires pertaining to loving and hating, being close and intimate, and spending time by oneself or with others. *Ego needs* are those for competence, knowledge, status, and respect. Wants and desires relating to self-esteem, self-confidence, achievement, reputation, and recognition are all included among the ego needs. A given kind of behavior can be controlled by incentives in any one of the three need-areas. For example, a student may enroll in a particular course because it is on the path to a degree and an economically secure life (physio-economic need); because his friends are also enrolling in it (social need); or because he is oriented toward the mastery of the subject matter of the course (ego need). We never know exactly what the active needs are that students bring with them to our classrooms, but we can be sure that they are not identical. The most viable and effective classrooms are those in which desirable behavior (work, or learning), from the point of view of the system, can lead to a variety of rewards. In other words, they are classrooms in which people with varied needs can all be rewarded for contributing to goals the teacher also values.

In universities, I have been impressed with the narrow range of rewards (those limited to the ego area) offered in most classrooms for effective performance. We offer recognition for knowledge and competence through grades, academic honors, and the personal respect of teacher and classmates. Some teachers and courses, by no means most, offer exciting opportunities for the intrinsic satisfactions to be taken from the growth and development of one's understanding and intellectual capacities. Very rarely do the formal learning systems of the university provide much in the way of social satisfactions, and those that have been available informally are being badly eroded by the size and bureaucracy of the universities. Affection and liking between students and teachers become impossible when they spend little time in face-to-face contact. The same is true for students in their relations with one another when work assignments are individual and when living arrangements are not communal.

In the survey which some of my students made of first-year students, the needs found to be the least well satisfied were social needs; my upperclass students have confirmed, in diaries I asked them to keep, that this deprivation is only partially made up after two or three years in the system. The social needs of students are relevant to the designer of classroom processes in two important ways. First, the goals of classroom design, as I have outlined them above, emphasize encounter as a significant educational goal. Learning that is low on encounter is not experienced by students as relevant and will not easily be applied to choices and actions in the real world. Educational systems fail significantly to approach the goal of encounter when students' relationships with teachers and one another are impersonal, lacking in emotional impact, and without important consequences for the individual's social needs. Second, such educational systems fail to motivate significant numbers of students whose social needs are more active and potent than their needs for the ego rewards traditionally offered in the classroom. Social needs of students must be attended to if only to revitalize the classroom and stimulate learning. This means that systems of rewards in classrooms should be designed so that the learning process will either be intrinsically socially rewarding or will lead to social rewards for the effective and highly motivated learner.

I have been treating needs as though they were to be met directly by rewards or, in reverse, by punishments or the withholding of rewards. Actually, however, goal-seeking operations vary not only as to the three basic need areas, but also as to the social processes that satisfy the needs. These processes will be assessed according to their levels of influence. Teaching, after all, is a process of influence.

COMPLIANCE

At a rather low level of need-satisfaction, the individual is prepared to enter into what Kelman (1958, 1961) has called *compliance* transactions with the environment. He is deprived enough and hungry enough to be concerned mainly with getting the next satisfier and avoiding the next punishment or deprivation. The distinguishing characteristic of compliance is that the person being influenced is oriented to external sources of reward and punishment, and behavior is consequently controlled by the outside agent who administers rewards and punishments. If external sources of satisfaction fail the individual, he has few resources of his own on which to fall back. He is often confused and lost. In the area in which his need is high, he is likely to have underdeveloped values and standards of ethical behavior and to take what he can get when and how he can get it. He is relatively unresistant to exploitation by others, and he will exploit them in turn when opportunity offers. He is oriented to the present and near future and finds it difficult to put off present wants for future advantage.

In the classroom we find dependent students responding to

rewards and punishments in both social and ego-need areas. Some students work hard for grades, fear failure, go to great lengths to impress the teacher with their willingness to work and their mastery of what he has assigned, and seldom take any risks that might result in punishments, such as disagreeing with opinions of the teacher. They are employing compliance-processes in the ego area. Other students exert themselves to be pleasing and likeable. They may amuse other students and the professor; they avoid conflict and controversy for fear of offending others; they may spend a great deal of time in socializing to the detriment of their work; their effectiveness as students may be at the mercy of whether the girl or boy friend or the roommates are at the moment accepting or rejecting them. They are functioning at the compliance level in the social area.

From the point of view of the learner, compliance management is most effective when the need is strong and when the individual has few resources of his own to use in achieving satisfaction independently of external sources of reward and punishment. It is least effective when the need is weak or currently well satisfied, and when the individual has readily available alternate sources of satisfaction. From the point of view of the classroom designer, compliance systems are most useful when the response desired from the learner can be closely specified and compliance observed. The effective administration of rewards and punishments depends on one's being able to specify, in advance, the response which one requires from the learner, and then to observe whether the response has been produced, and to reward or not accordingly. Compliance management lends itself to rote and instrumental learning. It does not work as well where discovery or invention, and hypothesis testing or application are the major learning processes, because, in these cases, it is precisely the external control of behavior from which one is trying to shake the learner loose. Nor does it work well when the teacher does not control rewards that will satisfy the active needs of his students. Influence through compliance is similar to Cytrynbaum and Mann's definition (in this volume) of the teacher as formal authority.

The progression from one level of need satisfaction to another seems to be a developmental process in which stages have to be gone through in a regular order. There are two processes relevant to this moving up and out from dependency and passivity. One is a moving away from others; the other a new kind of moving toward others. The moving away involves a counterdependent orientation in which the individual struggles to free himself from control by others. He shows a new willingness to endure deprivation in order to avoid domination, secure in his feeling that the deprivation is temporary and, at least to some extent, under his own control. He separates himself from the ideas, attitudes, and standards of others; after having been conforming, he becomes iconoclastic. In the ego area, we now find students rebelling against domination and dependency. Sometimes they avoid schoolwork for extracurricular activities where they can attain recognition, respect, and a feeling of growing competence without submitting to the control of assignments, examinations, and grades. Sometimes they seem to go on a sort of private strike, in which their productivity and their grades take a sudden nose dive. Sometimes they become argumentative and contentious, challenging the authority and competence of the teacher. In the social area, we find people who are emerging from dependency developing an increased willingness to take risks with love and friendship. They become more likely to fight with their friends and to violate the standards of acceptable behavior. They may exploit the exploiters by trying to see how many people they can have in love with them at the same time, or by using friendship to manipulate others.

IDENTIFICATION

It is possible to become fixated or stuck at any stage of development. Dependent and counterdependent orientations can become life styles for individuals or for whole groups and societies. If development proceeds naturally, however, the moving away of counterdependency is followed by the moving toward of *identification*. With identification, influence takes place through the influenced person's wanting to be like or to learn from a model. The influenced person seeks the influence, out of his own needs for self-definition, rather than complying in return for rewards or in fear of punishment or deprivation. Another aspect of identification is the establishment of relationships in which one finds identity and self-definition through the way others act toward him. If I am a member of a group that treats me as likeable and worthy of friendship and trust, I will be willing to meet its standards and requirements to maintain the identity the group confirms. If I belong to a group or organization holding an elite status in my profession, I will be willing to accept its influence in order to continue to see myself as elite. Any relationship contributing to a person's own sense of success, competence, or worthiness of love can be a source of influence through the person's desire to maintain that support for his identity. Identification processes are significant sources of influence in the classroom. In Cytrynbaum and Mann's typology, they are found in the teacher as ego-ideal and the teacher as person. The popular image of a good teacher is of a person who serves as a model for students, inspires them to the highest ideals, sets them a good example, brings out the best in them. These are ways we have in everyday speech of talking about influence through identification. Identification is also significant in the influences students exert upon one another. Students develop an image of the ideal student which is by no means the same as the faculty's image, which is less likely to embody social attractiveness than is the students'.

INTERNALIZATION

At a certain stage in the development of the individual, he may develop beyond being greatly dependent on others for the satisfaction of his needs. He may acquire a strong sense of his own identity and a correspondingly clear and strongly held set of values. In the normal course of development, most of us come to operate on the basis of internalized values and standards a large part of the time and in a number of areas. We are not honest just because we are afraid of being caught, but because we identify ourselves as reasonably honest persons; we do not give love only to receive it in return, but because we feel love and we see ourselves as warm, loving persons; we do not achieve just for the acclaim and respect of others, we work for the pleasure and satisfaction we find in a job well done. When we are operating from such values and from our abilities to give, create, and love we can truly be said to be self-directed and to own our own lives. People who are operating in such an inner-directed mode of need satisfaction tend to be rather unresponsive to coercive influences or to identification processes. If the rewards or the relationships offered to these inner-directed people reinforce their values and sense of self-identity, they respond, but their values take precedence when there is a conflict between inner and outer influences. If such persons can be subjected to massive and unrelieved environmental control, their values and sense of self can often be broken down and they can be made externally directed once again. For most of us, this can happen, to some degree, in times of personal stress or deprivation: when we are without money and hungry, or unloved and alone, or failing and unrecognized in our work. Some of the time, however, most of us operate more in accordance with our values than with our interests (the latter being defined as getting the most satisfaction for the least effort).

University students may be more subject to external coercion than are the adults they will become. Certainly they are more likely to be deeply involved in the processes of identity formation than they will be later. Many of them, however, operate much of the time upon strongly internalized values firmly rooted in a clear sense of identity. Unfortunately, because of the increasing gap between students' values and those embedded in the structure and operation of the university, the attempts at influence made by teachers are often irrelevant or counter to students' values. When this happens, particularly if the coercive pressures are great enough to make them feel really oppressed, students either do not respond or they resist. Even when the values of students and teachers are not conflicting, students do not like to have their self-direction taken away from them; they react as though the coercive pressures were being used to *de-develop* them. The self-directed student may then avoid direct involvement by playing the game while investing his real concerns and energies elsewhere, perhaps by trying to learn in his own way, while fending off control with whatever means of resistance he can muster; perhaps by trying to change the system by joining university reform movements, or by using the system to further his own needs and values if he can find ways of doing so; or by dropping out of the system. But he will not fit into the system and be a good, integrated member of it unless it offers him opportunities to direct his own activities in accordance with his own values.

The question for the classroom designer becomes, how does one exercise his responsibility for teaching and at the same time encourage self-direction on the part of students? Some part of the answer may be found in the use of the influence process which Kelman (1958, 1961) calls *internalization*. It has also been called *expert power* (French and Raven, 1959). Cytrynbaum and Mann (in this volume) call it *facilitation*. If we assume the individual's own values as a major driving force, we can still facilitate learning and influence behavior by inducing the individual to see new or different ways to maximize his values. This may be done through giving him information, or by introducing new concepts that help account for events and experiences he has not previously been able to integrate into his problem-solving. We do not directly offer the individual rewards and punishments as inducements to learning. We aid him in discovering ways in which he can increase his own satisfactions, assuming that his own needs will provide the stimulus for learning. We do not seek to inspire the student with a vision of what he can become. Instead, we assume that he knows what he wants to become and wants to learn whatever will bring him closer to his own ideals of being and doing.

Different characteristics of the teacher become important in influence through internalization. What is important is the credibility of the teacher and his ability to develop the student's trust in his own competence and motives. This is so because, if the teacher is successful in his influence attempt, the student will personally experience success or failure on his own responsibility. Influence through internalization never takes the responsibility away from the influenced person.

With internalization, the encounter between the student's values and the consequences of his actions is maximized. The teacher is responsible for his own competence and for his own honesty, but he stops short of making choices for the student as to what the latter should learn or how he should learn it. He serves as an aid to the student's own learning, not an instigator of it. Influence through internalization facilitates conceptual learning by discovery and hypothesis testing. The teacher facilitates conceptual learning not only through his personal relationship to the student, but also through his designs for learning. In fact, given the increasingly large classes and impersonalization of relationships between students and teachers, the most effective way to influence by internalization is by classroom design. This means that we design the classroom so that the student can act upon his own values and goals in the process of learning. Sometimes this means that he selects his own learning tasks, sometimes that he determines his own approach to some task which the teacher sets. The more freedom of choice and action the student has, the more opportunity there is to involve his own goals and values, and to own his learning experience.

Much of the remainder of this chapter explores the problems and difficulties we face when trying to move from the traditional com-

pliance-based influence systems in the classroom to designs which maximize internalization. The discussions are based on the hierarchical
model of learning, needs, and influence processes set forth above and
summarized in the table. "Lower," more concrete, externally directed
processes lead by stages of development to "higher," more abstract,
internally directed processes. Processes at a given level go together, fit
with one another and reinforce each other. Learning process, influence
process, and the level of need development at which the student is
operating are interdependent.

Compliance tends to result in rote learning and in instrumental
learning. Simpler, mechanistic learning processes are favored by deprivation and high need on the part of the students. High need levels
make students accept the dependency which accompanies influence
through compliance. Appropriate teaching styles and classroom design
for the effective use of compliance include clear specification of expectations and reliable reward for performance, frequent assessment of
performance, and a firm but fair style on the part of the teacher.

Identification presupposes a higher level of independence and
an active search for identity and values on the part of the student.
It leads to learning which is value relevant and likely to become integrated with the individual's values and goals. Identification depends
upon the knowledge and skill in design and personal qualities of the
teacher.

Internalization presupposes a degree of value development on
the part of the learner, to the point that he is willing and able to endure deprivation and postponement of immediate gratification in the
service of learning and of his values and standards. This ability to
operate independently of external rewards and punishments permits
self-directed exploration and manipulation of the environment. Internalization lends itself to conceptual learning by the methods of discovery and hypothesis testing.

A great deal of design ingenuity is required, particularly when
there are fixed principles, concepts, or skills which it is decided in
advance are to be taught. The teaching style which facilitates internalization is one of competence, trustworthiness, and honesty. The teacher
avoids judging the performance of the learner except against the latter's own standards. Instead, he provides accurate, objective but non-
evaluative feedback in which he simply describes what the effects of

A Hierarchical Model of Classroom Processes

Influence Processes	Ideal Teaching Style	Design Principles	Major Learning Processes	Level of Student Need Development Required
Compliance ("lower")	Firm but fair; clear and consistent about what he expects and what are the consequences of compliance and non-compliance.	Behavior and learning desired are clearly specified; success and failure are accurately and frequently assessed; rewards are reliably forthcoming for success, withheld for failure. Source of reward may be teacher or other students, but in either case standards of performance are made clear in advance.	Rote learning, including the mechanistic learning of concepts and theories without integration with the individual's values and goals. Instrumental learning through rewarding of correct behavior.	Subsistence: strong needs for rewards offered within the classroom, with little opportunity or ability to obtain alternate satisfiers of the same needs elsewhere. A level of need and lack of resources leading to willingness to endure a high degree of dependency.
Identification	When modeling: exciting, inspiring and admirable. Persuasive and charismatic. When engaged in self-defining relationships with students:	Maximum contact and interaction between student and identification models (teacher or students): thus, an emphasis on groups and collab-	Instrumental learning through modeling effective behavior. Conceptual learning through adoption of the ideas, values, theories of	Some confidence in own ability to satisfy own needs. The individual is engaged in the building of a sense of identity and self-worth within the

	empathetic and accepting. Treating the student as though he is what he would like to become, e.g. responding to the student's competence and likeability.	orative learning tasks. Need for finding and training persons with whom students can readily identify (other students, graduate students). Knowing and working within the values of the student culture.	valued and attractive others.	need area and is receptive to identification models and to adopting the ideas and standards of valued others or of others who value him.
Internalization ("higher")	Competent, trustworthy. Providing reliable information and useful ways of understanding experience. Providing nonevaluative feedback as to how he sees the student's behavior, abilities, accomplishments. Judging only against the student's own values and standards.	Learning designs which involve and activate students' own goals and values. Maximum opportunity to set own goals and make choices as to approaches to problems. Designs in which the consequences of thought and action for achieving or failing to achieve the student's own goals can be experienced.	Conceptual learning through discovery and hypothesis testing. High integration of learning with values and goals of the student.	Considerable confidence in ability to satisfy own needs, and a consequent willingness to endure deprivation for periods of time in the service of own values and standards. Strong sense of own identity, and well-developed values and standards. An ability to give as well as a need to receive need satisfactions.

the student's behavior are without praising or blaming. He provides information, ideas, and help in formulating concepts, rather than being a source of reward, punishment, and external control.

Much of this book is about the attempts of teachers to move toward the constellation of learning processes, and influence relationships we have identified as "higher" in the hierarchy. This is a difficult and risky enterprise, and for each of the reasonably successful projects reported here, there must be scores of attempts which result in the teacher giving up the task and reluctantly going back to more traditional classroom designs and teaching styles.

TRADITIONAL CLASSROOM

Classrooms contain students at a mixture of need-development levels. These students do not respond to influence in the same ways, but the teacher cannot usually choose his students; he must try to educate them all, or he must work with some and let the others get along as best they can. The vast majority of students have learned to get along somehow in learning situations where there is a good deal of influence by compliance in the ego area. Behavior is manipulated through grades; students are encouraged to compete; competence consists not only in meeting some standard, but in being better than one's fellows. Cooperation between students in their work is usually defined as cheating, either actual or borderline. Along with this basic compliance pattern is a less formal system of influence through identification. Teachers model the behavior they expect from students and do their best to inspire and draw out commitment to academic values. By and large, there are few opportunities for self-direction and influence through internalization. Those which exist are usually reserved for specially selected students who enter honors programs or independent study.

Side by side with the classroom learning system is the student culture, which is based largely on social needs and motives. The two cultures often conflict, especially where the competitive reward structure of the classroom interferes with the development of friendly, cooperative relationships among students. The style of adaptation to this "normal" classroom culture varies with the relative need strengths of the individual student between the areas of social and ego needs. The student culture has more influence over those with the stronger social needs.

Students who have strong needs for the rewards offered by the formal compliance system will tend to be controlled in the way the system is designed to control them. They will attend classes, take notes on lectures, complete assignments on time, study hard, and write examinations which reflect what they think the teacher wants. They will try to obtain the maximum rewards for the minimum work and may not show a great deal of concern as to the intrinsic value of academic activities.

Students whose level of development is above that of the most dependent relationship are usually in a state of at least partial conflict and defense against the compliance relationships in the classroom. They may try to manipulate or outfox the system, sabotage or rebel against it, or withdraw from it. If there are acceptable identification models available in the persons of the teacher or effective students, this conflict may be reduced. This occurs when the student is able to identify with the values associated with being a good student.

Most of the time, I think, most of our students are rather peripherally committed to formal academic activities and defend themselves against too much influence from the teacher or his classroom design. They respond to the occasional inspiring teacher, but they do not see the classroom as a place where their own values and goals can be pursued. They do not devote more energy and time to work than is necessary to get the rewards they need from the system. They comply, but they do not commit themselves. Instead, they keep their commitment to academic work low in order to devote themselves to activities which promise more opportunity for growth and identity development. Most students have learned to write the classroom off because it does not meet their needs very well.

The teaching experiences reported in this volume suggest that the normal classroom situation is not wholly favorable for the introduction of classroom designs relying on ego needs satisfied through internalization. Some few students quickly grasp the opportunity for self-directed learning and utilize it. Many others respond initially with some combination of anxiety, confusion, mistrust, resentment, or apathy. In this book, the chapters by Andrews, Cahn, and South, and especially the one by Torbert and Hackman, illustrate the problem. One major cause lies in the discrepancy between the social needs of students and the ego-based reward structure of the traditional classroom.

Having high levels of ego need, teachers tend to design their classrooms as though social needs do not exist or will not be aroused in the classroom. However, social needs are aroused as soon as students are in the presence of other students or the teacher. Classroom designs often go awry when we fail to take this into account. For example, in this volume it has been suggested that small work groups of students spend a fair amount of time "unproductively." The students themselves report that they feel guilty about the wasted time. I suspect that much of the time seen as wasted is spent in satisfying social needs. Because the satisfaction of these needs is not designed into the task, activities directed toward meeting them are tangential to work and are evaluated negatively. Another common example has to do with classroom participation. Students who are too active in demonstrating their knowledge in class often irritate others because they make them look stupid or lazy by comparison. Students know they may be disliked or avoided by others if they appear too bright in class, and for many whose social needs are strong, this inhibits their performance.

If social needs are not designed into the classroom, they will operate anyway, perhaps disruptively. Furthermore, students' relationships with their peers are a significant part of their life experience, their concerns, values, and goals. The classroom can hardly be said to be high on *encounter* for the student if we continue to operate so as to minimize the importance of any human relationships in the classroom except those between student and teacher. The classroom becomes at least partially irrelevant to the student's values and goals unless his relationships with other students can become a contribution and a vehicle for the learning process.

USING THE SOCIAL NEEDS

If the social needs of students are to become significant in the learning process, students must work together. In practice, this means that we shall want to use groups as learning settings. Groups are by no means without their disadvantages. To begin with, the opportunity to interact with others affords occasions for social punishments and deprivations (rejection, dislike, boredom, and so on) as well as for satisfactions. Furthermore, people in groups can be happy and satisfied without these feelings being connected in any way with learning. The task of the designer is to connect effective learning with the attainment of social satisfactions. Several times I have had the experience of designing a course around a term-long group project that counted for most or all of the grade in the course. If the group worked well and was satisfying to its members, all was well. But if the members of the group had interpersonal difficulties (disliked one another, struggled for power, and so on), members became discouraged part way through the course and began to withdraw from the group activity. This is always a danger when students are required to work collaboratively. Most have had little experience working in groups, since the traditional classroom emphasizes individual activity. They do not know how to work out the appropriate division of labor, or deal with competition, over- and under-participation, and unwillingness to work on the part of individuals.

Without making this chapter a treatise on group dynamics, I can make some practical suggestions for increasing the likelihood that learning groups will be productive and satisfying to their members and that an occasional failure will not be disastrous for the unlucky individuals in the failing group.

Try to compose groups so that competence is evenly distributed among groups. This can be done by grade-point average, by grades on previous tests or projects in the current course, and so on. In this way, each group will have some very good resources as well as some members who have to be helped or carried by the other members. The less effective students will be exposed to more effective ones who may serve as identification models for them. Most students will have had little contact with one another's work habits; working closely with effective students has been shown to have a good effect on the work of underachieving ones. Cahn (in this volume) gives a good example of the process of student modeling.

Try to compose groups so that there is as little interpersonal conflict as possible. Unless the group is formed for the study of group dynamics, energy that has to be spent in dealing with conflict, competition, and disagreement is subtracted from that available for the learning task. A good deal of work has been done to study the effects of grouping members who have different personal characteristics, and the author has reviewed some of this work in a recent paper (Harrison, 1965). Of particular interest is FIRO-B, the instrument described by Schutz (1958), which measures individual preferences for different kinds of interpersonal relationship. I have experimented successfully with groups composed on FIRO-B scores to try to reduce conflict and maximize cohesiveness and satisfaction of group members. For example, I distributed evenly among the groups people with low inclusion scores, so that no group would have too many members who did not really like being in groups. I identified highly dominant people and placed them with others who were more willing to accept influence. I gave each group some members who were not at the extreme on any of the scales. Another way of composing compatible groups is to allow members to select their own groups, preferably after they have had some experience of one another. Before deciding, they might discuss, in rotation, the qualities they would look for in a work-group member. People tend to be more committed to making a decision work if they have participated in it, and group members who have chosen their own group will not give up as quickly as they would if the choice were the teacher's. Of course, this method conflicts with the suggestion that groups be composed to have an even distribution of talent. One has to make a choice.

Let the group decide differences in individual rewards. Sometimes students have complained to me that group projects are unfair because everyone receives the same grade even though some students are unable or unwilling to do their share of the work. The project work is then completed at the last minute by one or two highly motivated group members, often working alone. Because it is against the informal standards of students to put pressure on one another to work harder, it is difficult for students to deal unaided with members' under-productivity. This problem is also reported by Culbert, South, and Torbert and Hackman (in this volume). I have successfully dealt with this problem by having the students distribute rewards (grades) within the group on the basis of individual contribution. Students worked together on a task in four- or five-man groups, producing a report to which I assigned a grade. The students then each ranked the others according to their individual contributions to the group product. The average of the group members' rankings was fixed as the grade I assigned to the group's product. Individual members' grades were adjusted higher or lower than this average according to the average rank they received from the other members rating their contributions. The students with whom I used this method accepted it as fair, and the group products were among the best I had received at that time.

Legitimize leadership in the group. Students are encouraged, by the traditional reward-structure of higher education, to compete with one another for grades, academic recognition, and entrance into graduate schools and the professions. They become unwilling to accept influence from their competitors; to preserve some friendliness and collaboration in the system, the peer culture develops strong norms in favor of leaving one another alone where scholastic matters are concerned. However, group work requires considerable mutual influence for its success. Since students do not readily develop arrangements for directing and coordinating the activity of group members by themselves, I usually give a push by prescribing or suggesting an authority structure in the group. I generally ask a new group to spend some of its early meeting time discussing what leadership functions need to be performed and how they would like them performed. Since most students prefer to operate under a chairman, I may ask them to discuss the characteristics they would like in a leader and then to select one of their number for the post. After such discussion, the group is more likely to select a leader who can be a model students can identify with. I have successfully tried channeling the distribution of grades to individuals through group leaders chosen by students. Again, a group grade, assigned by me to a project, set the average of individual grades, and the leader assigned higher and lower grades to reflect individual contribution. The leader's grade was set by the teacher. The purpose of channeling rewards through the group and legitimizing leadership is to make the compliance influences in the classroom support the effective functioning of the group. Otherwise, some students may correctly view the group as irrelevant to the goal of obtaining high individual grades.

Reduce the threatening aspects of group work. Students may correctly assess their effectiveness as group members to be low. The norms of the traditional classroom legitimize individual treatment of the student by the teacher. I have found that, to legitimize my group design, it helps to explain exactly why I feel the design is appropriate to the learning task and what benefits I expect students to derive from it. I solicit feedback and suggestions from students about the design, especially about the grading features, and modify it where there are strong objections. I give students as much participation in the decision about adopting the design as I can so that they will be committed to making it work. In addition, it is possible to provide options that reduce the fear of failure. Some tasks can be done either individually or in a group, and students can be given a choice. Group projects can be limited in duration and scope. I now usually use several projects, never longer than two to three weeks. Groups can be resorted for each new project, so that individuals have a fresh start each time. Runkel (in this volume) uses a different procedure for reducing threat and pressure: he gives term-long projects but permits them to be continued into the following term; the lack of a deadline decreases anxiety and stress.

I do not view the use of learning groups as a panacea for the defects of the traditional classroom. However, groups still offer the best vehicle for students to meet social needs through productive learning activity. Carefully designed and managed, learning groups can increase involvement of students in the classroom and provide them with opportunities to pursue significant values and goals in the learning situation.

If it were possible to make pure internalization-classrooms productive, this would be an ideal development. Unfortunately, it is usually beyond our reach. In such a classroom, there are no grades, no assigned projects, papers, or examinations. The teacher provides learning resources (readings, lectures, laboratory equipment, for example) but does not prescribe their use. Without rewards and punishments applied in the classroom, students who are highly oriented to external satisfiers of their ego needs tend to withdraw. They use their energy and time to obtain satisfaction in other course work where the traditional pattern continues. In present-day universities, where most students have to work hard to get good grades and to graduate, nearly everyone is somewhat responsive to coercive pressures. Consequently, attendance and effort drop off in noncoercive classrooms, except on the part of those few students who are genuinely self-directed or who are attached to the classroom by bonds of identification. From a practical point of view, the noncoercive classroom seems nearly unworkable unless students can be selected for it or strong identification relationships can be established early. It is as though students' time and energy are attracted to the area of greatest coercion. For this reason I take the somewhat controversial position that most classrooms where internalization is heavily relied upon must also have some coercive features. Usually this means that grades are given on the basis of some assigned work, but as far as the actual conduct of the work is concerned, the students are given quite a lot of freedom to choose projects, approaches, and learning resources. The power to reward and punish is used to fence in the students so that they will stay in contact with the learning situation and to fence out the competition and demands of other activities, both curricular and extracurricular. Students are given great freedom as to what they will do in the course, but the traditional rewards of grades are contingent on their applying themselves vigorously to the task of learning. Such designs, using mixtures of influence through compliance and internalization, create serious difficulties for many students. For the student who is quite dependent, who values grades but has little confidence in his ability to obtain them, these designs produce a great deal of confusion and anxiety, because they violate the principles for effective compliance-based learning. The student does not have a clear specification of the behavior desired. He knows he is expected to produce something that will be graded, but often he is not told what to produce, how to produce it, or with what criteria the work will be judged. His attempts to get clarification from the teacher may well be rebuffed. The dependent student may give up, feeling that his chances of getting a good grade are very low.

The mixture of compliance and internalization also creates difficulties for the majority of students whose development in the ego area is high enough for them to take some responsibility and self-direction. These students are usually engaged in some kind of defense against the coercive pressures of the classroom. To the extent that they need the rewards of the compliance system, they will play the game, trying to manipulate the system so as to get maximum rewards from minimum effort. To do this, they need the same kind of information that the dependent student requires: an exact specification of the way the rewards and punishments will be administered. Then they can meet the minimum requirements with little wasted time and effort. Often these students do not value and enjoy learning for its own sake, nor do they have well-developed skills for self-directed learning. They are not confident that, if they put themselves wholeheartedly into the process of self-directed learning, the result will be intrinsically satisfying or will be highly valued by the teacher. Furthermore, students often mistrust the motives and trustworthiness of the teacher. They ask themselves why this teacher suddenly takes an interest in the growth and freedom of students. They may not believe that the choice of project or approach is really free. They may feel, not always without reason, that the teacher who offers them choices is withholding a rather clear notion about what he will reward.

I have had the experience of getting students to make a provisional commitment to self-directed learning, only to lose their involvement midway through the course. It is discouraging. Once it occurred because I set students a group task beyond their ability to do well. When the reports were turned in, I graded them on the quality of the products, which was not high. The students had actually put in considerably more time and effort than the reports showed. They felt cheated and punished. They had committed themselves to do a difficult, ambiguous task, had done their best to develop approaches to it, and were now being punished because the projects did not come up to my private standard. The feeling of excitement and discovery that had existed at the beginning of the course for all of us was replaced by an apathetic despair which was never completely overcome.

USING IDENTIFICATION

Identification processes are midway between compliance and internalization and tend to be compatible with both. Identification seems to offer a key to the transition between the two extreme and antagonistic processes. Unfortunately, our ability to serve as identification models for students is often quite limited.

One of the significant changes which has taken place in higher education during the years since World War II is the progressive weakening of the influence of the teacher through identification. Part of this is caused by increasing class loads and the consequent depersonalizing of the relationship between teacher and student. With increased distance, the establishment of influence through identification depends on the teacher's ability to perform as an inspiring, charismatic lecturer. Skills in establishing self-defining relationships in face to face relationships become less relevant because fewer and fewer students spend significant amounts of time in direct interaction with teachers.

Part of this change can probably be traced to the increasing specialization and "technicalization" of the disciplines. The academic is increasingly restricted to being an ego-oriented model of the competent, knowledgeable professional (Cytrynbaum and Mann's teacher as socialization agent), rather than inspiring identification with himself as a person with warmth, understanding, concern and wisdom. A further consequence of technicalization is that more and more of the academic's time is spent in becoming and remaining competent in his discipline, and he is less and less oriented toward establishing and maintaining personal and mutually self-defining relationships with students.

In addition, the teacher is losing his potency as an identification model for students along with other members of his generation (parents, professionals, leaders in industry and government, etc.). The orientations of students who are coming to universities are changing from economic, achievement and intellectual goals toward more emphasis on the quality of life and experience and on the establishment and maintenance of satisfying human relationships. The teacher may well have sacrificed his own social satisfactions in the pursuit of academic excellence. He is often ill equipped by background and personal values to model the kind of person students want to become.

All these factors seem to conspire to reduce the effectiveness of identification with the teacher as an influence for learning in the classroom. The result is that students turn to other students for their models, developing a peer culture increasingly divergent and out of touch in values and attitudes with that of the faculty, and teachers fall back on compliance models of classroom management for lack of effective alternatives.

The remedies for these difficulties lie in the domains of reform of the university organization, redefinition of the role of teacher and redesign of the training of academics. Such questions are beyond the scope of this book. The question is, what can the innovative teacher do with the resources available to him: himself, his students and the authority and prestige of his role in the university?

To begin with, the teacher has some control over his own behavior in the classroom. He can choose to lead students toward internalization models or to keep them back in a compliance mode. As an identification model, the teacher elicits reciprocal behavior from his students. They expect him to determine the rules of his classroom game, even if only so they can break the rules. His behavior becomes pivotal for movement toward or away from an internalization model. In taking this stand I differ from Runkel's point of view that student reactions depend mostly upon the design of the learning situation. The structure of the course only provides the static conditions that permit or inhibit growth. The behavior of the teacher himself is at the center of the dynamics of what actually happens. Whether teacher behavior was semi-programmed (Horn, in this volume), or spontaneous and free (Springer, in this volume), it was always significant. Given the fact that most of us are not, in our persons, overly inspiring models for students, I believe we still have a good deal of choice as to the impact of our behavior on the transition to internalization models. Below, I compare and contrast compliance-oriented and internalization-oriented behaviors that affect students' freedom and risk-taking. In a second tabulation, I make the same kind of comparison for behaviors affecting the depth of encounter with students' goals and values. Each teacher and graduate assistant can apply at least some of the facilitative behaviors without appearing awkward or phony.

BEHAVIORS INFLUENCING SELF-DIRECTION AND RISK-TAKING BY STUDENTS

Compliance-Oriented

Making all the decisions about how the course is to be run. Ignoring or turning down attempts by students to change rules, assignments, deadlines, format or subjects. Adhering closely to rules and standards and showing neither fear nor favor in administering them. Avoiding or ignoring feedback from students as to their reactions and evaluations of the course and the teaching, and as to their needs and desires for change.

Internalization-Oriented

Finding ways to place alternatives and choices before students and to modify the content or conduct of the course in response to student influence. Being approachable and understanding in management of the classroom. Using rules and deadlines as ways of helping students manage their time and direct their effort. Being willing to revise or suspend rules when students come up with a better way or when to do so would encourage students to push ahead and take moderate risks. Soliciting and using student feedback during the course, as well as after.

Presenting ideas, facts, and opinion as though they are immutable, demonstrated truth. Win-

Questioning and speculating about one's own dogma and discipline. Being impressed or con-

BEHAVIORS INFLUENCING SELF-DIRECTION AND
RISK-TAKING BY STUDENTS (*continued*)

Compliance-Oriented

Internalization-Oriented

ning discussions and arguments with students through superior logic or academic authority. Being careful not to make mistakes or be wrong and not to expose or publicize one's own errors when they occur.

vinced by student thought, criticism, and argument. Showing students when they have made a point or changed one's thinking. Taking risks with ideas, admitting the possibility of being wrong. Exposing one's own mistakes, errors, and inadequacies of knowledge and competence without shame.

Presenting only neat, cleaned-up end results of thinking and research: positive conclusions, findings, facts. Focusing on what is known or authoritatively thought. Dealing with the content of the subject and excluding the processes of search, controversy, and speculation by which knowledge is generated, destroyed, and reconstituted.

Presenting the processes of thinking and learning in all their untidiness, contingency, and deviation from rule. Discussing controversy and search in the past and present, stressing the shifting, temporary nature of our conceptions of truth. Discussing one's own thinking and research, not in terms of results and certainties only, but in terms of the personal processes of search, choice, evaluation of ideas and findings, and deviation from formally accepted rules of scientific procedure.

Showing mistrust of students' abilities as self-directed learners. Providing instructions which prevent students' having to make choices under conditions of uncertainty. Providing guidelines, information, and answers

Showing confidence in students' abilities as self-directed learners: by leaving many choices open, providing guidelines and instructions that are incomplete and must be filled in by students, raising questions for

Compliance-Oriented

for any problems which students will face in completing assignments.

Internalization-Oriented

which answers are not provided. At the same time, standing ready to provide more support and structure when uncertainty and ambiguity threaten to immobilize students' abilities to act.

BEHAVIOR AFFECTING ENCOUNTER: THE INVOLVEMENT OF STUDENTS' VALUES AND GOALS

Compliance-Oriented

"Sanitizing" the subject matter by avoiding value issues, personal goals, and human relevance. Attempting a value-free, objective, and detached presentation of issues. Avoiding the action consequences of knowledge and opinion. Limiting students to talking and thinking, short of action.

Presenting one's own values, opinions, and goals as facts. Investing one's point of view with the weight of academic or personal authority. Using one's persuasiveness and ability in argument and controversy to make students feel inadequate in their own positions or to make them reluctant to expose their values and opinions openly.

Ignoring or rejecting the values, attitudes, and points of view of

Internalization-Oriented

Emphasizing the values, goals, and personal choices which are involved in or relevant to the subject matter. Being open about one's own attitudes and values regarding the subject matter. Comparing and contrasting one's own values with those of students, others in one's own field, and society as a whole, and encouraging students to do the same.

Owning up to one's own values, but without coercing students to adopt them. Being persuasive without being domineering. Reinforcing students when they question values and choices of the teacher and when they offer alternatives. Being sensitive to the level of persuasion that will stimulate students without shutting them off.

Learning the values, issues, and points of view of the student

BEHAVIOR AFFECTING ENCOUNTER: THE INVOLVEMENT OF
STUDENTS' VALUES AND GOALS

Compliance-Oriented	*Internalization-Oriented*
the student culture. Alienating the subject matter and oneself from the problems, aspirations, and goals of students. Dealing with intergenerational conflict as temporary differences between superior, wiser adults and less competent, immature youth. Arrogating special privileges and rights to the older generation.	culture. Relating these issues to course content wherever possible. Dealing with intergenerational conflict as a controversy between equals, with different goals, interests, and life styles, but with equal access to the truth and equal right to be served.

Some facilitative behaviors are possible for each of us, but no teacher can demonstrate them all. Sometimes, other students are better sources of the behavior than we are. There are several ways, varying greatly in formality, to use graduate and undergraduate students as learning models. At the informal extreme, several experiments seem to indicate that placing effective and ineffective learners together in work groups, discussion sections, or living arrangements results in the less effective students identifying with and adopting the behavior of the more effective ones. Students who are effective learners also seem, in general, to be more liked and esteemed by other students than those who are not. Graduate students used as teaching assistants vary greatly in their effectiveness as role models for students, because they are sometimes too strongly identified with the values of the academic world they are trying to enter. Instead of using the closeness of the graduate to the student culture, we usually try to strip it away. In doing so we make it likely that they will have the same difficulties we have in relating with students. If we can avoid this natural desire to perpetuate ourselves, we can train graduate students, in their teaching assignments, to take the role of a mature student rather than that of an immature professor. We can work through trained graduate or undergraduate assistants by establishing close relationships with them and having them, in turn, work closely with smaller groups of students. They can be most effective if we try to select for graduate assistantships studentlike graduates and then help them be sensitive, effective members of their own generation rather than stiff, awkward members of ours.

Our innovation in these matters has not, perhaps, progressed very far. The development of techniques and designs for using students to teach students is the most promising area for experiment in higher education. I believe this because both the economics of education (the shortage of teachers and their increasing preoccupation with the generation and application of new knowledge), and the increasing generation gap in values and needs makes us less effective identification models for our students. They are going to take one another for role models anyway; it is perhaps appropriate that they do so. In any event, this inevitable process can and should be developed in the service of learning. In this connection the reports of Runkel and Cahn (in this volume) are of particular interest. They show quite clearly how effective students can be in helping one another to learn while at the same time maintaining their own position as students.

ANXIETY AND FAILURE

Freedom and the opportunity to take risks reduce the certainty of reward and increase the possibility of failure. Students whose development toward internalization has not progressed far will experience anxiety and fear of failure when uncertainty and freedom are increased. Moderate anxiety stimulates effort and problem-solving activity; higher levels tend to immobilize students, make them withdraw from involvement, or become defensive and antagonistic. Defensive reactions interfere with learning and with the development of effective student-teacher relationships. Some ways of controlling anxiety and fear of failure through classroom design and teacher behavior are suggested below.

Although a high tolerance for ambiguity is a desirable personal characteristic for the innovative teacher, the production of extreme ambiguity for students is not. Most students need to feel that there is someone in the classroom who knows what he is doing. For example, I spend considerable time during the early days of an innovative course explaining the overall course design, the teaching goals I am working toward, what each project or exercise is supposed to accomplish, and what will be expected of students. Student assistants who have previously taken the course can also reduce anxiety (Runkel, in this volume). Just the fact that the students have volunteered to come back and help out is probably a powerfully reassuring message to the newcomers.

In the area of grades, students often need to know that there is some form of insurance against risk. One way of doing this is to set a floor under grades, a minimum level of reward which can be obtained for compliance with basic course requirements. This was done by some of our authors. Usually it takes the form of giving a middle grade for minimum performance, for example, for meeting all assignments. The teacher takes a risk that some students will be undermotivated to perform because of the low level of pressure. He hopes to make this up by the involving and intrinsically motivating characteristics of his design.

To reduce the likelihood of early failure, I give an early project that is fairly easy to do well, and grade it liberally. I indicate clearly where I think students could have been more effective on the task, but I do not give really low grades unless there is evidence of inadequate time and effort. Fortunately, students tend to have time, at the beginning of a term, for interesting projects before the coercive pressures of exams and papers in other courses catch up with them. I use the early part of the term for projects that require a lot of outside work and, as exam time approaches, I reduce the workload.

I have found that it is easier for students to apply and test concepts and theories than it is for them to build their own conceptual framework to explain experiences. At the beginning of a course, I usually present students with some concepts and assign to them the task of applying the concepts to data they gather. The project for which the class was asked to interview other students to test a theory of motivation is a case in point. If I want students to build their own theory inductively from experience, I usually hold that task until later in the course.

The concept of choosing one's own level of risk can be generalized to a design principle. Where possible, students should be able to choose among different degrees of structure, direction, and risk in dealing with the same subject matter. Some students might want to build theory, others to apply or test concepts, still others to take an examination on the material. Of course, following this principle can multiply the teacher's work enormously. It is most likely to be needed where there are wide differences in readiness. Students are more willing to commit themselves to self-direction and risk if they have some influence over the choice. When I am about to introduce a task that will make students anxious or violate their norms of the student culture, I usually submit it to debate in class. I explain what it is I want them to undertake and why, I invite them to suggest objections and modifications, and I accept these if I can. In extreme cases, I have abandoned a project because of student objections. The need for students to have influence does not stop when the decision is made. When things go wrong it is important to have rapid feedback. For example, I encourage students to let me know, well in advance, if they are going to have trouble meeting deadlines so that the problem can be discussed in class and the deadline changed if it is unrealistic.

If one is committed to the development of self-direction and the students' ownership of their learning, difficult choices have to be made about content. Unfortunately, it is possible to process a great deal more information in a mechanical and routine way than when the information is to be made relevant to the learner's experience. I have never found it possible to cover as much material in a design maximizing self-direction and involvement as my colleagues can by using more traditional designs. If a student is out interviewing, or observing, or messing about in the laboratory, he cannot be reading or memorizing at the same time. This has posed no conflict of goals in my classroom. I was not preparing people to be psychologists; I was training them to think psychologically. I did not feel that it was important that they be able to conduct rigorous research investigations, nor that they have a firm grounding in the basic facts and findings of my discipline. Where there is a good deal of material to be covered, teachers will be in conflict over the desire to train students to become active, involved learners and the pressure to get on with the job. This is particularly distressing when one's course is a prerequisite for others and there has been an organizational decision about what students should master at each level. Even if the teacher subscribes to the belief (as I do) that the higher learning of a limited number of concepts is generally preferable to the more mechanical learning of a large number of facts and relationships, he may not have a wholly free choice.

I have only limited help to offer in this dilemma. I believe that programmed and instrumental techniques increase the efficiency of rote and instrumental learning, and save time for higher educational processes. Students can go through texts and programs on their own.

Programmed units can be alternated with projects designed for more active learning. Perhaps passing subject-matter tests can serve as the entrance requirement for the more involving activities. In the project units, the focus would shift from the superficial acquisition of a lot of learning to the exploration in depth of a few ideas and concepts. Horn (in this volume) has shown how programmed instruction itself can be made involving and self-directed. However, his approach would also run afoul of a departmental decision to cover a fixed syllabus since it permits the breadth or depth of focus to be determined by the individual learner. I believe it is important to separate routine, compliance-based learning activities from self-directed projects so as to preserve the integrity of the latter. Students who are under pressure to work on routine mechanical material to be tested and graded will find it difficult to commit themselves, at the same time, to more ambiguously defined self-directed tasks. External pressures should always be reduced when self-directed activities are called for. In this way, some measure of internalization can be preserved even in classrooms where there is pressure to cover a lot of ground.

SUMMARY

In setting forth some goals for the university classroom, that it maximize freedom, encounter, and learning how to learn, we have examined the processes by which learning may take place; and have seen that the goals can best be met, by conceptual learning, through discovery and through testing of concepts and theories. Rote learning and the simpler forms of instrumental learning tend to constrict the student's freedom. Material so learned is often isolated from the values and goals of the individual. We have discussed the levels of development from dependency on external rewards, through the search for values and a stable identity, toward the full expression of one's potential based on internalized values and standards. At each level, students respond to different kinds of influence processes. Dependent students respond to influence by compliance: giving and withholding relatively tangible rewards. As students free themselves from dependency, they become responsive to influence through identification with the behavior and values of the teacher or other students. As the identity, values, and standards of students become more stable, they become less easily influenced by external rewards and students have less need for identification models. Influence through internalization processes then becomes effective; the teacher becomes more a consultant to the student's learning activities and less a director or inspirer of learning.

The classroom contains a mixture of students: a highly dependent minority; a majority seeking values and identity; and another minority that is independent and self-directing. This mixture is managed by compliance, with supplementary reliance on identification. The minority of dependent students are effectively influenced through this system, while the majority respond with a mixture of defense and compliance. The learning processes stimulated by this system fall far short of the ideal of high freedom, high encounter, and learning how to learn.

It appears that identification, as a transitional process, can alleviate the strains of the mixture of compliance and internalization in the ordinary classroom. Unfortunately, acceptability of teachers as identification models has been reduced by social trends and organizational developments in the modern university. However, it is still possible to suggest how teachers can use their own behavior to facilitate movement toward higher learning processes. We can also design classrooms where graduate and undergraduate students can serve as identification models for others. The social needs of students can be used to facilitate learning. A natural vehicle is the learning group. We have examined some ways of designing and managing such groups.

Classroom innovation can benefit from a conceptual framework and from some practical guidelines. The examples of our colleagues who have helped to write this book can give inspiration to those who wish to engage in this risky, exciting enterprise. In the end, however, the innovative teacher is engaged in a self-directed learning experience of his own. Though he can share important parts of the journey with colleagues and students, the most difficult stages will be the loneliest ones. We hope these chapters suggest some ways less hard and long. That is all any guide can do. The choices and their consequences belong to the traveler.

BIBLIOGRAPHY

ABRAMS, L. "The Student Abroad." In S. Baskin (Ed.), *Higher Education: Some Newer Developments*. New York: McGraw-Hill, 1965.

ADELSON, J. "The Teacher as a Model." In N. Sanford (Ed.), *The American College*. New York: Wiley, 1962.

ANDERSON, D. G. "Self-Assigned Grades." *Counselor Education and Supervision*, 1966, *6*, 75–76.

ARGYRIS, C. "Explorations in Interpersonal Competence." *Journal of Applied Behavioral Science*, 1965, *1*, 58–83.

ARNOLD, J. *1956 Summer Session Notes*. Cambridge: Creative Engineering Laboratory, Mechanical Engineering Department, Massachusetts Institute of Technology, 1956.

AXELROD, J., FREEDMAN, M. B., HATCH, W. R., KATZ, J., and SANFORD, N. *Search for Relevance: The Campus in Crisis*. San Francisco: Jossey-Bass, 1969.

BASKIN, S. "Independent Study: Methods, Programs and for Whom?" In *Current Issues in Higher Education*. Washington: American Association for Higher Education, 1962.

BASKIN, S. "Innovations in College Teaching." In C. B. T. Lee (Ed.), *Improving College Teaching*. Washington: American Council on Education, 1967.

BEACH, L. R. "Use of Instructionless Small Groups in a Social Psychology Course." *Psychological Reports*, 1962, *10*, 209–210.

BENNET, L. *Before the Mayflower*. Baltimore: Penguin Books, 1966.

BENNIS, W. G. *Changing Organizations*. New York: McGraw-Hill, 1966.

BENNIS, W. G., SCHEIN, E. H., BERLEW, D. E., STEELE, F. I. (Eds.), *Interpersonal Dynamics*. Homewood, Ill.: Dorsey, 1964.

BENNIS, W. G., and SHEPARD, H. A. "A Theory of Group Development." In W. G. Bennis, K. D. Benne, and R. Chin (Eds.), *The Planning of Change*. New York: Holt, 1961.

BIBER, B. "A Learning-Teaching Paradigm Integrating Intellectual and Effective Processes." In E. M. Bower and W. G. Hollister (Eds.), *Behavioral Science Frontiers in Education*. New York: Wiley, 1967.

BIDWELL, P. W. *Report on Undergraduate Education in Foreign Affairs*. New York: Columbia University Press, 1962.

BLOOM, B. S., and WEBSTER, H. "The Outcomes of College." *Review of Educational Research,* 1960, *30,* 321–333.

BOWER, E. M. "The Confluence of Three Rivers: Ego Processes." In E. M. Bower and W. G. Hollister (Eds.), *Behavioral Science Frontiers in Education*. New York: Wiley, 1967.

BRADFORD, L. P. "Membership and the Learning Process." In L. P. Bradford, J. R. Gibb, and K. D. Benne (Eds.), *T-Group Theory and Laboratory Method: Innovation in Re-education*. New York: Wiley, 1964.

343

BRADFORD, L. P., GIBB, J. R., and BENNE, K. D. (Eds.), *T-Group Theory and Laboratory Method: Innovation in Re-education*. New York: Wiley, 1964.

BROWNING, F., and TYSON, V. (Eds.), *Course Survey Bulletin*. Eugene, Ore.: Student Projects Inc., 1968.

BUGENTAL, J. F. T. *Challenges of Humanistic Psychology*. New York: McGraw-Hill, 1967.

CASSIRER, E. *The Logic of the Humanities*. C. S. Howe (Trans.). New Haven: Yale University Press, 1961.

CHAMBERLAIN, M. N. "The Professional Adult Educator: an Examination of his Competencies and of the Programs of Graduate Study which Prepare him for the Field." Unpublished doctoral dissertation. University of Chicago, 1960–1961.

CHICKERING, A. W. *Education and Identity*. San Francisco: Jossey-Bass, 1969.

CUBAN, L. "Not 'Whether?' but 'Why?' and 'How?': Instructional Materials on the Negro in the Public Schools." *Journal of Negro Education*, 1967, *36*, 434–436.

CULBERT, S. A., and CULBERT, J. "Sensitivity Training Within the Educational Framework: A Means of Mobilizing Potential." *Journal of Creative Behavior*, 1968, *2*(1), 14–30.

DELLA-PIANA, G. M., and GAGE, N. L. "Pupils' Values and the Validity of the Minnesota Teacher Attitude Inventory." *Journal of Educational Psychology*, 1955, *46*, 167–178.

"A Declaration of Educational Independence." *Moderator*, November 1966.

DENNIS, L. E., and JACOB, R. M. (Eds.) *The Arts in Higher Education*. San Francisco: Jossey-Bass, 1968.

DIXON, W. R., and MORSE, W. C. "The Prediction of Teaching Performance: Empathic Potential." *Journal of Teacher Education*, 1961, *12*, 322–329.

DOBBINS, C. G., and LEE, C. B. T. (Eds.) *Whose Goals for American Higher Education?* Washington: American Council on Education, 1968.

EVANS, R. I., and LEPPMANN, P. K. *Resistance to Innovation in Higher Education*. San Francisco: Jossey-Bass, 1967.

FELDMAN, K. A., and NEWCOMB, T. M. *The Impact of College on Students*. San Francisco: Jossey-Bass, 1969. 2 vols.

FISHMAN, J. A., and PASANELLA, A. K. "College Admission-Selection Studies." *Review of Educational Research*, 1960, *30*, 298–310.

FLAVELL, J. *The Developmental Psychology of Jean Piaget*. New York: Van Nostrand, 1963.

FOOTE, C., MAYER, H., and associates. *The Culture of the University*. San Francisco: Jossey-Bass, 1968.

FRANKEL, C. "Rights and Responsibilities in the Student-College Relationship." In L. E. Dennis and J. F. Kauffman (Eds.), *The Col-*

lege and the Student. Washington: American Council on Education, 1966.

FREEDMAN, M. B. *The College Experience.* San Francisco: Jossey-Bass, 1967.

FRENCH, J. R. P., JR., and RAVEN, B. "The Bases of Social Power." In D. Cartwright (Ed.), *Studies in Social Power.* Ann Arbor: University of Michigan Institute of Social Research, 1959.

GARDNER, J. W. As quoted in *The Chronicle of Higher Education,* 1969, *3*(15), 1.

GIBB, J. "Climate for Trust Formation." In L. Bradford and others (Eds.), *T-Group Theory and Laboratory Method: Innovation in Re-education.* New York: Wiley, 1964.

GORDON, W. J. J. "Operational Approach to Creativity." *Harvard Business Review,* 1956, November–December.

GREENE, M. *Existential Encounters for Teachers.* New York: Random House, 1967.

GRIMES, J. W., and ALLINSMITH, W. "Compulsivity, Anxiety, and School Achievement." *Merrill-Palmer Quarterly,* 1961, *7,* 247–271.

GROVES, W. E. "The New Plights and Pleas of Students." Address to the Moderator Drop-In, New York, June 1967.

HAINES, D. B., and MCKEACHIE, W. J. "Comparative Versus Competitive Discussion Methods in Teaching Introductory Psychology." *Journal of Educational Psychology,* 1967, *58,* 386–390.

HARRINGTON, M. *The Other America: Poverty in the United States.* New York: Macmillan, 1962.

HARRISON, R. "Group Composition Models for Laboratory Design." *Journal of Applied Behavioral Science,* 1965, *1,* 409–432.

HARRISON, R., and HOPKINS, R. L. "The Design of Cross-cultural Training: An Alternative to the University Model." *Journal of Applied Behavioral Science,* 1967, *3,* 431–460.

HEATH, D. H. *Growing Up in College.* San Francisco: Jossey-Bass, 1968.

HEFFERLIN, JB L. *Dynamics of Academic Reform.* San Francisco: Jossey-Bass, 1969.

HEIST, P. (Ed.) *The Creative College Student.* San Francisco: Jossey-Bass, 1968.

HOCKING, W. E. "History and the Absolute." In L. S. Rouner (Ed.), *Philosophy, Religion, and the Coming World Civilization.* The Hague: Martinus Nijhoff, 1966.

HORN, R. E. "Learner-controlled Use of Information Retrieval Systems." *Programmed Instruction,* 1964, *4*(2), 5, 11–12.

HORN, R. E., and SPOCK, M. "The Development of Validated Museum Exhibits." Proposal submitted to the United States Commissioner of Education, March 1965.

ISAACSON, R. L., MCKEACHIE, W. J., MILHOLLAND, J. E., LIN, Y. G., HOFELLER, M., and ZINN, K. L. "Dimensions of Student Evaluations of Teaching." *Journal of Educational Psychology,* 1964, *55,* 344–351.

JACKSON, P. W. "The Conceptualization of Teaching." Paper presented at meeting of American Psychological Association, Philadelphia, August 1963.

JACOB, P. E. *Changing Values in College: An Exploratory Study of the Impact of College Teaching.* New York: Harper, 1957.

JENCKS, C., and RIESMAN, D. *The Academic Revolution.* New York: Doubleday, 1968.

"Joint Statement on Student Rights and Freedoms." *AAUP Bulletin,* 1968, *54,* 258–261.

JORGENSON, C. "Outreach: Outcomes and Evaluation." Symposium presented at meeting of American Psychological Association, September 1966.

KATZ, J., and associates. *No Time for Youth: Growth and Constraint in College Students.* San Francisco: Jossey-Bass, 1968.

KEAN, R. (Ed.) *Dialogue on Education.* New York: Bobbs-Merrill, 1967.

KELMAN, H. C. "Compliance, Identification and Internalization: Three Processes of Attitude Change." *Journal of Conflict Resolution,* 1958, *2,* 51–60.

KELMAN, H. C. "Processes of Opinion Change." *Public Opinion Quarterly,* 1961, *25,* 57–58.

KENNAN, G. F. (Ed.) *Democracy and the Student Left.* Boston: Little, Brown; New York: Bantam Books, 1968.

KNAPP, R. "Changing Functions of the College Professor." In N. Sanford (Ed.), *The American College.* New York: Wiley, 1962.

KNOWLES, M. S. "Andragogy, not Pedagogy!" *Adult Leadership,* 1968, *16,* 350–386.

KNOWLES, M. S. "How Andragogy Works in Leadership Training in the Girl Scouts." *Adult Leadership,* 1968, *17,* 161–194.

KNOWLES, M. S. *The Modern Practice of Adult Education.* New York: Association Press (in press).

KRIS, E. *Psychoanalytic Explorations in Art.* New York: International Universities Press, 1952.

KUBIE, L. S. "Unsolved Problems of Scientific Education." *Daedalus,* 1965, *94,* 564–587.

LANGMEYER, D. "An Exploratory Study of Group Effectiveness Using Two Tasks and Three Populations Differing in Organizational History." Unpublished doctoral dissertation, University of Oregon, 1968.

LAWRENCE, P. R., and SEILER, J. A. *Organizational Behavior and Administration.* Homewood, Ill.: Irwin, 1965.

LEE, C. B. T. (Ed.) *Improving College Teaching.* Washington: American Council on Education, 1967.

LEONARD, G. B. *Education and Ecstasy.* New York: Delacorte Press, 1968.

MCFARLAN, F. W., MCKENNEY, J. L., and SEILER, J. A. *The Harvard Business School Management Simulation.* New York: Macmillan, 1969, in press.

MCKEACHIE, W. J. "Research on Teaching at the College and University

Level." In N. L. Gage (Ed.), *Handbook of Research on Teaching*. Chicago: Rand McNally, 1963.

MCKEACHIE, W. J. "Student Power Motives, Discussion Teaching, and Academic Achievement." Ann Arbor: University of Michigan, 1967. Mimeograph number VI-A-3-1.

MCKEACHIE, W. J. "Student Ratings of Teacher Effectiveness." Paper presented at the American Psychological Association, September 1965.

MCKEACHIE, W. J. *Teaching Tips.* (5th ed.) Ann Arbor: Wahr, 1968.

MCKEACHIE, W. J., LIN, Y. G., MILHOLLAND, J., and ISAACSON, R. L. "Student Affiliation Motives, Teacher Warmth, and Academic Achievement." *Journal of Personality and Social Psychology*, 1966, *4*, 457–461.

MANION, J. P. "Recent Developments." In E. H. Hopkins (Ed.), *Innovation in Higher Education*. Washington, D.C.: U.S. Department of Health, Education and Welfare, 1967.

MANN, R. D., and others. *Interpersonal Styles and Group Development*. New York: Wiley, 1967.

MANN, R. D., AND OTHERS. *The College Classroom: Conflict, Change and Learning*. New York: Wiley, 1970.

MARTIN, W. B. *Conformity*. San Francisco: Jossey-Bass, 1969.

MASLOW, A. H. *Motivation and Personality*. New York: Harper, 1954.

MASLOW, A. H. *Toward a Psychology of Being*. Princeton: Van Nostrand, 1962.

MAYHEW, L. B. *Colleges Today and Tomorrow*. San Francisco: Jossey-Bass, 1969.

MEAD, G. H. *The Social Psychology of George Herbert Mead*. Anselm Strauss (Ed.). Chicago: University of Chicago Press, 1956.

MILHOLLAND, J., and STOCK, B. "Course Grades in Psychology 101." In W. J. McKeachie (Ed.), *Research on the Characteristics of Effective Teaching*. Washington, D.C.: U.S. Office of Education Report 05950, 1968.

OSBORN, A. F. *Applied Imagination: Principles and Procedures of Creative Thinking*. New York and London: Scribners, 1954.

PEARL, A., and RIESSMAN, F. *New Careers for the Poor*. New York: Free Press, 1965.

RIESSMAN, F. *The Culturally Deprived Child*. New York: Harper, 1962.

ROGERS, C. R. *On Becoming a Person: A Therapist's View of Psychotherapy*. Boston: Houghton Mifflin, 1961.

ROGERS, C. R. "The Facilitation of Significant Learning." In L. Siegel (Ed.), *Contemporary Theories of Instruction*. San Francisco: Chandler, 1966 (a).

ROGERS, C. R. "Graduate Education in Psychology: A Passionate Statement." In W. G. Bennis and others (Eds.), *Interpersonal Dynamics*. Homewood, Ill.: Dorsey, 1964.

ROGERS, C. R. "The Interpersonal Relationship in the Facilitation of Learning." Lecture given at Harvard University, April 1966 (b).

ROSSMAN, M. "Notes on the Implications of the Movement Regarding Educational Reform." Washington, D.C.: U.S. National Student Association, 1966. Mimeographed.

RUNKEL, P. J., HARRISON, R., and RUNKEL, M. (Eds.) *The Changing College Classroom.* San Francisco: Jossey-Bass, 1969.

RUNKEL, P. J., LAWRENCE, M., OLDFIELD, S., RIDER, M., and CLARK, C. "Stages of Group Development: An Empirical Test of Tuckman's Hypothesis." *Journal of Applied Behavioral Science,* in press.

SAMPSON, E. E., and KORN, H. A. *Student Activism and Protest.* San Francisco: Jossey-Bass, 1969, in press.

SANFORD, N. (Ed.) *The American College: A Psychological and Social Interpretation of Higher Learning.* New York: Wiley, 1962.

SANFORD, N. "The Development of Cognitive-Affective Processes Through Education." In E. M. Bower and W. G. Hollister (Eds.), *Behavioral Science Frontiers in Education.* New York: Wiley, 1967 (a).

SANFORD, N. *Where Colleges Fail.* San Francisco: Jossey-Bass, 1967 (b).

SCHUTZ, W. C. *FIRO: A Three-Dimensional Theory of Interpersonal Behavior.* New York: Holt, 1958.

SCHUTZ, W. C., and ALLEN, V. L. "The Effects of a T-Group Laboratory on Interpersonal Behavior." *Journal of Applied Behavioral Science,* 1966, 2, 265–286.

SEILER, J. A. "Laboratory in the First Year." *Harvard Business School Alumni Bulletin,* 1967 (b), *43*(6), no paging.

SEILER, J. A. *Systems Analysis in Organizational Behavior.* Homewood, Ill.: Irwin-Dorsey, 1967 (a).

SLATER, P. E. *Microcosm: Structural, Psychological, and Religious Evolution in Groups.* New York: Wiley, 1966.

SMITH, G. K. (Ed.) *Agony and Promise.* San Francisco: Jossey-Bass, 1969.

SMITH, G. K. (Ed.) *Stress and Campus Response.* San Francisco: Jossey-Bass, 1968.

STEINBERG, D. "A Proposal for Action Curriculum." Washington, D.C.: U.S. National Student Association, 1966. Mimeographed.

STERN, G. G. "Environments for Learning." In N. Sanford (Ed.), *The American College.* New York: Wiley, 1962.

STICKLER, W. H. (Ed.) *Experimental Colleges: Their Role in American Higher Education.* Tallahassee: Florida State University, 1964.

STONE, J. C. *Breakthrough in Teacher Education.* San Francisco: Jossey-Bass, 1968.

STONE, J. C. *Teachers for the Disadvantaged.* San Francisco: Jossey-Bass, 1969.

SUNDERLAND, S. "Changing Universities: A Cross-Cultural Approach." *Journal of Applied Behavioral Science,* 1967, *3*, 461–488.

TANNENBAUM, R., and DAVIS, S. A. "Values, Man, and Organization." Paper read at McGregor Conference on Organization Development, Sloan School of Management, Massachusetts Institute of Science, October 1967.

THELEN, H. A. "Group Interactional Factors in Learning." In E. W. Bower and W. G. Hollister (Eds.), *Behavioral Science Frontiers in Education*. New York: Wiley, 1967.

TOFFLER, A. *The Future as a Way of Life*. New York: Harper, 1965.

TRENT, J. W., and MEDSKER, L. L. *Beyond High School*. San Francisco: Jossey-Bass, 1968.

TROW, W. C. "Role Functions of the Teacher in the Instructional Group." in N. B. Henry (Ed.), *NSSE Yearbook*. Chicago: University of Chicago Press, 1960, *59,* 30–60.

TUCKMAN, B. W. "Development Sequence in Small Groups." *Psychological Bulletin,* 1965, *63,* 384–399.

WEIR, J. R. "Sensitivity Training in the Classroom." *Human Relations Training News,* 1968, *12*(1), 5–6.

WILSON, O. M. "Teach Me, and I Will Hold My Tongue." In C. B. T. Lee (Ed.), *Improving College Teaching*. Washington, D.C.: American Council on Education, 1967.

WISPÉ, L. G. "Evaluating Section Teaching Methods in the Introductory Course." *Journal of Educational Research,* 1951, *45,* 161–186.

Index

DATE DUE

6. 7.'84	
JUN 15 1987	

BRODART, INC.   Cat. No. 23-221